"This is a superb treatment of ⸺ ⸺ ecclesiology. It is clear, concise, and biblical. This will be a valuable resource in the years ahead as we seek to think theologically and practically about the church."

—DANIEL L. AKIN
President, Southeastern Baptist Theological Seminary

"Very accessible and readable. . . . Merkle bases his conclusions solely upon Scripture and is ready to make changes, where necessary and biblical, to the way things have always been done."

—JIM NEWHEISER
Pastor, Grace Bible Church, Escondido, CA
Director, Institute for Biblical Counseling and Discipleship

"This work is lucid, biblically grounded, and well argued. Scholars, pastors, and serious readers will profit from this work, which is clearly relevant to how we organize our churches."

—THOMAS R. SCHREINER
James Buchanan Harrison Professor of New Testament Interpretation,
The Southern Baptist Theological Seminary

"An unfortunate dichotomy often exists between theology and practice in the local church. This dichotomy is absent from the Bible and, thankfully, it does not exist in *40 Questions About Elders and Deacons*. This book should be required reading for all who aspire to execute biblically defined and motivated leadership in line with the gospel."

—DANIEL MONTGOMERY
Pastor, Sojourn Community Church, Louisville, KY

"Merkle clearly possesses a mastery of the subject matter and the important literature. He also writes clearly and is easily understood. It is a delight to read a book that combines competency and readability such as we find in *40 Questions About Elders and Deacons*. The format is a popular and useful one for surveying important questions on church leadership in the New Testament. Even those who will disagree at times with his conclusions will appreciate the clarity of the argument and find the presentation of the pros and cons of the issues useful and succinct.

"In sum, he has written a work on an important and much discussed subject in the church that is well written and organized. Pastors, students, and lay leaders of the church will find it most useful."

—ROBERT H. STEIN
Senior Professor of New Testament Interpretation,
The Southern Baptist Theological Seminary

40 QUESTIONS ABOUT
Elders and Deacons

Benjamin L. Merkle

Kregel
Ministry

40 Questions About Elders and Deacons

© 2008 by Benjamin L. Merkle

Published by Kregel Publications, a division of Kregel, Inc., P.O. Box 2607, Grand Rapids, MI 49501.

ISBN 978-0-8254-3364-1

Printed in the United States of America

5 6 7 8 9 / 17 16 15 14 13

*To the elders at
Grace Bible Church of North County
for first teaching me what it means
to be an elder.*

Contents

Foreword

It is a great privilege and joy as Christians to be able to gather together as the body of Christ and to worship our God. Too often we forget what a great gift it is to worship together. Dietrich Bonhoeffer rightly says, "It is by the grace of God that a congregation is permitted to gather visibly in this world to share God's Word and sacrament. Not all Christians receive this blessing. The imprisoned, the sick, the scattered lonely, the proclaimers of the Gospel in heathen lands stand alone."[1] He goes on to say,

> It is true, of course, that what is an unspeakable gift of God for the lonely individual is easily disregarded and trodden under foot by those who have the gift every day. It is easily forgotten that the fellowship of Christian brethren is a gift of grace, a gift of the Kingdom of God that any day may be taken from us, that the time that still separates us from utter loneliness may be brief indeed. Therefore, let him who until now has had the privilege of living a common Christian life with other Christians praise God's grace from the bottom of his heart. Let him thank God on his knees and declare: It is grace, nothing but grace, that we are allowed to live in community with Christian brethren.[2]

As believers we so easily forget what an unspeakable privilege it is to be part of the community of the saints, the church of Jesus Christ.

Jesus Christ is the head of the church, and we derive our instructions from Him. The church is not a human institution or idea. The ordering of the church is not a matter of our wisdom or preference. The church is not a business where the brightest executives brainstorm on how it should be

---

1. Dietrich Bonhoeffer, *Life Together*, trans. John W. Doberstein (San Francisco: HarperSanFrancisco, 1954), 18.
2. Ibid., 20.

organized. Too many conceive of the church as a human organism where we innovatively map out its structure. God has not left us to our own devices. He has given us instructions on the nature and design of the church in His inspired and authoritative Word. To jettison what God says about the church and supplant it with our own ideas is nothing less than astonishing arrogance. As members of the church we do not give others our own wisdom, but what we have learned from Jesus Christ our Lord.

The problem is that many believers lack understanding. They have never studied or been taught what the Scriptures say about the organizing of the church. I remember attending a meeting of a church search committee where I was interviewing to be the pastor. They were apparently concerned and worried about the report that I believed the church should have elders, for it was one of their first questions. They simply did not know that the word "elder" is the most common term for leaders in the New Testament. How few Christians know that the word "pastor" (Eph. 4:11) only occurs once in the New Testament! I am not arguing here that we must use the word "elder" and abandon the title "pastor." My point is that many Protestants who claim to be devoted to the Scriptures are often abysmally ignorant of what the Scriptures actually teach. We all too easily exalt human traditions over the Word of God.

This book by Ben Merkle admirably fills a void in the literature on church leadership. The question and answer format makes it accessible for the busy pastor or student of Scripture who may only have time for bite-sized chunks of reading. Still, the book is not superficial. Merkle has deeply studied the Scriptures and has researched the subject thoroughly. Even if one disagrees with him, one will find that his discussion is fair, and he presents evidence on both sides of issues. The book is not only biblically grounded but also full of practical advice, answering the questions pastors and others commonly ask regarding church leadership. This is a gem of a book, for it is scripturally profound and full of commonsense wisdom. I pray the Lord will use it so that we, the church of Jesus Christ, will glorify Him.

THOMAS R. SCHREINER
James Buchanan Harrison Professor of New Testament Interpretation
The Southern Baptist Theological Seminary

Introduction

In recent years the importance of having a biblical church government has become a central issue in many churches. Pastors study the New Testament and realize that their churches do not reflect what they find in Scripture. Church members likewise read their Bibles and wonder why their churches do not have elders or why the deacons rule the church instead of serve the church. In my opinion this awareness is both a good sign and a bad sign. It is a good sign because it is healthy when God's people desire to be faithful and committed to His Word. The Bible should be our standard for all faith and practice. But it is also a bad sign because it reveals that we have drifted from God's model for the church and demonstrates that the church has lost confidence in the sufficiency of Scripture. Instead, we have patterned our churches after the successful, corporate model. Consequently, a return to a biblical model of government is desperately needed in the church today.

Until I began seminary I had not given the topic of church government or, more specifically, eldership, much thought. It was not the seminary, however, that caused me to begin thinking about this issue. Rather, it was the local church I joined while completing my studies. The church did not have *a* pastor but six pastors or, as they preferred to be called, "elders." For three and a half years I watched and learned from them. Although I was not an elder of the church, as an intern I was permitted to attend some of the elder meetings. Because their concept of church leadership seemed so different from that of other churches, I began to study the issue in depth to see what the Scriptures taught. This experience instilled in me a passion and desire to see God's church return to a biblical model of leadership.

My interest with church polity was later reignited when I wrote my doctoral dissertation titled "The Elder and Overseer: One Office in the Early Church." In this dissertation, I examined the relationship between the two Greek terms *presbuteros* ("elder") and *episkopos* ("overseer") and determined that the two terms are used to represent the same office in the church.

Although this conclusion is commonly accepted among evangelicals, it is not consistently applied in the context of the local church. After writing and publishing my dissertation, I was challenged to write a more general and comprehensive book on elders.

Many quality books related to the topic of biblical leadership and the offices of elder and deacon have been written already. Yet, there are two main reasons why this book is unique. The first reason is its question-and-answer format. I spent a lot of time thinking about the approach I would take in writing this book. After teaching the Pastoral Epistles many times as a seminary course and giving seminars on biblical leadership in local churches, I realized that students and church members were asking many important questions that needed to be addressed. This was true whether I was teaching in America or in Southeast Asia. Other books on biblical leadership or church polity often provide excellent exegesis of the relevant passages from Scripture but seldom synthesize their results. Often, readers have to scan the entire book to find specific answers to questions they have. In this book, my approach is to pose a question and provide a concise, yet thorough, response. By asking and answering key questions, I directly address issues that often are only alluded to or dealt with in only a cursory manner in other works. Thus, the format is more user-friendly, and key issues that often are overlooked are answered directly.

A second reason why this book is unique is that I address each question primarily from a biblical perspective. While nearly every author on this topic appeals to the Bible in defense of a position, others often write primarily from a historical or practical perspective. My area of expertise, however, is biblical studies, not historical or practical theology. Therefore, my aim is to answer the proposed questions based on a sound interpretation of Scripture. Although we can learn from history and are unwise to ignore the insights of those who have gone before us, this book does not provide historical background to the issues. I do not trace the history of particular denominations or cite creeds in defense of my positions. Likewise, this book is not written from a practical perspective. There are already many good books written by pastors who have "been there and done that" and write from their personal experiences. While such books offer great practical advice, there is the danger of defending a certain style of church government simply because "it worked for me." My approach is not to answer the questions primarily from the perspective of what is practical, but from what is biblical. I should note, however, that having biblical leadership is extremely practical because God's way is always the best way. The question is whether we trust God enough to follow what we find in His Word.

The basic layout of the book is straightforward. I ask forty key questions and offer a biblical response to each one. The forty questions are divided into three parts. Part 1, "Offices in General," provides an overview to many of the central issues related to church government. This section discusses various forms of government and defends congregationalism in particular. It also identifies the offices of elder and deacon as the two church offices that are applicable for today's church.

Part 2, "The Office of Elder," is divided into four sections due to the amount of New Testament material and the current interest in this office. The first section provides background information related to the terms "elder" and "overseer" and also discusses the role and authority of elders. The second section explains the specific qualifications needed for elders. The qualifications that an elder must be the "husband of one wife" and must have "believing children" are discussed in greater detail. Finally, this section provides an in-depth discussion regarding the question of whether or not women should serve as elders. The third section covers issues related to the plurality of elders. It discusses the biblical basis for multiple elders, the number of elders a congregation should have, the relationship among the elders, the advantages of having a plurality of elders, and how a church can make a transition to a plural eldership model. The fourth section explains the selecting, ordaining, paying, and removing of elders.

Part 3 addresses the office of deacon. It examines the background, qualifications, and role of the diaconal office. It also describes the proper relationship between the deacons and elders. This section also discusses the question of whether women should be permitted to fill the office of deacon. Finally, the necessity of using the titles "elder" and "deacon" is considered.

Abbreviations

AThR	*Anglican Theological Review*
BDAG	Frederick W. Danker, *A Greek-English Lexicon of the New Testament and Other Early Christian Literature*, 3rd ed. Chicago: University of Chicago Press, 2000.
BJS	Brown Judaic Studies
BNTC	Black's New Testament Commentaries
BSac	*Bibliotheca sacra*
ECC	Eerdmans Critical Commentary
EDT	W. A. Elwell (ed.), *Evangelical Dictionary of Theology*
ESV	English Standard Version
ExpTim	*Expository Times*
GTJ	*Grace Theological Journal*
HCSB	Holman Christian Standard Bible
HDR	Harvard Dissertations in Religion
ICC	International Critical Commentary
JBL	*Journal of Biblical Literature*
JETS	*Journal of the Evangelical Theological Society*
JSNTSup	Journal for the Study of the New Testament: Supplement Series
JTS	*Journal of Theological Studies*
KJV	King James Version
NAC	New American Commentary
NASB	New American Standard Bible
NIBCNT	New International Biblical Commentary on the New Testament
NICNT	New International Commentary on the New Testament
NIGTC	New International Greek Testament Commentary
NIV	New International Version
NKJV	New King James Version

NLT	New Living Translation
NRSV	New Revised Standard Version
NTS	*New Testament Studies*
ResQ	*Restoration Quarterly*
RSV	Revised Standard Version
SBT	Studies in Biblical Theology
SecCent	*Second Century*
TDNT	Gerhard Kittel, ed. *Theological Dictionary of the New Testament.* Trans. Geoffrey W. Bromiley. 10 vols. Grand Rapids: Eerdmans, 1964.
TJ	*Trinity Journal*
TNTC	Tyndale New Testament Commentaries
WBC	Word Biblical Commentary
ZNW	*Zeitschrift für die neutestamentliche Wissenschaft*

PART 1

Offices in General

Why Is It Important to Have a Biblical Form of Church Government?

The organizational structure of a church is an important issue. It is not, however, the most important issue. There are many other issues that have priority over this one. The deity of Christ, justification by faith alone, the inspiration, infallibility, and sufficiency of Scripture, and the substitutionary atonement of Christ are just a few examples of issues that are more crucial to the Christian faith. Moreover, although some aspects of church government are clearly set forth in Scripture (e.g., teaching is the responsibility of the elders and not the deacons), other aspects are less clear (e.g., how church leaders should be selected). As a result, at certain points we must allow for some flexibility, while acknowledging that our personal preferences should not be put on par with Scripture. It is necessary, therefore, that we approach the issue of church government with humility and with a teachable spirit.

But just because a topic may not be the most important does not make it unimportant. As we will see, the form of church government that a local congregation employs is extremely relevant to the life and health of the church. As the body and bride of Christ, the church should seek to be pure and spotless. If certain biblical patterns and principles are ignored or abandoned, then the church will reap negative consequences. It is beneficial for the church, therefore, to follow the wisdom of God as recorded in Scripture.

Church government is important not because outward structures are important, but because outward structures directly affect who can be a leader in the church, what each leader does, and to whom each leader is accountable. Thus, when we speak of church government or church polity, we are really speaking of the roles, duties, and qualifications of those who lead the body of Christ. The following discussion represents a few reasons why church government is important.

It Affects Who Can Be a Leader

One reason a *biblical* form of church government is so important is that church government directly affects who is qualified to lead or rule the church. Depending on the style of a church's polity, prospective leaders may or may not be held to the biblical requirements listed in 1 Timothy 3 and Titus 1. If a church emphasizes a candidate's professional accomplishments over his personal character and family life, it can result in the church of Jesus Christ being led by someone who is biblically unqualified. In other cases, a particular church may add qualifications to those listed in the New Testament. For example, in some churches a person will not be considered for leadership unless he has a minimum educational level (usually a Master of Divinity). Other relevant questions relate to whether a candidate must be a certain age or gender, or whether a leader can be single, divorced, or remarried. Thus, a church's polity and related doctrine often determines who can be a leader.

The selection process of a leader also will differ depending on the church's organizational structure. In some congregations, leaders are chosen by the majority vote of the congregation. In other churches, the presiding leader or leaders are responsible for making the final decision of adding new staff members. Still, in other models the bishop, who stands above the congregation, appoints a leader for the church. Therefore, a church's governmental structure relates not only to the qualifications needed to be a leader but also to the particular method of selecting a leader.

It Affects What a Leader Does

The organizational structure of a church also will affect the particular role of a church leader. This aspect is important because the duties of a church leader often have eternal consequences. Leaders, especially pastors or elders, are not merely responsible for running an organization but also have the crucial role of shepherding, teaching, and equipping the congregation. In addition, church leaders are examples to the rest of the flock.

Church Leaders Are Shepherds

Having a biblical form of church government is important because church leaders are given the task of shepherding the congregation. The author of

Hebrews exhorts his readers to obey their leaders and submit to them, "for they are keeping watch over your souls" (Heb. 13:17). What could be a more important and, at the same time, more frightening job description? Leaders in the church (elders in particular) are given the task of making sure those in their charge have a healthy relationship with God. Their calling is not to run an organization or to help people maximize their potential in the world. Rather, their calling is to come beside their fellow brothers and sisters and lead them to the Great Shepherd. But shepherds not only lead; they also must protect. In Acts 20, Paul warns the Ephesian elders that after he is gone, savage wolves will come in among them and will not spare the flock (v. 29). Godly church leaders are needed to shepherd the flock and to protect the flock against false teachers who would seek to lead the sheep astray.

Church Leaders Are Teachers

Biblical church government is crucial because church leaders are given the task of teaching the congregation the Word of God. The Bible is our standard for life and godliness (2 Peter 1:3). As such, it is crucial that those who teach the Word are adequately gifted and trained to accurately handle the Word of Truth (2 Tim. 2:15). The truth is always under attack. False teachers and false teachings are rampant outside and inside the church. Paul warned Timothy that certain false teachers have the devastating affect of "upsetting the faith of some" (2 Tim. 2:18), which means that some had actually abandoned the apostolic faith and embraced another gospel. It was for that very reason that Paul sent Timothy to Ephesus. Paul feared that false teachers were in danger of leading the congregation away from the pure gospel. But Paul not only sent Timothy to Ephesus and left Titus behind in Crete; he also sent letters to these associates (and to the churches they served) in order to protect the truth of the gospel. In a similar manner, church leaders are entrusted with the responsibility "to contend for the faith that was once for all delivered to the saints" (Jude 3). It is the elders of the church who are needed not only "to give instruction in sound doctrine" but also "to rebuke those who contradict it" (Titus 1:9).

Church Leaders Are Equippers

Paul writes that Christ gave gifts to the church, including apostles, prophets, evangelists, and pastor-teachers (Eph. 4:11). These leaders are given "to equip the saints for the work of ministry, for building up the body of Christ"

(Eph. 4:12). Godly leaders are needed to equip the congregation to do the work of the ministry and to help the congregation become mature in its faith. Without such leaders, congregations become like children who are "tossed to and fro by the waves and carried about by every wind of doctrine, by human cunning, by craftiness in deceitful schemes" (Eph. 4:14). God has designed the body of Christ to be led by those who are gifted to help the congregation become stable and mature. Therefore, the specific roles given to leaders in the church are crucial for the body of Christ to reach maturity.

Church Leaders Are Examples

Because church leaders are examples to the congregation and to those in their community, they have a great responsibility. Their testimony can either help or hurt the cause of Christ and His gospel. Peter exhorts the elders to be "examples to the flock" (1 Peter 5:3). The author of Hebrews encourages his readers to imitate the faith of their leaders (Heb. 13:7). The type of church government a local congregation embraces often determines who its leaders are and what its leaders do. Because leaders are called to be examples to the flock and because the flock is encouraged to follow the example of its leaders, employing a biblical model is vital. Paul indicates that elders, or overseers, must not only manage their own household well but also must "be well thought of by outsiders" (1 Tim. 3:7). If a church's polity allows certain unqualified people to become leaders, their negative example will affect not only those in the church but also those outside the church, possibly causing some to despise the gospel.

It Affects to Whom a Leader Is Accountable

The organizational structure of a church is also important because it determines to whom the church leaders are accountable. In some systems, the senior pastor is given unmatched authority and is accountable to no one in particular. Only a congregational vote is given more authority or power. In other models, the senior pastor is accountable to the deacons, who really are responsible for business of the church. The senior pastor does only what the deacons tell him to do. Other structures do not have one leader but a number of leaders who are given equal authority. In this case, the pastor or minister is not accountable to the congregation but to other selected leaders who are on the church council. Finally, in some structures the church leader does not report to the congregation, the deacons, or fellow council members but to the one who appointed him to his position. In this model, the church leader is accountable to someone outside the local congregation. Thus, the various forms of church government determine the accountability structure of the leaders.

Summary

The church as the body of Christ is composed of believers who have been redeemed by the precious blood of Christ. It is for this reason that those who are called to lead the church under God's guidance are given such an important task. Because the outward structure of a congregation directly relates to who leads the church, what a leader does, and to whom a leader is accountable, church government becomes an extremely important issue in the life and health of a church.

Reflection Questions

1. Do you agree that it is important to have a biblical form of church government?
2. What do you think is the strongest reason for a biblical form of church government presented in this chapter? Why?
3. What problems might result if a church does not have a biblical form of church government?
4. Do you think your church has a biblical form of church government? Why or why not?
5. What could be done to improve your church's leadership structure?

What Are the Various Forms of Church Government?

There are four main approaches or styles of church government. Although each approach is complex and has many variations, the following summary presents a simplified overview, beginning with the most structured.

Episcopal

This form of church government is hierarchical-autocratic and is practiced by Episcopalians, Anglicans, Methodists, Eastern Orthodox churches, Roman Catholics, and some Lutherans. The term "episcopal" comes from the Greek word *episkopos*, which means "bishop" or "overseer." Although the various denominations that follow the episcopal model disagree on important details, they all share the central concept that authority resides in the office of the bishop. The bishop is distinct from, and superior to, the officials at the level of the local church. Thus, the bishop is responsible for ordaining and appointing leaders (known as priests or rectors) to the local congregations and is usually responsible for several local churches (known as a "diocese") rather than merely one local congregation. Episcopal government is based on the belief that Christ, as the head of the church, has entrusted the leadership of the church to the bishops, who are the successors of the apostles.

Methodists have the simplest form of episcopacy, having only one level of bishops. Other denominations, such as the Anglican and Episcopal churches, also have archbishops who have authority over many, or all, of the bishops. Roman Catholics have the most developed episcopal system, having not only archbishops but also a pope (who is the bishop of Rome and is above the archbishops). The pope is considered to have absolute and ultimate authority over the church. Appeal for episcopal authority is based on apostolic succession, whereby the function of the apostles is passed on to the bishops they ordained by the laying on of hands. Consequently, this style of church organization is hierarchical in that it has various levels of authority. The various levels of leadership are chosen from above and not from below. In other words, the congregation does not vote on or choose its leader; rather someone in a higher position (the bishop) appoints the leader for the congregation. Thus, authority rests not in the congregation, or even in the congregational leadership (the priest or rector), but with the bishops.

Presbyterian

This form of church government is hierarchical-representative and is practiced by Presbyterians and other Reformed denominations. The term "presbyterian" comes from the Greek word *presbuteros*, which means "elder." Although this style of church organization is hierarchical in that it has various levels of authority above the local church (often used as a court of appeal: session/consistory, presbytery/classis, synod, General Assembly), the local congregation (under the leadership of the elders) chooses those who will lead them. In each congregation there is only one level of local leadership, the elder. Yet, one elder does not rule alone. Rather, the church is led by a group of elders (usually known as the "session" [Presbyterian] or "consistory" [Reformed]). Thus the elders, who are elected or appointed, have the authority in the church as representatives of the congregation.

According to presbyterianism, there are two types or kinds of elders: teaching elders and ruling elders. The teaching elder is usually the paid minister who is seminary trained, ordained, and has been thoroughly examined by the presbytery (session members from several local churches). This elder does most, if not all, of the preaching and teaching. He is also in charge of officiating other sacred tasks, such as the sacraments of baptism and Holy Communion. The ruling elders are essentially "lay" elders, not being ordained or needing seminary training. They provide leadership in the church by helping set church policies and supervising various ministries. This twofold distinction is based on 1 Timothy 5:17: "Let the elders who rule well be considered worthy of double honor, especially those who labor in preaching and teaching."

Congregational

This form of church government is local-democratic and is held by most Baptists, Congregationalists, independent or Bible churches, and most Lutherans. As the name indicates, the final authority does not rest with the bishops (episcopalianism) or the elders (presbyterianism) but rather with the local assembly of believers. This authority is usually exercised in the form of the majority vote of the congregation. The basis of this democratic style of governance is based on the doctrine of the priesthood of all believers. Thus, although the church is usually led by a pastor (often with deacons in a supporting role), ultimate authority lies with the individual members of the congregation.

By nature congregational churches do not have a denominational hierarchical structure but are *autonomous* (literally, "self-law"), self-governing bodies. Thus, each local congregation, under the authority of Christ and His Word, governs itself and is independent of other congregations. No ecclesiastical authority exists outside the local church. Often such churches will form loose denominational associations for cooperative ministry, but these associations are voluntary.

Because congregationalists practice the autonomy of the local church, a wide variety of governing structures is found. Perhaps the most common, however, is the model of a single elder (usually called the "pastor" or "senior pastor") who is chosen by the congregation to be the spiritual leader of the church. He is responsible for setting the vision of the church and does most of the preaching and teaching. This pastor may have a pastoral staff and is often assisted by the deacons. Other churches maintain that a plurality of elders is the biblical model and therefore insist that one person should not be singled out as *the* pastor (or senior pastor). Rather, each of the elders is given equal authority. Unlike in presbyterianism, these elders do not have any authority outside their local church, and no distinction is made between teaching and ruling elders. That is, all elders should both teach and rule.

Nongovernmental

This form of church government is held by some Brethren and Quaker congregations. The need for a formal church structure is minimized, and stress is placed on the leading of the Holy Spirit who influences and guides believers in a direct manner (and not so much through an organization). According to this position, imposed, external structures usually degenerate into formalism, which quenches the Spirit. While great emphasis is placed upon the priesthood of all believers, often there are still elders who help lead the congregation. Preaching and teaching, however, are not limited to the elders, but freedom is given to allow the Holy Spirit to prompt others to share God's Word.

Summary

Which of the above traditions, if any, is correct? This question is not as easy as might appear due to the limited information we have in the New Testament related to church organizational structure. For example, in the Pastoral Epistles (especially 1 Timothy and Titus), we are told more about what a church leader should *be* than what a church leader should *do*. Furthermore, most of the information we have is descriptive, rather than didactic in nature. In other words, most of the material is not found in teaching sections but is located in narratives that describe what took place. Thus, we need to make interpretive decisions as to whether what is said is normative for us today. For example, we learn in Acts that the apostles cast lots to determine who would replace Judas as the twelfth apostle (Acts 1:26). This passage is descriptive in that it describes what happened in history. But we must decide whether this passage is teaching us how *we* ought to choose our leaders. Most modern scholars agree that the method the apostles used to choose Matthias is *not* how we should choose our leaders today.

Some maintain that all forms of church government are permissible since the Bible does not advocate a single, coherent view but rather presents a progression and development of various traditions.[1] While there is some truth in this statement, we also must attempt to align our churches as closely as possible to the model(s) found in the New Testament.[2] Peter informs us that God's "divine power has granted to us all things that pertain to life and

---

1. So Peter Toon, "Episcopalianism," in *Who Runs the Church? 4 Views on Church Government*, ed. Paul E. Engle and Steven B. Cowan (Grand Rapids: Zondervan, 2004), 2–41.

2. I disagree with Peter Toon's view of church tradition. Although he argues that the New Testament is unclear as to what model is the most biblical, he maintains that episcopalianism is the preferred model since that was the model the church embraced in the second through the fifth centuries. He comments, "That the *episcope* of the church in the earliest times should have settled in the form of monoepiscopacy (rather than in the form of presbyteral episcopacy) is a fact that one cannot set aside. As a minimum we surely have to say that it was allowed, if not directed, by the Holy Ghost." He continues, "It is difficult to believe that Almighty God, the Father of our Lord Jesus Christ, would have allowed the church in its formative years of growth and expansion in Europe, Africa, and Asia to go so seriously wrong as to make a major mistake in terms of its general polity and church government" ("Episcopalianism," 26). Such a position is dangerous because God often allows His people to make decisions that are contrary to His will. For example, God allowed the nation of Israel to select Saul as king although it was not God's ideal for the nation (1 Sam. 8). Samuel Waldron offers a forceful critique of Toon's position when he states that Toon "cannot insist that a normative church government was so unimportant to God that he did not even bother to reveal it in the Bible, and then insist that it is so important to God that it is inconceivable that he would have allowed the early church to have erred on the subject" ("A Plural-Elder Congregationalist's Response," in Engle and Cowan, *Who Runs the Church?* 61).

godliness" (2 Peter 1:3), which includes church government. Similarly, Paul states, "I am writing these things to you so that . . . you may know how one ought to behave in the household of God, which is the church of the living God, a pillar and buttress of truth" (1 Tim. 3:14–15; also see 2 Tim. 3:15–17). We are not left in the dark regarding how to organize the local church.

It is essential that any form of church government recognize that Jesus Christ is the head of the church. Paul states in Colossians that Jesus "is the head of the body, the church" (Col. 1:18). There is only one true leader of the church—Jesus Christ. He is the "chief Shepherd" (1 Peter 5:4), and all other shepherds/pastors are undershepherds. That is, they shepherd God's flock under the authority and direction of Jesus and His Word. The authority of any church leader is always a derivative authority. Jesus administrates His church by means of the Word and the Spirit, and all human leaders are subject to these.

Reflection Questions

1. What are the strengths and weaknesses of the episcopal model of church government?
2. What are the strengths and weaknesses of the presbyterian model of church government?
3. What are the strengths and weaknesses of the congregational model of church government?
4. What are the strengths and weaknesses of the nongovernmental model of church government?
5. Do you think it is acceptable to use any of these forms of church government? Why or why not?

Does the Jerusalem Council in Acts 15 Support Episcopalianism or Presbyterianism?

Both the episcopal and presbyterian models of church government adhere to some form of ecclesiastical hierarchy in distinction to the congregational model, which maintains that each local church should be autonomous, or self-governed. Thus, what this question is asking is whether or not Acts 15 provides a biblical example of a hierarchical structure. For those who claim that church tradition is as authoritative as the biblical witness, no such example is needed. But for those who claim that the Bible alone is our authoritative guide for the church, this question takes on extreme relevance. The reason this question specifically mentions Acts 15 and the so-called "Jerusalem Council" is because this event is the most common example (and sometimes the only example) given in support of denominational hierarchy.[1] Another text that is sometimes cited is Matthew 18:15–20, but because this verse clearly teaches that the final step in church discipline is to "tell it to the church" (which does not mean the church as represented by the elders), we will concentrate all our discussion on the Acts passage.

In Acts 15, Luke records that the church in Antioch was facing a serious problem because some men had come down from Judea and were teaching that one had to be circumcised according to the custom of Moses in order

---

1. So Peter Toon, "Episcopalianism," in *Who Runs the Church? 4 Views on Church Government*, ed. Paul E. Engle and Steven B. Cowan (Grand Rapids: Zondervan, 2004), 28; Robert L. Reymond, "The Presbyterian-Led Church: Presbyterian Church Government," in *Perspectives on Church Government: Five Views of Church Polity*, ed. Chad Owen Brand and R. Stanton Norman (Nashville: Broadman and Holman, 2004), 96; L. Roy Taylor, "Presbyterianism," in Engle and Cowan, *Who Runs the Church?* 45, 80. Taylor writes, "Certainly the Acts 15 passage just mentioned provides the prime example in the New Testament of Presbyterian-representative-connectional church government" (ibid., 80).

to be saved (v. 1). This crisis forced the church in Antioch to appeal to the Jerusalem church to call a council meeting so that this issue could be dealt with authoritatively. According to advocates of a hierarchical system, various churches sent representatives to Jerusalem. For example, we read that Paul and Barnabas were "appointed" and sent as representatives of the church in Antioch (v. 2). The council discussed this matter in great detail (vv. 6–7) and heard the testimony of Peter (vv. 7–11), as well as that of Barnabas and Paul (v. 12). After these events transpired, James (who was presumably the head of the Jerusalem church and thus head of the council) made an authoritative decree that Gentiles who turn to God do not need to be circumcised to be saved (v. 19). But the decree did not stop there. James also declared that a letter should be sent to the churches in Antioch, Syria, and Cilicia stating that the Gentiles should "abstain from the things polluted by idols, and from sexual immorality, and from what has been strangled, and from blood" (v. 20). Paul and Barnabas, along with Judas and Silas, were commissioned by the council to deliver the message of this authoritative decree to the various churches in the specified regions (vv. 22–23). When they arrived in Antioch, they proclaimed the decree to the church, which joyfully accepted it (vv. 30–31). Based on the above description of this council meeting, many argue that each church is not an independent body but is part of, and accountable to, a larger ecclesiastical structure. As a result, local churches are bound to accept the decisions of their respective denominational councils.

There are, however, at least three problems with the interpretation of Acts 15 given above. The Jerusalem Council is not a good model for episcopalianism or presbyterianism because (1) it was not representational, (2) it involved unique circumstances, and (3) it included decisions that were not binding.

The Jerusalem Council Was Not Representational

There is no indication that every church sent a representative (or representatives) to Jerusalem.[2] As a matter of fact, we are told of only one church that sent delegates to Jerusalem—the church at Antioch. It is a mischaracterization of Acts 15 to claim that all the churches sent representatives in

---

2. Taylor argues, "The 'whole church' included not just the church of Jerusalem but elders from other churches as well" ("Presbyterianism," 167). This statement, however, has *no* support from the context of Acts 15. Nowhere does it mention that elders from other congregations attended this council. Later Taylor admits, "It is true that there is no reason to believe that elders from the churches of Cyprus and Asia Minor which Paul and Barnabas had established on the first missionary journey attended the council of Jerusalem" (ibid., 235).

a manner similar to ecclesiastical council meetings that occur in our day. Some claim that the churches in Phoenicia and Samaria also sent representatives because Luke mentions that Paul and Barnabas passed through these regions on their way to Jerusalem. But such a position is looking for evidence that cannot be supported. Luke merely informs us that they passed through these areas "describing in detail the conversion of the Gentiles" (Acts 15:3). There is no mention that the churches in Phoenicia and Samaria sent representatives along with Paul and Barnabas to Jerusalem. After the decree was written, it was to be sent, not only to the church in Antioch, but also to the churches in Syria and Cilicia. Again, nowhere do we read that churches from these regions participated in the proceedings. To assume that churches in Syria and Cilicia sent representatives to Jerusalem is begging the question. Furthermore, the decision of the church in Antioch to send Paul and Barnabas to Jerusalem was completely voluntary in nature. They were not summoned by the Jerusalem church. Rather, it was the church in Antioch that initiated the meeting.

The Jerusalem Council Involved Unique Circumstances

A second objection to the argument that Acts 15 supports a hierarchical ecclesiastical structure is based on the uniqueness of the event. In the first place, the topic of discussion could not have been more important. Although the outward expression of the debate involved circumcision, the deeper, more critical question was whether Gentiles had to become Jews before being received as the people of God. The implications of this question were therefore much broader than just circumcision. Not only would the requirement of circumcision have greatly hindered the evangelistic work of Paul and Barnabas among the Gentiles, but it also would have irreconcilably divided the Gentile church from the Jewish church. But, more importantly, for the Jerusalem church to accept the position of the Judaizers would have meant the mother church of the Christian faith had accepted a false gospel (Gal. 1:6–7).

Another unique element was the presence of the apostles. This was no ordinary gathering of church leaders. At this early stage in the life of the church, the apostles were still involved in helping the church find its way under the direct guidance of the Holy Spirit. In Acts 15 the phrase "the apostles and the elders" occurs five times in reference to the council meeting. It is clear that the apostles take a leading role in that they are always mentioned before the elders. Thus, because of the apostles' presence, there are elements of the council meeting that are nonrepeatable (such as the authority the apostles gave to the decree).[3]

Furthermore, this gathering was not the planned annual meeting of a denomination. Rather, it was an emergency session needed to answer the important question of whether Gentiles needed to obey the Law of Moses (esp. circumcision) to be considered among the people of God (i.e., saved). Why was this meeting held in Jerusalem? This crisis was dealt with in Jerusalem, not so much because the Jerusalem church was the center of ecclesiastical power, but because that was where the problem originated. We read in Acts 15:1 that some men came down from "Judea" (i.e., Jerusalem and the surrounding area) and were teaching that Gentile Christians needed to be circumcised. Where were these "Judiazers" teaching such doctrine? According to Acts 15:2 it was in Antioch because that is where Paul and Barnabas were disputing and debating with them. Thus, the council meeting in Jerusalem was prompted by the church in Antioch, who sent Paul, Barnabas, and others to speak with the apostles and elders in Jerusalem about this matter. In essence, then, this was not a gathering of representatives from various churches but one church asking another church for advice and clarification. After all, the Jerusalem church appeared to be the source of the very problem the church in Antioch was seeking to overcome (Acts 15:1, 24; cf. Gal. 2:12).

The Jerusalem Council Included Nonbinding Decisions

A third problem with interpreting Acts 15 as a pattern of church hierarchy is that the decision made by the council (and presented by James) that the Gentiles need to avoid certain foods is best understood, not as a binding decree set by an ecclesiastical authority, but as a plea for sensitivity to the Jewish people.[4] The decision that Gentiles did not need to be circumcised was not

---

3. Writing from a Reformed (Presbyterian) perspective, Berkhof admits that the Acts 15 "council was composed of apostles and elders, and therefore did not constitute a proper example and pattern of a classis or synod in the modern sense of the word" (Louis Berkhof, *Systematic Theology* [Grand Rapids: Eerdmans, 1941], 591). Earlier Berkhof writes, "Scripture does not contain an explicit command to the effect that the local churches of a district must form an organic union. Neither does it furnish us with an example of such a union. In fact, it represents the local churches as individual entities without any external bond of union" (ibid., 590).

4. Robert Stein comments, "The issue at stake, according to Luke, is . . . social intercourse between Jew and Gentiles. The decree does not add a requirement for Gentiles who are seeking salvation. Rather, they are directions given by the Spirit (Acts 15:28) which seek to promote sensitivity on the part of Gentile Christians with respect to issues that were especially offensive to Jews"

open to dispute (Acts 15:19). This question needed to be answered clearly because it involved one's salvation. Were the four prohibitions, however, given as binding law for the churches in Antioch, Syria, and Cilicia? If so, are these "decrees" binding on Christians today? The difficulty of answering these questions has to do with the nature of the second prohibition—abstaining from sexual immorality. Of course, this prohibition was binding. We know this because other texts in the New Testament clearly teach that sexual immorality is a sin (Rom. 13:13; 1 Cor. 6:9, 13, 18; 10:8; 1 Thess. 4:3). The other three prohibitions, however, should be viewed as a plea for sensitivity to the religious scruples of Jewish people because it is clear that Christians are not bound by certain food laws (Acts 10:15; 11:9; Rom. 14:14; 1 Cor. 6:12–13; Col. 2:16–17).[5]

This thesis is supported by the context of the prohibitions in Acts 15. Verse 21 gives us the reason why James included the prohibitions: "For [*gar*] from ancient generations Moses has had in every city those who proclaim him, for he is read every Sabbath in the synagogues." Notice, the reason given is *not* that God's Holy Word requires obedience to these Old Testament food laws. Rather, the reason given is that there are Jewish people (including Jewish Christians) in cities all over the world who still feel bound to the Law of Moses. After all, the two elements of Gentile lifestyle that greatly offended the Jewish population were their sexual immorality and their diet. What James, and the council, is saying is that while Gentiles do not need to be circumcised to be saved, it would be extremely helpful for relations between Jews and Gentiles if the Gentiles would live sexually moral lives and be sensitive to the Jewish food laws. "The four requirements suggested by James

---

("Jerusalem," in *Dictionary of Paul and His Letters*, ed. Gerald F. Hawthorne, Ralph P. Martin, and Daniel G. Reid [Downers Grove, IL: InterVarsity Press, 1993], 471). Reymond states, "James requested only that Gentiles be instructed, not for their salvation's sake but for the sake of the church's peace and harmony between them and their Jewish Christian brothers, that they should abstain from 'food polluted by idols, from sexual immorality, from the meat of strangled animals [which would have been a specific example of "blood"] and from blood' (15:13–21), which could be interpreted as saying in effect no more than the Gentiles should not remain content with the pagan standards of life to which they were accustomed but which more than likely intended that Gentile Christians should indeed avoid eating practices in the presence of Jewish Christians that might offend them" ("Presbyterian-Led Church," 101). John B. Polhill notes, "Gentile sexual mores were lax compared to Jewish standards, and it was one of the areas where Jews saw themselves most radically differentiated from Gentiles" (*Acts*, NAC [Nashville: Broadman and Holman, 1992], 26:331).

5. It is also possible that the prohibition to abstain from sexual immorality was related to ritual laws (see Polhill, *Acts*, 331).

were thus all basically ritual requirements aimed at making fellowship possible between Jewish and Gentile Christians."[6] F. F. Bruce accurately summarizes: "Therefore without compromising the Gentiles' Christian liberty, James gave it as his considered opinion that they should be asked to respect their Jewish brethren's scruples by avoiding meat which had idolatrous associations or from which the blood had not been properly drained, and by conforming to the high Jewish code of relations between the sexes instead of remaining content with the lower pagan standards to which they had been accustomed."[7]

It is also misleading to view James as the bishop (in the modern sense of the term) of the church(es) in Jerusalem.[8] He was among the elders of the congregation and, as such, a leader in the Jerusalem church. He also was probably considered an apostle (Acts 15:13–21; 1 Cor. 15:7–9; Gal. 1:19; 2:9; James 1:1). But notice that James does not simply hand down a decree on his own authority. He acted in concert with the elders and the rest of the congregation.

Summary

Although it is often cited as *the* basis for a hierarchical form of church government, the so-called "Jerusalem Council" in Acts 15 does not provide a compelling foundation for building a hierarchical structure among local congregations. Unlike certain denominational meetings today, representatives were not sent from every church. Apparently the only church that sent delegates was the church at Antioch. Furthermore, the council of Acts 15 was formed because of unique circumstances. This event was not an ordinary, planned gathering of churches but was an emergency meeting needed to address a specific, historical crisis. It was also unique because the apostles were involved in the meeting. Finally, the decision made by the council that the Gentiles needed to avoid certain foods is best understood, not as a binding decree set by an ecclesiastical authority, but as a plea for sensitivity to the Jewish people.

---

6. Ibid. Polhill rightly notes the question before the council: "If Gentiles were not being required to observe the Jewish ritual laws, how would Jewish Christians who maintained strict Torah observance be able to fellowship with them without running the risk of being ritually defiled themselves?" (ibid., 330).

7. F. F. Bruce, *Commentary on the Book of Acts* (Grand Rapids: Eerdmans, 1980), 311.

8. D. A. Carson maintains, "The position of James in Acts 15 is peculiar, but the evidence is being stretched when interpreters conclude that James chaired the proceedings" ("Church, Authority in the," in *EDT*, ed. Walter E. Elwell [Grand Rapids: Baker, 1984], 229).

Reflection Questions

1. What were the circumstances that made the Jerusalem Council necessary (Acts 15)?
2. Who attended this meeting?
3. Why was the meeting held in Jerusalem?
4. Do you think the council's decision recorded in Acts 15:20 is binding on all Christians today (cf. 15:21)?
5. Is it appropriate to use this meeting as a justification for a denominational hierarchy?

What New Testament Evidence Is There in Support of Congregationalism?

B y "congregationalism" we are referring to the idea that a local assembly of believers should govern themselves (under the lordship of Christ) and that the church is therefore not hierarchical in nature. This question addresses the authority of the local church. For example, should each congregation be able to act independently of any denominational constraints, or should it be subject to the decisions made by the hierarchical structure of a denomination? Should a church be able to call its own pastor, determine its own budget, and purchase its own property independently of any outside authority? Or is it closer to the biblical model to limit the freedom of each congregation and subject it to a higher authority in a denominational structure? In the following discussion, we will offer several reasons why congregationalism is closest to the New Testament model of church government.

Congregations Choose Their Leaders

The book of Acts provides a compelling, although perhaps not conclusive, basis for affirming congregationalism or the autonomy of the local church. The first piece of evidence is found in the account of Judas's successor as the twelfth apostle. The apostles, along with many other "brothers" (about 120 persons in all), were gathered in Jerusalem awaiting the coming of the Spirit. Peter stood up and declared that a replacement for Judas was in order, alluding to David and quoting the book of Psalms. After the qualifications were given by Peter, we read that "they put forward two, Joseph . . . and Matthias" (Acts 1:23). It is worth noting that Peter, who some claim to be the chief apostle and the first "pope," did not himself choose the replacement of Judas.

Rather, "they" (i.e., the assembly of 120) put forth two candidates (v. 23) and "they prayed" (v. 24) and let God choose through the casting of lots. All of those who were present played a role in deciding Judas's successor, and not just the eleven apostles or the apostle Peter himself.

A second example from the book of Acts is found in chapter 6 with the choosing of seven men to serve in a diaconal-type role in the church. Because the Hellenistic (i.e., Greek-speaking Jewish) widows were being neglected, a complaint was made that reached the ears of the twelve apostles (v. 1). Upon hearing this news, "the twelve summoned the full number of the disciples and said, 'It is not right that we should give up preaching the word of God to serve tables. Therefore, brothers, pick out from among you seven men of good repute, full of the Spirit and of wisdom, whom we will appoint to this duty'" (vv. 2–3). Again, notice that the Twelve did not simply choose seven men but brought the need before the entire congregation ("the full number of the disciples," v. 2) and let them choose seven men whom they believed met the given qualifications. In this particular case, the congregation chose the men, but the apostles "appointed" them to their office (vv. 3, 6). This pattern is important because we later read in Acts 14:23 that Paul and Barnabas "appointed elders" in the churches of southern Galatia (Antioch, Iconium, Lystra, and Derbe). The assumption is sometimes made that Paul and Barnabas chose the leaders from among the congregation and then appointed them to their new leadership positions. But based on the pattern found in Acts 6, it is also possible that the respective congregations chose men from among themselves and then Paul and Barnabas "appointed" them as elders publicly.[1] Thus, the pattern in the early church was that the congregation (or a body larger than the apostles) chose the leaders, but the apostles officially recognized and publicly appointed them to their leadership positions.

The important role of the congregation is also found in the sending forth of Paul and Barnabas as missionaries. In Acts 13 the Holy Spirit commanded the church in Antioch to set apart Barnabas and Saul for missionary work. Verse 3 says, "Then after fasting and praying they laid their hands on them and sent them off." In this context we are not told precisely to whom this

---

1. This interpretation is also favored by Erickson (Millard J. Erickson, *Christian Theology*, 2nd ed. [Grand Rapids: Baker, 1998], 1092). John B. Polhill mentions that the NIV footnote indicates "that the congregation may have elected the elders, with Paul and Barnabas confirming this by laying their hands on them" (*Acts*, NAC [Nashville: Broadman and Holman, 1992], 319n. 74).

command was given and who laid hands on Barnabas and Saul. It is possible that "they" refers only to those mentioned in verse 1 (i.e., Barnabas, Simeon, Lucius, Manaen, and Saul). But since Barnabas and Saul would not be the ones commissioning themselves, that leaves only three other people (Simeon, Lucius, and Manaen). Some suggest this passage indicates that the leaders of the various churches in Antioch had "formed themselves into a local presbytery."[2] This interpretation is not convincing for at least two reasons. First, verse 1 not only mentions the five people noted above but also mentions that they were part of "the church at Antioch." Second, the Holy Spirit spoke to them "while they were worshiping the Lord and fasting" (v. 2). The reference to them worshiping indicates that this was not just a handful of people but the whole congregation.[3] Consequently, it is better to interpret "they" in verse 3 ("they laid their hands on them and sent them off") as referring to the entire congregation, not just the three other prophet-teachers.

This interpretation finds support in the subsequent relationship that Paul and Barnabas had with the church in Antioch. In Acts 14:27, for example, we are told that after their first missionary journey, Paul and Barnabas returned to Antioch to give a report of their missionary activities. The writer, Luke, indicates that they did not share only with the leaders of the church, but they "gathered the church together" so that all could hear and rejoice in the work that God had done through His servants.[4] Similarly, when the need arose to send Paul and Barnabas to Jerusalem to inquire about the problem of the Judaizers, Luke informs us that they were "sent on their way by the church" (Acts 15:3). The involvement of the entire congregation is also found later in Acts 15. After James stated his position rejecting the need for Gentiles to be circumcised in order to be saved, "it seemed good to the apostles and the elders, *with the whole church*, to choose men from among them and send them to Antioch with Paul and Barnabas" (v. 22, emphasis added). Apparently, the council meeting did not take place behind closed doors but was attended by the "whole church," who, along with the apostles and elders, also affirmed the position of James. The pattern in Acts is that the entire congregation, not

---

2. Robert L. Reymond, "The Presbyterian-Led Church: Presbyterian Church Government," in *Perspectives on Church Government: Five Views of Church Polity*, ed. Chad Owen Brand and R. Stanton Norman (Nashville: Broadman and Holman, 2004), 96.

3. So Polhill, *Acts*, 290.

4. Reymond is reading into the text his presbyterianism when he states, "Much more likely the leaders of the many house churches came together to hear their missionaries' report" ("Presbyterian-Led Church," 81).

just the leaders, was involved in important decisions, and its consent was vital to the unity and mission of the wider Christian community (also see 2 Cor. 8:19, where a delegate was appointed by the churches to travel with Paul).

Congregations Exercise Discipline

More evidence for the autonomy of the local church is garnered from the key role the congregation is given in the process of church discipline. In Matthew 18 Jesus gives us the proper steps for dealing with a believer who sins. The first step is to approach that person alone and "tell him his fault" (v. 15). If he refuses to listen, the second step is to "take one or two others along with you" in order to have other credible witnesses (v. 16). If he still refuses to listen, the final step is to "tell it to the church" (v. 17). If he refuses to listen to the church, he is to be treated as a Gentile and a tax collector (i.e., as an unbeliever). Mark Dever is correct when he writes, "Notice to whom one finally appeals in such situations. What court has the final word? It is not a bishop, a pope, or a presbytery; it is not an assembly, a synod, a convention, or a conference. It is not even a pastor or a board of elders, a board of deacons or a church committee. It is, quite simply, the church—that is, the assembly of those individual believers who are the church."[5] Because the final step in the church disciplining process is given to the church, this indicates that the local congregation is to deal with its own problems and does not need a higher ecclesiastical body making decisions for it. As believers who are filled with the Holy Spirit and gifted according to God's wisdom, they are capable of following God's Word and God's will.

This same pattern is also found in the writings of the apostle Paul. Concerning the unrepentant man who was sleeping with his father's wife (i.e., his stepmother), Paul rebukes the Corinthians' toleration of this sin and states, "Let him who has done this be removed from among you" (1 Cor. 5:2). This command to expel, or excommunicate, this professing believer is given to the entire congregation and not just to the leaders of the church. This analysis is confirmed in the introduction of the letter, where Paul addresses the church as a whole (1 Cor. 1:2, "to the church of God that is in Corinth"). Furthermore, Paul specifically mentions that church discipline is to be done "when you are assembled in the name of the Lord Jesus" (1 Cor. 5:4), which

---

5. Mark Dever, *Nine Marks of a Healthy Church*, expanded ed. (Wheaton, IL: Crossway, 2004), 221.

indicates that the whole congregation is present. More support is found in 2 Corinthians, where Paul mentions a brother who caused him much pain and was subsequently punished "by the majority" (i.e., by the congregation, 2 Cor. 2:6). It was not Paul who disciplined this person, or even the elders or the pastor. Rather, he was punished by the congregation as a whole.[6]

Congregations Receive Apostolic Letters

Paul's pattern of addressing his letters to entire congregations is further evidence that churches should be self-governed. As we have seen already in 1 Corinthians, Paul always addressed his letters to churches to the entire congregation rather than to the leaders of the church (Rom. 1:7; 1 Cor. 1:2; 2 Cor. 1:1; Gal. 1:2; Eph. 1:1; Phil. 1:1; Col. 1:2; 1 Thess. 1:1; 2 Thess. 1:1).[7] Schreiner rightly concludes, "The congregation as a whole is addressed because the congregation ultimately determines the direction of the church."[8] Paul wrote four letters to individuals (1–2 Timothy, Titus, Philemon), but three of these, the Pastoral Epistles (1–2 Timothy, Titus), were written for public dissemination even though they are addressed to individuals.[9] This conclusion is confirmed by the closing benediction in each of these letters, where Paul writes, "Grace be with you" (1 Tim. 6:21; 2 Tim. 4:22) and "Grace be with you all" (Titus 3:15). In each case the "you" is not singular (i.e., Timothy or Titus) but plural (i.e., the congregation in Ephesus or Crete). It

---

6. Paul Barnett notes, "Possibly Paul's use of a vocabulary of 'majority' implies a deliberative session of the Corinthian assembly, with some voting mechanism" (*The Second Epistle to the Corinthians*, The International Commentary on the New Testament [Grand Rapids: Eerdmans, 1997], 125n. 18). David Garland writes, "Paul's concern about the punishment of the offender presents the picture that the church members presided as judges over the person involved and pronounced a sentence" (*2 Corinthians*, NAC [Nashville: Broadman and Holman, 1999], 29:125). Charles Hodge states that church discipline "is . . . clearly recognized as belonging to the church. It is also clear . . . that this right belongs to each particular church or congregation. The power was vested in the church of Corinth, and not some officer presiding over that church. The bishop as pastor was not reproved for neglect of discipline; but the church itself, in its organized capacity" (*An Exposition of the First Epistle to the Corinthians* [Grand Rapids: Eerdmans, 1956], 83).

7. The one deviation that Paul makes from this pattern is in Philippians, where he not only addresses "all the saints in Christ Jesus" but also mentions "the overseers and deacons" (Phil. 1:1).

8. Thomas R. Schreiner, *Paul, Apostle of God's Glory in Christ* (Downers Grove, IL: InterVarsity Press, 2001), 385. He later adds, "If the Pauline letters were addressed only to leaders, we might conclude that leaders were to enforce their will on congregations" (ibid.).

9. William D. Mounce writes of Titus: "While written in the form of a personal letter addressed to an individual, the content of this letter is for public dissemination" (*Pastoral Epistles*, WBC [Nashville: Nelson, 2000], 46:392).

is also significant that the last book of the Bible, Revelation, is addressed "to the seven churches that are in Asia" (Rev. 1:4).

Congregations Are Full of Priests

The doctrine of the priesthood of all believers likewise contributes to the notion that the local church should be self-governed. According to the New Testament, all believers have direct access to God and, as priests, serve one another (1 Peter 2:5, 9; Rev. 1:6; 5:10; 20:6). As such, the burden of responsibility does not fall only on the leaders of the church but on the church as a whole. For example, in 1 Corinthians 11 Paul rebukes the entire congregation for its abuse of the Lord's Supper (11:17–34). Galatians 1:8–9 places the responsibility of protecting the purity of the gospel in the hands of the local congregations. In 1 Thessalonians, each believer is called upon to "test everything" (5:21; cf. 1 John 4:1, which challenges each believer to "test the spirits to see whether they are from God"). According to 1 John, each believer is anointed by the Holy Spirit and is able to understand all truth (2:27). In addition, congregations are told to admonish or instruct one another (Rom. 15:14; 1 Thess. 5:14). Finally, Jude encourages all believers to "contend for the faith that was once for all delivered to the saints" (v. 3). Notice that the "faith" was delivered not merely to the leaders of the church (pastors/elders/overseers or deacons) but to all the "saints" (i.e., those who are called, beloved, and preserved, v. 1).

Congregations Are to Be Governed by Servants

Finally, the idea of a hierarchical ecclesiastical system seems to run contrary to Jesus' statements about leadership. In Luke 22:25–27 Jesus says,

> The kings of the Gentiles exercise lordship over them, and those in authority over them are called benefactors. But not so with you. Rather, let the greatest among you become as the youngest, and the leader as one who serves. For who is the greater, one who reclines at table or one who serves? Is it not the one who reclines at table? But I am among you as the one who serves.

The disciples were arguing about who would be the greatest. They were thinking in terms of rank and position. Jesus rebukes them because they were thinking according to the philosophy of the world and not according to the principles of the kingdom. They wanted a title, but Jesus tells them that true leaders are not those with more authority but those who humbly serve.

Summary

Based on the considerations above, the New Testament seems to favor a self-governing model for the church. In the early church, many important decisions—such as selecting leaders (Acts 1:23; 6:2–3), sending missionaries (Acts 13:3; 14:26–27), affirming theological positions (Acts 15:22), carrying out church discipline (Matt. 18:17), and performing excommunication (1 Cor. 5:2)—were the responsibilities of the local congregation. Additional support is found in the fact that Paul's letters to churches were addressed to entire congregations and not just to officeholders in the church. Finally, the priesthood of all believers and the teaching of Jesus also lend evidence in favor of congregationalism.

The principle of the autonomy of the local church does not, however, rule out cooperation of local churches in ministry for a common purpose. Indeed, such cooperation among congregations is found in the New Testament. Perhaps the clearest example is Paul's effort to raise money among the Gentile churches for the famine victims in the Jerusalem church (see esp. 2 Cor. 8:1–15). Independent churches today often pool their resources in order to support missions, train church leaders, and perform community projects. Such cooperation is important because it displays the truth that each congregation is not an isolated, self-absorbed entity but is part of the larger body of Christ. Such cooperation should be viewed not merely as a practical strategy but as a theological necessity. Churches need to demonstrate to themselves and to the world that they are part of a larger organism (not merely an organization). It is simply a poor testimony to the world when local congregations have no fellowship with other congregations. Yet, such cooperation should be voluntary and the organizational structure needed to funnel such resources should not have authority over the internal affairs of the local church.

Reflection Questions

1. How do Acts 1:23; 6:3; and 13:3 support congregationalism?
2. How do Matthew 18:15–17; 1 Corinthians 5:2; and 2 Corinthians 2:6 support congregationalism?

3. Paul's letters to churches were always addressed to the entire congregation rather than the leaders. Does this fact support congregationalism?
4. Why did Paul address some of his letters to individuals (like Timothy and Titus)?
5. Does the doctrine of the priesthood of all believers support congregationalism? Why or why not?

Are the Offices of Apostle, Prophet, Evangelist, and Priest for Today?

The answer to this question will determine much of how one believes a local church should be organized. Because various denominations have different answers to this question, let us proceed by answering the question one office at a time.

Is There an Office of Apostle?

Usually when we think of apostles, we think of Jesus' twelve disciples who became known as the twelve "apostles." In the New Testament, however, the Greek term for "apostle" (*apostolos*) has both a technical and a nontechnical or general usage. In its technical usage it refers specifically to those who were chosen and commissioned by Jesus. The nontechnical usage refers more generally to a "messenger" or an "accredited representative." For example, in the Greek of Philippians 2:25, Epaphroditus is called an apostle (or messenger) because he was sent by the church at Philippi to minister to Paul on its behalf. A second example of the nontechnical usage is found in the Greek of 2 Corinthians 8:23, where those traveling with Titus are likewise called "apostles [i.e., messengers] of the churches." When considering whether or not the office of apostle is still in operation today, however, the type of apostle in question relates to the technical meaning.

According to the New Testament, there were specific qualifications that were needed in order for one to qualify as an apostle in the technical sense. First, one needed to be an eyewitness of Jesus' resurrection. When the apostles determined that Judas needed to be replaced, Peter mentioned that the one who was chosen must be "a witness to his [i.e., Jesus] resurrection" (Acts 1:22; also see Acts 1:2–3; 4:33). When Paul was forced by the Corinthians to speak of his rights (which he reluctantly did), he stated, "Am I not free?

Am I not an apostle? Have I not seen Jesus our Lord?" (1 Cor. 9:1; also see 15:7–9).

Second, in order to be an apostle, one needed to be specially commissioned by Jesus. Jesus called the twelve disciples to follow Him and later commissioned them to go preach the gospel to the world. Paul was also called and commissioned by Jesus but not during Jesus' earthly ministry. On his way to persecute the church in Damascus, Paul was given a special post-resurrection and postascension call and commission from Jesus (Acts 9:5–6, 15–16; 26:15–18; cf. Gal. 1:1). Recognizing that his apostleship was somewhat unique, Paul writes, "Last of all, as to one untimely born, he [i.e., Jesus] appeared also to me. For I am the least of the apostles, unworthy to be called an apostle, because I persecuted the church of God" (1 Cor. 15:8–9). In most of his letters, Paul makes it clear that he did not choose to be an apostle and consequently did not give himself the title, but he was called and set apart by the will of God.[1]

It is also evident that some of Paul's coworkers were given the title "apostle." For example, Barnabas is called an apostle in Acts 14:14 (cf. Acts 14:4). Although not directly named as an apostle, Apollos is possibly included in Paul's reference to "us apostles" in 1 Corinthians 4:9 (cf. 1 Cor. 4:6), and Silas may be included in Paul's reference to "apostles of Christ" in 1 Thessalonians 2:6 (cf. 1 Thess. 1:1). It is debated as to whether Andronicus and Junia were well-known "among the apostles" or well-known "by the apostles" (Rom. 16:7). The latter interpretation, which does not recognize them as apostles, is to be preferred.[2] There is also the possibility that James the brother of Jesus was considered an apostle (Acts 15:13–21; 1 Cor. 15:7–9; Gal. 1:19; 2:9; James 1:1).

Are there still apostles like the Twelve and Paul today? Theologically and historically this question must be answered negatively. There are not people today who have witnessed the physical resurrection of Jesus and have been personally commissioned by Him to be apostles. But some might respond, "Doesn't the New Testament indicate that the office of apostle was given to the church?" There are two important texts that are used to support the notion that the office of apostle is still valid for today. In 1 Corinthians 12:28,

---

1. Rom. 1:1; 1 Cor. 1:1; 15:7–9; 2 Cor. 1:1; Gal. 1:1, 12, 15–16; Eph. 1:1; Col. 1:1; 1 Tim. 1:1; 2:7; 2 Tim. 1:1, 11.
2. See Daniel B. Wallace and Michael H. Burer, "Was Junia Really an Apostle?" *NTS* 47 (2001): 76–91 (the same article also appeared in the *Journal for Biblical Manhood and Womanhood* 6.2 [2001]: 4–11).

Paul states, "God has appointed in the church first apostles, second prophets, third teachers." The other text is Ephesians 4:11, which reads, "And he [i.e., Jesus] gave the apostles, the prophets, the evangelists, the pastors and teachers." Based on these two verses, many claim that it is wrong to say there is no office of apostle (or prophet) since Paul specifically teaches that there is. Such a conclusion, however, fails to grasp the purpose of the apostolic ministry and flattens out the progressive nature of God's plan in redemptive history. For example, Paul plainly tells us the apostles (and prophets) were given to the church as a foundational office. He explains that the household of God is "built on the foundation of the apostles and prophets, Christ Jesus himself being the cornerstone" (Eph. 2:20). By definition, foundations are not repeatedly laid down but are used to give the initial footing that a building needs to stand secure. Thus, the apostles' foundational work is found in the first preaching of the gospel and in their writing of the Scriptures. Judas was replaced by another apostle because the early church believed there was significance in Jesus choosing *twelve* apostles. But there is no indication in the New Testament that when the Twelve began to die off (or were martyred), they were replaced by others. As noted above, Paul felt awkward calling himself an apostle because the apostles were already set. That is why he refers to himself as "one untimely born" (1 Cor. 15:8). He also mentions that Jesus appeared to him "last of all" (1 Cor. 15:8), suggesting that no more appearances are to be expected.

It seems clear from Scripture that the office of apostle was a foundational office and is therefore not meant for the church today. Some, however, claim that God has restored the office of apostle to the modern church (most likely sometime in the 1990s). As a result, in many (usually charismatic) churches there are people who refer to themselves as "apostles." While they do not usually claim to have the same authority as the Twelve or Paul, they are using the term in the technical sense. When others hear the term "apostle," they also tend to associate the term with the technical usage of the New Testament. In my opinion, the attempt to restore the apostolic office is based on a misunderstanding and misuse of Scripture. There is no indication in Scripture that God would restore this office in the twentieth century.

Others, often in missiological circles, use the term *apostle* to refer to a church planter. They reason that because Paul's main duty as an apostle was to plant churches (Rom. 15:20), anyone who is doing this same work can rightly be called an apostle. There are a number of problems with such usage, however. First, what made Paul an apostle (in the technical sense) was not that he was a church planter, but that he was uniquely called and commissioned by Jesus. There is no clear indication that the Twelve were engaged in church planting, but that did not make any one of them any less of an apostle than Paul. Paul was definitely involved in planting churches; not because he was an apostle, but because he was an apostle to the Gentiles. Second, although the nontechnical usage of *apostle* can refer to one who is sent out, the one being sent out was not necessarily sent out as a missionary or as a church planter. As was already mentioned, Epaphroditus was sent out by the Philippian church to help Paul while he was under house arrest in Rome (Phil. 2:25). Consequently, it is misleading to use the term *apostle* to refer to a church planter or even a missionary.[3]

Nevertheless, even if this office were still functioning today, it would not be considered a "church" office. The apostles were not bound to one church but filled a supracongregational role. That is, their authority to teach and to discipline was not limited to one congregation but applied to all the churches.[4]

Is There an Office of Prophet?

In the Old Testament the prophets functioned mainly as God's spokesmen. Although they sometimes predicted the future, by far the majority of their prophetic words involved calling the people of Israel to repent and wholeheartedly embrace God (and God alone) for their salvation. During the intertestamental period there was silence from God, and no prophets were given to speak God's message to the people. With John the Baptist, however, the silence was broken as John called the people of Israel to repent and be baptized.

Prophets are rarely mentioned in the life of the early church. Most of the

---

3. Wayne Grudem comments, "Though some may use the word *apostle* in English today to refer to very effective church planters or evangelists, it seems inappropriate and unhelpful to do so, for it simply confuses people who read the New Testament and see the high authority that is attributed to the office of 'apostle' there." He continues, "If any in modern times want to take the title 'apostle' to themselves, they immediately raise the suspicion that they may be motivated by inappropriate pride and desires for self-exaltation, along with excessive ambition and a desire for much more authority in the church than any one person should rightfully have" (*Systematic Theology: An Introduction to Biblical Doctrine* [Leicester: InterVarsity Press; Grand Rapids: Eerdmans, 1994], 911).

4. For example, see 1 Cor. 5:9–13; 7:25–28; 2 Cor. 2:1–11; Gal. 5:2–3; Phil. 3:1–21; 4:2. D. A. Carson writes, "Their [i.e., the apostles'] authority extended beyond the local congregation, even beyond congregations they had been instrumental in founding" ("Church, Authority in the," *EDT*, ed. Walter E. Elwell [Grand Rapids: Baker, 1984], 228).

references are found in the book of Acts. For example, Acts 11 mentions that prophets from Jerusalem came to the church at Antioch. One of these prophets, named Agabus, "stood up and foretold by the Spirit that there would be a great famine over all the world" (11:28). Later in Acts, we are told the names of some of the "prophets and teachers" who were in the church at Antioch: "Barnabas, Simeon who was called Niger, Lucius of Cyrene, Manaen a member of the court of Herod the tetrarch, and Saul" (13:1). After the decision of the Jerusalem Council was written, it was delivered to Antioch, Syria, and Cilicia by Paul and Barnabas, along with two prophets, Judas and Silas (15:22–23). Luke records that in Antioch, "Judas and Silas, who were themselves prophets, encouraged and strengthened the brothers with many words" (15:32). Finally, in Acts 21 we meet the prophet Agabus again. While Paul was in Caesarea, Agabus came down from Judea and prophesied what would happen to Paul. After taking Paul's belt and binding his own hands and feet, he said, "Thus says the Holy Spirit, 'This is how the Jews at Jerusalem will bind the man who owns this belt and deliver him into the hands of the Gentiles'" (21:11).

We also know that the church at Corinth had prophets. While instructing the church concerning proper order in the worship service, Paul says, "Let two or three prophets speak, and let the others weigh what is said" (1 Cor. 14:29). According to Paul, it is clear that God gave prophets to the church. Again, in 1 Corinthians 12:28 he states, "And God has appointed in the church first apostles, second prophets, third teachers." In Ephesians 4:11 he writes, "And he [Jesus] gave the apostles, the prophets, the evangelists, the pastors and teachers."

It is one thing, however, to claim that the early church had prophets and another thing to maintain that the *office* of prophet is still functioning today (the *gift* of prophecy is another question). As noted above, the primary function of the prophet was to proclaim God's Word to His people. Before the New Testament was completed, this was essential for the life of the early church. After the New Testament was written, however, the need for such immediate revelation from God diminished (cf. Heb. 1:1–2). This position is confirmed by Ephesians 2:20, which indicates that the church was built on the foundation of the apostles and prophets. It is also worth noting that Paul mentions the office of prophet only in his early writings (i.e., 1 Corinthians and Ephesians), whereas his later writings are completely silent, possibly indicating that the office was already fading out in Paul's day.

Is There an Office of Evangelist?

The term "evangelist" is a derivative of the Greek verb *euangelizō*, meaning "to announce good news," and is used only three times in the New Testament. The first reference is to Philip, who was one of the seven chosen in Acts 6. He is called "Philip the evangelist" later, when Paul visited Caesarea and stayed with him (Acts 21:8). The second reference is found in Ephesians 4:11, where "evangelists" is listed after apostles and prophets. Finally, Paul encourages Timothy to "do the work of an evangelist" (2 Tim. 4:5). Although not much is known about them, evangelists often accompanied the apostles or were sent on special tasks. As the name itself indicates, their primary task was sharing the gospel with others. Because this office is not referred to as a foundational office (like "apostles" and "prophets" in Eph. 2:20), and because this office was not linked with the giving of special revelation, many assume that this office is still valid for today.[5] Yet, this office is not a church office in the sense that those who function in this role do not minister so much in the church but outside the church as they evangelize the lost.[6] Or, it could be, as Knight argues, that the evangelist should be regarded as a specialized manifestation of the office of elder.[7] The function of the evangelist can be distinguished from that of the pastor-teacher (Eph. 4:11), but being an evangelist is also a mark of those who, like Timothy, are called to preach the Word (2 Tim. 4:1–5).

Is There an Office of Priest?

In the Old Testament the priests were responsible for the temple and the temple sacrifices. The priests stood between God and the people as

---

5. Some theologians, such as John Calvin and Louis Berkhof, argue that the office of evangelist was an extraordinary and thus temporary office.
6. F. F. Bruce, *The Epistles to the Colossians, to Philemon, and to the Ephesians*, NICNT (Grand Rapids: Eerdmans, 1984), 347. Bruce notes that the evangelists likely would have continued the gospel-preaching aspect of the apostolic ministry so that the church would continue to grow in succeeding generations after the apostles were no longer alive.
7. George W. Knight, "Two Offices (Elders/Bishops and Deacons) and Two Orders of Elders (Preaching/Teaching Elders and Ruling Elders): A New Testament Study," *Presbyterion* 11 (1985): 9. Knight offers a possible reason why the term "evangelist" was separated from that of pastors and teachers in Eph. 4:11. He writes, "Because the activity of evangelists, as important as it is to the work of the church and the eldership, is not so intrinsically a part of the work of the eldership in reference to its role as pastors of the flock that it should be given as an aspect of pastoring as teaching was. . . . Evangelists are gaining lost sheep, not caring for saved and gathered ones. So the apostle has placed that aspect of the teaching eldership, evangelists, in a separate category and recognizes that some have special gifts for that task" (ibid., 11).

mediators. Because the people were sinful and God was holy, someone had to offer sacrifices so that God's righteousness would be upheld and His wrath diverted. We also know that the priests had to come from the tribe of Levi and the high priest had to come from the lineage of Zadok (Ezek. 43:19; 44:15; 48:11). Thus, the priesthood was limited to a select group of people whose duty it was to bring peace between God and His people.

In the New Testament, however, there is a noticeable shift. According to Peter, all of God's people are the stones that make up a spiritual house, and as such they make up "a holy priesthood" that is able "to offer spiritual sacrifices acceptable to God through Jesus Christ" (1 Peter 2:5). A few verses later, Peter adds that Christians are a "royal priesthood" (v. 9). Furthermore, John states that Jesus has "made us a kingdom, priests to his God and Father" (Rev. 1:6; also see Rev. 5:10; 20:6). These verses teach us that all believers are priests to God, having direct access to God through faith in Jesus Christ (Heb. 10:19–20). There is only "one mediator between God and men, the man Jesus Christ" (1 Tim. 2:5). Because of the sacrifice of Jesus Christ, we no longer need to go to someone else to offer sacrifices on our behalf. Jesus Christ was the perfect sacrifice who paid the penalty for our sins. As a result, all believers are priests of God with direct access to the Father through the work of the Son.

Consequently, it would be misleading and confusing to call a worker in the church a "priest."[8] Nowhere in the New Testament is a Christian leader given such a title. In the context of the early church, the only person given such a title is Jesus, who is often called our High Priest in the book of Hebrews. Thus, because believers all are classified as priests of God and because no church leader is ever called a priest, it is unfitting to give a leader in the church such a title.

---

8. Paige Patterson comments, "In simplest of terms, if every believer is a priest, the necessity of an official priesthood is negated" ("Single-Elder Congregationalism," in *Who Runs the Church? 4 Views on Church Government*, ed. Paul E. Engle and Steven B. Cowan [Grand Rapids: Zondervan, 2004], 141). Paul F. M. Zahl, himself an Anglican, admits that the usage of the term "priest" for ordained ministers is unfortunate. He notes that it was not until the term became incorporated in the 1979 version of the Book of Common Prayer that it became used almost universally. He comments, "It is the unscriptural importation of a superannuated *Old Covenant* idea into Christian church-speak. It does violence to the identity of Christian ministers as followers in the train of the one High Priest" ("The Bishop-Led Church: The Episcopal or Anglican Polity Affirmed, Weighed, and Defended," in *Perspectives on Church Government: Five Views of Church Polity*, ed. Chad Owen Brand and R. Stanton Norman [Nashville: Broadman and Holman, 2004], 227–28).

Summary

Although there is some debate over the offices of apostle and prophet, most scholars agree that these offices were foundational offices and are no longer given. While certain "apostolic" or "prophetic" gifts might still be functioning, the corresponding offices ended in the first century. The office of evangelist is still accepted by many churches and usually relates to the proclamation of the gospel to unbelievers. As such, it is not usually considered a *church* office since those who hold this office minister outside the church. Finally, it is inappropriate to use the title "priest" as a designation for an officeholder because all God's people are priests. Furthermore, this title is never used of Christian leaders in the New Testament and is best reserved for Jesus, who is our "High Priest."

Reflection Questions

1. What are some of the reasons you have heard for maintaining that there are still apostles (in the technical sense) today? Are these reasons legitimate?
2. Does Ephesians 2:20 imply that the (technical) office of apostle is not meant for today?
3. Is there any scriptural evidence that God would restore the offices of apostle and prophet in the twentieth century?
4. What do Acts 21:8; Ephesians 4:11; and 2 Timothy 4:5 teach us about the office of evangelist?
5. Why is it inappropriate for a Christian leader to be called a priest?

How Many Church Offices Are There Today?

This question is difficult to answer due to the diverse nature of the New Testament data. For example, sometimes leaders are mentioned but are given no title. This phenomenon seems to be especially true during the earliest period of the church, which possibly suggests that at first formal offices were not fully developed. In Galatians 6:6, Paul states, "One who is taught the word must share all good things with the one who teaches." In other words, it is the responsibility of those receiving instruction to provide for the physical sustenance of their teachers. This verse suggests that there was a class of instructors or catechizers who taught the Word to such an extent that they needed to be financially supported for their work. But if such people held a particular office, we are not told. In 1 Thessalonians 5:12–13, Paul exhorts the congregation: "We ask you, brothers, to respect those who labor among you and are over you in the Lord and admonish you, and to esteem them very highly in love because of their work." Here, Paul makes a distinction between the "brothers" and those they are to "respect" because of the work they do in teaching the congregation. No formal title is used, but it is clear that some were given positions of leadership in the church. The author of Hebrews likewise makes a distinction between the leaders and those who should obey them: "Obey your leaders and submit to them, for they are keeping watch over your souls, as those who will have to give an account" (Heb. 13:17; cf. 13:7). If a leader must give an account, he needs to know not only that he is a leader (which implies some formal position recognized by the church) but also who he is accountable to lead (which implies a distinction between the leaders and the followers). Although we do not know what particular "office" these leaders may have held, we do know that the author has in mind a distinct group of individuals.

There Are Two Church Offices: Elder/Overseer and Deacon

By the time the Pastoral Epistles (1–2 Timothy; Titus) were written, how-ever, it appears that there were two established offices in the church—overseers (or bishops) and deacons. In fact, overseers and deacons are also mentioned in Paul's earlier letter to the Philippians. In his opening greeting he addresses "all the saints in Christ Jesus who are at Philippi, with the overseers and deacons" (Phil. 1:1). In 1 Timothy 3, Paul gives qualifications for the two offices. In verse 1 he writes, "If anyone aspires to the office of overseer, he desires a noble task." The following verses then give the qualifications for those who would hold such an office. Then in verse 8 Paul shifts to the office of deacon: "Deacons likewise must . . ." Paul's letter to Titus, however, refers only to overseers, mak-ing no mention of deacons (Titus 1:5–9). This omission possibly indicates that the church in Crete was less developed than the church in Ephesus.

It also should be noted that the term "overseer," or "bishop," (*episkopos*) refers to the same office as that held by the person given the title "elder" (*pres-buteros*, e.g., Acts 14:23; 1 Tim. 5:17). These two terms were used to represent the same office (see question 9). Evidence for this conclusion is found in the interchangeable use of the two terms (Acts 20:17, 28; Titus 1:5, 7; 1 Peter 5:1–2). The primary role of the elders/overseers was ruling and preaching/teach-ing (Acts 20:28; 1 Tim. 3:2, 4–5; 5:17; Titus 1:9; 1 Peter 5:2–3), whereas the deacons were involved with other ministries (such as benevolence), which allowed the elders/overseers to focus on their primary calling.

Is There an Office of Pastor?

Although this term is commonly used in our modern church context, the noun "pastor" (or "shepherd") is used only one time in the New Testament in reference to a church leader (although the verb "to shepherd" and the noun "flock" are occasionally found).[1] In Ephesians 4:11, we are told, "He [Jesus] gave the apostles, the prophets, the evangelists, the pastors and teach-ers." "Pastor" is coupled with "teacher" here, and together they denote one order of ministry. In other words, the Greek construction favors interpreting this phrase as one office: the pastor/teacher. There is not one office of pastor and a separate office of teacher.[2]

---

1. The verb "to shepherd" (*poimainō*) occurs in Matt. 2:6; John 21:16; Acts 20:28; 1 Peter 5:2; Jude 12; Rev. 2:27; 7:17; 12:5; 19:15. The noun "flock" (*poimēn*) occurs in Matt. 26:31 and John 10:16. In Luke 12:32; Acts 20:28–29; and 1 Peter 5:2–3, the diminutive form (*poimnion*) is used.
2. In the Greek there is one article governing the two nouns, which indicates one group of people (*tous de poimenas kai didaskalous*, "the pastors and teachers"). Although the Granville Sharp

What then is the relationship between the office of pastor and that of the elder/overseer? Does the term "pastor" represent a separate and distinct office to that of the elder or overseer? There are at least two reasons to take these terms as representing the same office. First, elders/overseers, like pastors, are given the tasks of shepherding and teaching. In Acts 20:17 we read that from Miletus Paul "sent to Ephesus and called the *elders* of the church to come to him" (emphasis added). After these elders came, Paul instructed them "to shepherd [or 'pastor'] the church of God" (Acts 20:28, my translation). A similar passage is found in 1 Peter 5:1–3. In the first verse, Peter exhorts the "elders" of the churches. Then, in verse 2, he admonishes them to "shepherd the flock of God that is among you." According to these texts, the primary calling of an elder is to shepherd, or pastor, God's people.

Both elders/overseers and pastors are also given the task of teaching. In Ephesians 4:11, the term "pastor" is linked with the term "teacher," indicating that the primary method by which a pastor shepherds his flock is teaching them God's Word. Teaching is also the primary role of the elder/overseer. In 1 Timothy 3:2 a distinct qualification of the overseer is that he must be "able to teach." Later, Paul tells Timothy that the elders who rule well should be considered worthy of double honor, "especially those who labor in preaching and teaching" (1 Tim. 5:17). In a similar manner, Paul instructs Titus that an overseer must hold firm to the trustworthy Word he has been taught, "so that he may be able to give instruction in sound doctrine and also to rebuke those who contradict it" (Titus 1:9). Thus, because pastors and elders/overseers have the same function (i.e., shepherding and teaching), the two terms should be viewed as referring to the same office.

Second, as we mentioned earlier, the Greek term for "pastor" is found only once in the New Testament as a designation for a church leader. If this office is separate from the elder/overseer, what are the qualifications needed for those who hold this office? Paul gives us the qualifications for the elder/overseer but never for the pastor. Perhaps the reason for this omission is because in giving the qualifications for the elder/overseer, he is giving the qualifications for those who also can be called "pastor." Waldron rightly summarizes the data: "The inevitable conclusion is that there is no warrant for a distinction between the office of pastor and the office of elder in the New Testament."[3]

---

rule does not apply here since we are dealing with plural nouns, it is best to take this as a twofold designation referring to one group (the pastor-teacher).

3. Samuel E. Waldron, "Plural-Elder Congregationalism," in *Who Runs the Church? 4 Views on Church Government*, ed. Paul E. Engle and Steven B. Cowan (Grand Rapids: Zondervan, 2004), 216.

Is There an Office of Senior Pastor?

This question is raised primarily because the idea of having a "senior" pastor is so common today that many assume it has a scriptural basis. The senior pastor is usually the professional "clergyman" who has the most authority, does most of the preaching, and is the driving force behind the direction of the church. But if the term "pastor" refers to the same office as the elder, making a distinction between an elder and a pastor or senior pastor is unwarranted. That is, it is unhelpful and misleading to speak of someone being a pastor *and* an elder. By creating a "professional" class of elders (i.e., pastors or senior pastors), we create an unhealthy and unbiblical distinction. Nowhere in the Bible are elders who work "full time" for the church given a different title than those elders who also hold a "secular" job. Such a distinction creates an unhealthy dichotomy between the full-time and part-time elders, as well as between the clergy and laity. By speaking of a "senior pastor," in essence, we have created a third office, similar to what took place in the second century with the development of the monarchical bishop. L. Roy Taylor, himself a Presbyterian, rightly criticizes churches that "originate with congregational church government" but "develop a *de facto* episcopal government whereby the senior pastor is the primary decision-maker on major issues." He then adds, "While some may regard this as novel, it is actually a replication of the older monoepiscopacy of the second century."[4]

From a New Testament perspective, a separate office of senior pastor is a foreign concept. The early churches were not governed by one person but were led by a group of leaders. For example, every time the term for "elder" is used in the New Testament, it occurs in the plural form ("elders"), except when it is used generically (1 Tim. 5:19), or refers to a specific elder (such as Peter [1 Peter 5:1] or John [2 John 1; 3 John 1]). There is no instance of anyone ever being called "the pastor" of a local church, much less "the senior pastor." Actually, there is one reference to someone being called the "senior pastor." In 1 Peter 5:4, Jesus is called the "chief Shepherd" (i.e., Senior Pastor). Perhaps it is best to reserve this title for Jesus since all other shepherds are "undershepherds"?

---

4. L. Roy Taylor, "Presbyteriansim," in *Who Runs the Church?* 74.

Summary

From the very beginning, the early church had recognized leaders. Although we are not always aware of the specific titles they were given, it is clear that some were distinguished as leaders in the church and as such were worthy of respect and honor. By the time the Pastoral Epistles were written, two offices clearly had emerged: elder/overseer and deacon (cf. Phil. 1:1; 1 Tim. 3:1–13). "Pastor" refers to the same office as the elder or overseer, since the duty of the pastor is the same as the elder/overseer—shepherding and teaching. Finally, a separate office (or designation) of "senior pastor" has no warrant in Scripture since that title is used only of Jesus (1 Peter 5:4). It is not necessarily wrong to use such a title, but it might lead some to unduly give one man more authority than is biblical, thus creating another office.

Reflection Questions

1. How many offices does your church have?
2. Are these offices taught in the New Testament?
3. What scriptural evidence is there to support the teaching that "pastor" refers to the same office as elder or overseer?
4. Are there any examples of someone being called a "senior pastor" in the Bible?
5. What are the possible dangers of having extrabiblical offices?

PART 2

The Office of Elder

Section A
Questions Related to Background Issues

What Is the Background of the Terms "Elder" and "Overseer"?

Elders in the Old Testament

In the Old Testament, the term for "elder" (*zaqēn*) refers to (1) someone who has entered old age or (2) a leader of the community who performs various functions. Of the more than 180 occurrences of this term in the Old Testament, about two-thirds refer to a respected community leader, whereas only one-third are used as a reference to age. The establishment of the elders as a distinct group of leaders is nowhere delineated in the Old Testament; it is simply presupposed. Because "the elders" ruled as a collective body, the term is almost always found in the plural. Those who were known as "the elders" were not appointed to such a position by a higher authority but were ascribed authority by the people of the community, who deemed them worthy of respect and honor. Thus, a man became an elder by his moral authority, which was acquired by heredity, experience, knowledge, or wealth.

The elders of Israel functioned in a variety of roles. First, they were a representative body. The elders often represented the people in religious or political activity (Exod. 3:18; 12:21; 1 Sam. 8:4; 2 Sam. 5:3). Second, they were a governing body. Especially after the exile, the elders, often in concert with the governor, were the ruling body of the Jerusalem community (Ezra 5:5; 6:7, 14). Earlier, the elders were sometimes part of the royal council giving advice to the king (2 Sam. 17:4, 15). Third, they were a judicial body. According to Deuteronomy, the elders of the city often made decisions regarding the punishment of lawbreakers (19:12; 21:3; 22:15). In sum, the "elders served as national, political, and religious representatives and leaders."[1]

The material for this question is simplified and adapted from my earlier work, *The Elder and Overseer: One Office in the Early Church* (New York: Peter Lang, 2003), 23–44, 56–62.

1. David Mappes, "The 'Elder' in the Old and New Testaments," *BSac* 154 (1997): 82.

In Numbers 11, God directed Moses to gather seventy of the elders of Israel whom the Lord would appoint to help Moses rule the people. Because the burden was too great for Moses to bear, these elders were designated to assist Moses in leading the people. Thus, at an early stage in Israel's history, the elders began to take on official status. Subsequently, Numbers 11 became the model for the Sanhedrin and was later used to justify rabbinical ordination.

The translators of the Septuagint favored the term *presbuteros* to translate the Hebrew *zaqēn*, rendering it as such 127 times.[2] Because *zaqēn* often refers to leaders with some sort of official capacity and is not simply a designation of honor, it seems that a more official term (besides *presbuteros,* which generally was used as a designation for age in Greco-Roman society) might have been expected in the Septuagint.[3] Deissmann suggests that the translators of the Septuagint were influenced by the official use of *presbuteros* in Egypt, where the Septuagint was translated. He writes, "The Alexandrian translators have appropriated a technical expression which was current in the land."[4] Therefore, for those Christians familiar with the Greek Old Testament, the use of *presbuteros* as a designation for an official leader of the community would not have seemed strange at all. Indeed, the Septuagint was the Bible of choice not only for the majority of New Testament writers but also for their readers. Since the Septuagint had a profound impact on the thought and vocabulary of the early Christians, it seems reasonable to assume that the New Testament usage of *presbuteros* reflects the nuance of the Septuagint more than the typical Greco-Roman usage.

Elders in the New Testament

The Greek term *presbuteros* ("elder") and its cognates appear sixty-six times in the New Testament. It can refer to an old person (man or woman; e.g., John 8:9; Acts 2:17; 1 Tim. 5:1–2) or can be used in the comparative sense

2. *Zaqēn* is also translated twenty-five times by *presbutēs,* twenty-six times by *gerousia* (mostly in Deuteronomy), and three times each by *gerōn* and *anēr.* In each case where *zaqēn* is translated by *gerousia,* the former is always in the plural while the latter is in the singular. This suggests that the elders were seen as a corporate body with official status.

3. G. Adolf Deissmann notes, "We usually find [*presbuteros*] in places where the translators appear to have taken the [*zaqēn*] of the original as implying an official position" (*Bible Studies: Contributions Chiefly from Papyri and Inscriptions to the History of the Language, the Literature, and the Religion of Hellenistic Judaism and Primitive Christianity,* trans. Alexander Grieve [Edinburgh: T and T Clark, 1901; reprint, Peabody, MA: Hendrickson, 1988], 154).

4. Ibid., 155. Later he comments, "[*presbuteros*] was, till late in the imperial period, the technical term in Egypt for the occupant of an office in civil communities,—a usage by which the LXX did not fail to be influenced" (ibid., 233).

of one who is older than another (Luke 15:25). More commonly, *presbuteros* denotes officials in both Judaism (members of the Sanhedrin or synagogue) and the church. In a few places *presbuteros* has the meaning of "forefathers" (Matt. 15:2; Mark 7:3, 5; Heb. 11:2).

Similar to the Old Testament usage, we find various designations associated with elders: elders of the people (Matt. 21:23; 26:3, 47; 27:1; Luke 22:66; Acts 4:8), elders of the Jews (Luke 7:3; Acts 25:15), and elders of the church (Acts 20:17; James 5:14). There were elders in the churches of Jerusalem (Acts 11:30; 15:2, 4, 6, 22, 23; 16:4; 21:18), Galatia (Acts 14:23), Ephesus (Acts 20:17; 1 Tim. 5:17, 19), Crete (Titus 1:5), Asia Minor (1 Peter 5:1), and other Jewish Christian assemblies (James 5:14).

Most uses of *presbuteros* in the Gospels occur in association with the chief priests and/or scribes who were antagonistic to the ministry of Jesus. The uses in Acts in reference to leaders are mixed. The first four and the last four occurrences refer to those associated with the Jewish leaders who are opposed to the church (Acts 4:5, 8, 23; 6:12; 22:5; 23:14; 24:1; 25:15). The middle ten occurrences refer to the elders of the Christian church (Acts 11:30; 14:23; 15:2, 4, 6, 22, 23; 16:4; 20:17; 21:18). The first time "elders" is used in reference to a Christian group is in Acts 11:30, where the church in Antioch sends Barnabas and Paul to the elders in Jerusalem, with money to aid in the famine relief. It is interesting that the term appears in this new context without any explanation given by Luke. Eight of the ten references to Christian elders in Acts refer to the elders in Jerusalem, and in six of those references they are mentioned in association with the apostles. The two occurrences in Acts that do not refer to the Jerusalem elders are 14:23 and 20:17. In Acts 14:23, we are told that Paul and Barnabas "appointed elders . . . in every church" in the cities of Antioch, Iconium, Lystra, and Derbe. Acts 20:17 is in the context of Paul's farewell speech to the elders of Ephesus. The remainder of the New Testament references to "elders" occur in 1 Timothy 5:17, 19; Titus 1:5; Hebrews 11:2 (i.e., "forefathers"); James 5:14; 1 Peter 5:1, 5; 2 John 1; 3 John 1; and twelve occurrences in the book of Revelation (4:4, 10; 5:5, 6, 8, 11, 14; 7:11, 13; 11:16; 14:3; 19:4).

Overseers in the Old Testament

In the Septuagint, the term *episkopos* ("overseer") occurs fifteen times, two of which refer to God (Job 20:29; Wisdom 1:6). In reference to men, *episkopos* can refer to a variety of offices. In Numbers 31:14 and 2 Kings

11:15, military leaders are called "officers of the army" (NKJV) and in Judges 9:28, Abimilech is said to have appointed Zebul his "officer." Likewise, in 1 Maccabees 1:51, Antiochus appoints "overseers" (my translation) as governors over Israel. Nehemiah refers to the "overseers" of Benjamin (Neh. 11:9, 14). Finally, Isaiah 60:17 parallels "overseers" with "rulers" (my translation). About half of the references in the Septuagint are variously associated with religious activities. In Numbers 4:16, Eleazar the priest was made *episkopos* over the tabernacle and all the vessels in it. Although it is inaccurate to equate the use of *episkopos* with that of priest, it is interesting that the term is used in a religious context. In 2 Kings 11:18 we read, "The priest appointed overseers over the house of the LORD" (my translation). Second Kings 12:11 and 2 Chronicles 34:12, 17 explain that money raised to repair the temple was given to the "overseers" (my translation), who functioned as supervisors, paying the various laborers. And Nehemiah 11:22 calls Uzzi the "overseer" of the Levites.

In the Greco-Roman sources, from at least the classical period, *episkopos* can refer to the gods (personified forces) who watch over the persons or objects committed to their patronage.[5] When referring to people, this term likewise can refer to one's protective care over someone or something, but it also can be used as a title to denote various offices. The most common use, however, applies to local officials or to officers of societies or clubs.

Overseers in the New Testament

"Although the word [*episkopos*] had such a rich background, and was to enjoy an even richer development on Christian soil, it occurs only five times in the NT."[6] In Acts 20:28 Paul tells the Ephesian elders that the Holy Spirit has made them "overseers" who are to shepherd the church of God. The emphasis here is on their function and not office. That is, as elders their duty was to oversee and shepherd the flock. Yet, it is worth noting that the two terms ("elder" and "overseer") are used somewhat interchangeably. In his opening greeting to the church at Philippi, Paul addresses all the saints, including the "overseers" and "deacons" (Phil. 1:1). The use of the plural indicates that there was more than one overseer at Philippi. It also seems likely that this reference is more than simply a functional designation but is titular. In both

---

5. For an excellent survey of the usage of *episkopos*, see Livingstone Porter, "The Word ἐπίσκοπος in Pre-Christian Usage," *AThR* 21 (1939): 103–12.

6. H. W. Beyer, "ἐπίσκοπος," in *TDNT*, 2:615.

1 Timothy 3:2–7 and Titus 1:7–9, we read of the qualifications required for one to hold the office of "overseer." Finally, 1 Peter 2:25 refers to Christ as "the Shepherd and Overseer of your souls."

The related term, *episkopē*, occurs four times in the New Testament. Twice it refers to God's visitation in judgment (Luke 19:44; 1 Peter 2:12), and twice it refers to officeholders (Acts 1:20; 1 Tim. 3:1). In Acts 1:20, when the apostles decided to replace Judas, Peter justifies this action by quoting Psalm 109:8, which reads, "Let another take his office [*episkopē*]." Also, in 1 Timothy 3:1, Paul states, "If anyone aspires to the office of overseer, he desires a noble task." Finally, the verb form, *episkopeō* ("to oversee"), is found only twice (Heb. 12:15; 1 Peter 5:2), while the cognate verb *episkeptomai* occurs eleven times and is usually translated "visit."[7]

Summary

In the Old Testament, the term for "elder" can refer to an older person or to a senior community leader. About two-thirds of the references are used of the latter category, who, as a collective group, often functioned as a representative, governing, and judicial body. The translators of the Septuagint favored the term *presbuteros* to translate the Hebrew term *zaqēn*. In the New Testament, elders occur in both Jewish and Christian contexts.

The term for "overseer" (*episkopos*) occurs less often than the term for "elder" in both the Septuagint and the New Testament. In the Old Testament, it is used to represent a variety of different leadership positions. Of the five New Testament references, four refer to the Christian office, and one is a designation of Christ.

Reflection Questions

1. What are the two main meanings of the term for "elder" in the Old Testament?
2. What were the functions of elders in the Old Testament?
3. How is the term for "elder" mainly used in the New Testament?
4. How is the term for "overseer" used in the Old Testament?
5. What are the similarities and differences in the usage of the term for "overseer" in the Old Testament and the New Testament?

---

7. Matt. 25:36, 43; Luke 1:68, 78; 7:16; Acts 6:3; 7:23; 15:14, 36; Heb. 2:6; James 1:27.

What Is the Origin of the Christian Elder or Overseer?

Origin of the Christian Elder

Did the early church consciously borrow the title "elder" from a previously existing model of eldership? In other words, why were some leaders in the early church referred to as "elders"? Today, many scholars simply assume that the origin of the New Testament elder has a direct correlation to the synagogue elder. The assumption is that since most of the early Christians were Jews who formerly worshiped in the synagogue, it would be natural for them to adopt the type of government that the synagogue used and with which they were familiar. Although there is some truth to such reasoning, there is insufficient evidence to claim that the office of elder was borrowed directly from the synagogue.

Actually, at least four possible sources of the Christian elder have been proposed: (1) the Old Testament; (2) the Sanhedrin; (3) the synagogue; and (4) the culture. In the following paragraphs it will be argued that except for the title and the authority that goes with it, the New Testament office of elder is unique, not based on any previous models.

The Christian Elder Originated from the Old Testament

This position claims that the earliest Christians named their leaders "elders" because of the prominence of the term in the Old Testament. It must be admitted that the Old Testament (Septuagintal) usage of the term *presbuteros* ("elder") had some influence on why the early church referred to its leaders or officeholders as elders. To some extent, then, the term *presbuteros* was borrowed from the Greek Old Testament. One clear similarity is that

The material for this question is simplified and adapted from my earlier work, *The Elder and Overseer: One Office in the Early Church* (New York: Peter Lang, 2003), 44–56, 62–65.

both Testaments consistently use the term in the plural when referring to officeholders. While the Old Testament usage of the term clearly had some influence on the early church, it would be wrong to say the New Testament church patterned its leaders after these ancient predecessors. Although their functions overlap at times, there is not a one-to-one parallel. Harvey rightly concludes that there was no "*institution* in the Old Testament times which could be regarded as the forerunner . . . of the Christian presbyterate."[1]

The Christian Elder Originated from the Sanhedrin

Another view is that the early church borrowed the term from the Sanhedrin. Although the elders of the Old Testament often represented the people, they were not formally organized as a court like the later Sanhedrin. It was not until the Persian era that something resembling the Sanhedrin began to take shape.[2] According to the New Testament, the Sanhedrin had three classes of members. The high priest was the leader of the Sanhedrin; the scribes were professional lawyers; and the elders consisted of other members, priestly and lay, who belonged to neither of the first two groups. The Sanhedrin had a total of seventy-one members. It is clear that the Sanhedrin "elder" did not serve as the prototype for the Christian church because, as an institution, the function of the Sanhedrin was primarily judicial—it was a court and its members were mainly judges. Because of the differences in membership and function, almost no one affirms that the early church elders were patterned after the Sanhedrin. Again, Harvey rightly concludes, "There would be grave difficulties in regarding the Sanhedrin as a whole as the prototype of the Christian presbyterate."[3]

The Christian Elder Originated from the Synagogue

A third and widely held option is that the New Testament church adopted the structure of the synagogue and with it came the office of elder. J. B. Lightfoot was an early proponent of the view that Christian elders were

---

1. A. E. Harvey, "Elders," *JTS* 25 (1974): 320.
2. Emil Schürer, *The History of the Jewish People in the Age of Jesus Christ [175 B.C.–A.D. 135]*, ed. Geza Vermes, Fergus Millar, and Matthew Black, rev. ed. (Edinburgh: T and T Clark, 1979), 2:200–202; and Joachim Jeremias, *Jerusalem in the Time of Jesus*, trans. F. H. Cave and C. H. Cave, 3rd ed. (London: SCM, 1969), 223.
3. Harvey, "Elders," 323. He continues, "The word 'elders', when applied to the Sanhedrin, was either the technical name for a specific class of aristocratic laymen, or was a more general word, with strong Pharisaic overtones, which was used to refer to scribes both inside and outside the Sanhedrin. In neither case is there any easy analogy with Christian presbyters" (ibid., 323–24).

intentionally patterned after the synagogue elders. Whereas the diaconate presented the church with an altogether new office created by the apostles, the presbyterate came from the synagogue.[4] He states, "With the synagogue itself [the Christian congregations in Palestine] would naturally, if not necessarily, adopt the normal government of a synagogue, and a body of elders or presbyters would be chosen to direct the religious worship and partly also to watch over the temporal well-being of the society."[5] Burtchaell likewise comments, "It is impossible to understand primitive Christian worship unless in continuity with Jewish worship. So much of what we might consider to be distinctively and creatively Christian was in fact an outgrowth of its Jewish antecedents."[6] Thus, contends Lightfoot, "The name and office of the 'presbyter' are essentially Jewish."[7]

---

4. J. B. Lightfoot, *St. Paul's Epistle to the Philippians* (London: Macmillan, 1881), 187–95. He writes, "There is no reason for connecting [the diaconate] with any prototype existing in the Jewish community. The narrative [in Acts 6] offers no hint that it was either a continuation of the order of Levites or an adaptation of an office in the synagogue.... It is therefore a baseless, though very common, assumption that the Christian diaconate was copied from the arrangements of the synagogue" (ibid., 89–90).

5. Ibid., 192. Earlier Lightfoot writes, "It was not unnatural therefore that, when the Christian synagogue took its place by the side of the Jewish, a similar organization should be adopted with such modifications as circumstances required; and thus the name familiar under the old dispensation was retained under the new" (ibid., 96).

6. James T. Burtchaell, *From Synagogue to Church: Public Services and Offices in the Earliest Christian Communities* (Cambridge: Cambridge University Press, 1992), 190. He offers numerous examples of overlap between the two: "The blending of word and gesture into sacrament, the weekly holy day, the calendar of feasts, the daily rhythms of prayer, the reading of scriptures followed by exposition, the sacred meal, ritual initiation through baptism, anointing, the laying-on of hands: this and so much else derive from the Jewish tradition.... Fasting, charismatic prophecy, burial practices, ethical norms and ethical inquiry, veneration of the tombs of the saints, catechesis ... the centrality of Jerusalem, dedicated celibacy, [and] impediments to marriage" (ibid., 190–91). He later adds, "The *synagogue* and the *ekklesia* both typically met in plenary sessions of prayer, to read and expound and discuss the scriptures, to share in ritual meals, to deliberate community policy, to enforce discipline, to choose and inaugurate officers. Both maintained a welfare fund to support widows and orphans and other indigents among their memberships. Both accepted the obligation to provide shelter and hospitality to members of sister communities on their journeys. Both arranged for burial of their dead, and maintained cemeteries" (ibid., 339).

7. Lightfoot, *Philippians*, 96. Those agreeing with Lightfoot include Hans von Campenhausen, who writes, "There had for a long time been elders at the head of every Jewish congregation, especially in Palestine, and the idea of organising themselves in a similar way must have suggested itself to the Jewish Christian community. The system of elders is therefore probably of Judaeo-Christian origin" (*Ecclesiastical Authority and Spiritual Power in the Church of the First Three Centuries*, trans. J. A. Baker [Stanford: Stanford University Press, 1969], 77). Also see A. M. Farrar, "The Apostolic Ministry in the New Testament," in *The Apostolic Ministry: Essays on the History and Doctrine of Episcopacy*, ed. Kenneth E. Kirk (London: Hodder and Stoughton, 1957), 142; G. Bornkamm, "πρέσβυς," in *TDNT*, 6:663; and David Mappes, "The 'Elder' in the Old and New Testaments," *BSac* 154 (1997): 90n. 58.

There are, however, noticeable differences between the church and the synagogue with regard to the terms that are used. For example, the New Testament offers no parallels to the other offices that were connected to the synagogue. There are no parallels to the "senior elders" (*gerousiarchēs*), the Levitical priests, the "notables" (*archontes*), and other minor officers. The use of the title "elders" appears to be the only title the early church used in its structure that also was used in the synagogue. There are other terminology differences as well. The New Testament writers used "church" (*ekklēsia*) instead of "synagogue" (*synagōgē*); "deacon" (*diakonos*) instead of "assistant" (*hypēretēs*); "overseer" (*episkopos*) instead of "ruler/president of the synagogue" (*archisynagōgos*).

There is no doubt that the function of synagogue elders and Christian elders overlapped. David Mappes notes that the similarities include "the responsibility of the elders for the well-being of the people; the authority of the elders within the community, the desired moral qualities of the elders, and the elders' responsibility to communicate and take care of the Scripture."[8] The differences, however, should not go unnoticed. For example, Emil Schürer has convincingly argued that the elders did not lead the synagogue meeting.[9] The "ruler of the synagogue" (*archisynagōgos*) was the officeholder of the synagogue who was responsible for the specifics of the meeting. He himself did not lead in worship but was responsible for finding someone from the congregation to read the Scriptures and pray and for inviting suitable persons to preach.[10] Generally speaking, his goal was to insure that nothing improper occurred in the meeting (cf. Luke 13:14). Another synagogue official, the "assistant" (*hypēretēs*), was in charge of bringing out and returning the sacred Scriptures, blowing a trumpet to announce the beginning and end of the Sabbath, punishing those condemned to be scourged, and even teaching the children to read.

---

8. Mappes, "'Elder' in the Old and New Testaments," 91–92. Mappes, however, does note some difference between the two. He writes, "Differences between synagogue elders and church elders include the following: emphasis on the church elders' teaching role, lists of significant moral requirements for eldership, the lack of New Testament analogy to the [*archisynagōgos*], and the lack of civil or political power" (ibid., 92).

9. Schürer, *History of the Jewish People*, 2:427–54. He notes that one function of the elders in the synagogue involved disciplinary acts (i.e., the pronouncement of excommunication or exclusion from the congregation).

10. Cf. Acts 13:15: "After the reading from the Law and the Prophets, the rulers of the synagogue [*archisynagōgoi*] sent a message to them, saying, 'Brothers, if you have any word of exhortation for the people, say it.'" Also see Bernadette J. Brooten, *Women Leaders in the Ancient Synagogue: Inscriptional Evidence and Background Issues*, BJS 36 (Chico, CA: Scholars Press, 1982), 28–29.

This is not to say, however, that the elders had no influence in the synagogue. In Jewish society there was not a separation between the civil and the religious. Just as the elders had a great influence over the civil affairs, they also exercised authority over the religious life of the community, of which the synagogue was a major part.[11] Thus the elders were in charge of the affairs of the congregation in general. That is, as leaders of the community they were also leaders of the synagogue. Therefore, because synagogue elders "had no responsibility for the worship of the synagogue (this belonged to the [archisynagōgos]) nor for the custody of right doctrine or the exposition of scripture. . . . Synagogue elders provide at best a shadowy model for the Christian presbyters."[12]

The Christian Elder Originated from the Culture

This position maintains that Christian elders are identical to Jewish elders because, in both contexts, the title is used as an unofficial designation, referring only to one who was honored or respected in the community. It is argued that because "elder" is not the title of an office (in the Old Testament,

---

11. Schürer states, "There is no lack of positive evidence to the effect that the civic community as such also conducted the affairs of the synagogue. . . . [A] separation of political and religious communities would have been quite artificial. It would have been altogether contrary to the nature of post-exilic Judaism, which recognizes the political community only in the form of the religious. . . . It seems likely, therefore, that the synagogue congregations existed independently side by side with the political community only in cities with a mixed population. In purely Jewish districts, the elders of the locality will also have been elders of the synagogue" (*History of the Jewish People*, 2:428–29). He continues, "The powers of the elders of the congregation in religious matters must be envisaged as analogous to their authority in civic affairs. Thus as the city administration and jurisdiction lay entirely in their hands, so presumably did the direction of religious matters" (ibid., 2:431). Harvey writes, "It follows that the 'elders,' even if they had no place in the liturgical activity of the synagogue, nevertheless had the important function of forming an administrative and judicial council concerned with the whole life of the community" ("Elders," 324–25). R. Alastair Campbell similarly comments, "The elders ran the synagogues, but it was not as the elders of the synagogue that they did so. They ran the synagogues because they ran the community. . . . The synagogues existed not as independent congregations but as expressions of the life of the community to which they belonged" (*The Elders: Seniority Within Earliest Christianity*, Studies of the New Testament and Its World [Edinburgh: T and T Clark, 1994], 54).

12. Harvey, "Elders," 325–26; Thomas M. Lindsay comments, "Synagogue organization has some points in common with that of the early Christian communities, and these were probably taken over into Christianity, but the differences were so great that it is impossible to say that the one organization comes from the other" (*The Church and the Ministry in the Early Centuries* [London: Hodder and Stoughton, 1902], 131). He later writes, "It must always be remembered that Christian 'elders' had functions entirely different from the Jewish, that the vitality of the infant Christian Communities made them work out for themselves that organization which they found to be most suitable, and that in this case nothing but the name was borrowed" (ibid., 153).

Sanhedrin, or synagogue) but a designation of honor, the usage of the term is merely a cultural designation of one who is respected in the community. R. A. Campbell, a proponent of this position, notes that Israelite society was tribal and patriarchal. Consequently, at each level of the society (tribes, clans, and extended families), senior males were given leadership. The head of the house represented his family in the local village councils. These leaders were collectively described as "the elders." When an *individual* elder is referred to, he is likely to be called "head" or "prince" but not "elder." As a result, Campbell states that "'the elders' is a *collective* term for the leadership of the tribe, or of the ruling class under the monarchy and thereafter, but that it was never the title of an office to which an individual might be appointed."[13] Although heredity played an important role in becoming an elder, it was also based on one's character or moral authority. Campbell posits that the household, and not the synagogue, is the key to understanding the early churches' development. The house churches of the New Testament are not simply buildings but are "extended families with built-in authority patterns of their own."[14] Thus, the head of the house where the church met also became the head of the church. Although this position rightly recognizes weaknesses in other views, it also is untenable. As we have demonstrated, the term *presbuteros* is often used as the title of an officeholder and thus goes beyond a simple designation of honor.

Summary

It is difficult to determine the precise relationship between Christian elders and elders of the Old Testament, Sanhedrin, and synagogue. From the outset, one must acknowledge both similarities and differences. Yet, in each case the differences are substantial enough to reject any direct correlation.[15] We must reject the notion that the early church adopted the office of synagogue elder since it appears that these elders were not formal officeholders in the synagogue but were officials of the community. It is also relevant that the leaders in the Old Testament communities were called *presbuteroi* ("elders") in the Septuagint. It would seem more likely that the church based its leadership model on the Old Testament, which it wholeheartedly embraced, rather

---

13. Campbell, *Elders*, 26.
14. Ibid., 118.
15. See David W. Miller, "The Uniqueness of New Testament Church Eldership," *GTJ* 6 (1985): 315–27, who argues that New Testament eldership is purposefully distinct from Hellenistic societies and Jewish organizations.

than on the synagogue, which it tentatively rejected.[16] Furthermore, it is insufficient to claim that the term "elder" was never a title of an officeholder but merely an honored person in the community. It appears, therefore, that the Christian office of elder was not directly borrowed from any of its predecessors. The New Testament church borrowed the title, and the official status that came along with that title, but defined for itself the specific duties that those who held this title performed.

Origin of the Christian Overseer

As with the elder (*presbuteros*), it is difficult to identify the precise origin of the Christian overseer (*episkopos*). The three most common views are that this office originated from (1) the Old Testament, (2) Greek societies, or (3) the Jewish *mᵉbaqqēr*.

The Christian Overseer Originated from the Old Testament

Although *episkopos* is used in the Septuagint to denote a variety of official positions—from a military officer to a cultic administrator—many early Christians appealed to the Old Testament as a basis for the Christian overseer. For example, both Clement and Irenaeus appealed to Isaiah 60:17b ("I will give your rulers peace and your overseers [*episkopoi*] righteousness," my translation) to justify the office of "overseer"—a usage that indicates the early church felt a need to base its organizational structure on the Old Testament.[17] L. Porter explains, "Such Old Testament validation might appear especially necessary for the title of [*episkopos*] since it was applied, in contemporary as well as in more ancient usage, to the gods of the Greek pantheon, to mythical demi-gods, and to various other imaginary supernatural creatures."[18]

The Christian Overseer Originated from Greek Societies

Others have insisted that the *episkopos* of Greek societies or clubs provides the origin for the early Christian leaders. Commonalities between private clubs and Christian churches have been noted. Ellis, for example, com-

---

16. Campbell writes, "How likely it is that those who left synagogues to join the church, and Gentiles who had never belonged to them, would have wanted to reproduce their structures when they decisively rejected their whole basis of membership and initiation" (*Elders*, 119). I take the use of *synagōgē* in James 2:2 as a reference to a Christian meeting (so James B. Adamson, *The Epistle of James*, NICNT [Grand Rapids: Eerdmans, 1976], 105; and Douglas J. Moo, *The Letter of James*, TNTC [Leicester: InterVarsity Press; Grand Rapids: Eerdmans, 1985], 16:89).

17. *1 Clement* 42:4–5; Irenaeus *Adversus haereses* 4.26.5.

18. Livingstone Porter, "The Word ἐπίσκοπος in Pre-Christian Usage," *AThR* 21 (1939): 104.

ments that the private clubs "held regular meetings, usually with religious ceremonies, elected officers and sometimes a patron, and exercised a certain discipline over their members . . . they provided their membership with banquets and other festive and leisurely activities and, at the end, an honorable burial."[19] Yet, while Ellis affirms a correlation between clubs and Christian churches as social entities, he admits that the specific terminology (such as the terms *episkopos* and *presbuteros*) "are used quite broadly in a number of similar contexts and have no necessary or special connection with clubs, where in fact they appear relatively infrequently and usually with a different connotation than they have in Christian contexts."[20] Beyer also notes, "None of the offices denoted by the [*episkopos*] in the Greek-speaking world has so much in common with the Christian office of bishop as to enable us to affirm the possibility of a historical connection."[21] Likewise, Harvey writes, "We seem forced to admit that we can find no convincing models for Christian bishops . . . in Hellenistic organizations."[22]

The Christian Overseer Originated from the Jewish M^{e}baqqēr

Still others maintain that the Christian "overseer" was modeled after the *m^{e}baqqēr* (i.e., the spiritual leader) of the Qumran community. Bill Humble, for example, identifies the following parallels between the Jewish *m^{e}baqqēr* and the Christian *episkopos*:[23] (1) both were overseers, according to the root meanings of each title; (2) both were teaching officers; (3) both showed a fatherly concern for the group; (4) both offices were described using the analogy of the shepherd; (5) both received and administered funds for benevolent work; and (6) both heard allegations of offenses and administered discipline.[24] For these reasons Jeremias states, "The title *m^{e}baqqēr* corresponds literally with the Greek [*episkopos*], and . . . the positions and the

19. E. Earle Ellis, *Pauline Theology: Ministry and Society* (Grand Rapids: Eerdmans, 1989), 126.
20. Ibid., 136.
21. H. W. Beyer, "ἐπίσκοπος," in *TDNT*, 2:618.
22. Harvey, "Elders," 318. He later asserts, "Christians did not borrow these titles [*episkopos* and *diakonos*] from existing pagan institutions, but created them themselves" (ibid., 319).
23. It should be noted that Humble himself states that a verbal parallel between the Hebrew *m^{e}baqqēr* and the Greek *episkopos* "does *not* mean that the church 'borrowed' its organization from the Dead Sea community" (Bill J. Humble, "The M^{e}baqqēr in the Dead Sea Scrolls," *ResQ* 7 [1963]: 37).
24. Humble, "The M^{e}baqqēr," 37–38. Also see B. E. Thiering, "M^{e}baqqēr and Episkopos in Light of the Temple Scroll," *JBL* 100 (1981): 69–74; Campbell, *Elders*, 155–59; Jerome D. Quinn and William C. Wacker, *The First and Second Letters to Timothy*, ECC (Grand Rapids: Eerdmans, 2000), 267–71.

function of the *mᵉbaqqēr* are identical with those of a bishop in the Syrian *Didaskalia*."[25] B. E. Thiering also claims, "There appears now to be even better reason for supposing that the earliest Christian church adopted the office of bishop from the Essene lay communities."[26]

There is not, however, enough evidence to claim that the early church used the organizational structure of the Qumran communities. Although there are great similarities, there are also some notable differences. First, while there was only one *mᵉbaqqēr* at each camp, Christian churches apparently had a plurality of *episkopoi* (Phil. 1:1; Acts 20:28). Second, the *mᵉbaqqēr* at Qumran remained unmarried, while the *episkopoi* were married with families. Third, while the property and possessions were controlled by the *mᵉbaqqēr*, it was the apostles and the Seven who handled such funds, and not the *episkopoi*. Finally, if the *mᵉbaqqēr* was the model for the Christian *episkopos*, one would expect to find this term associated primarily with Jewish Christian congregations instead of Gentile congregations, as is the case. Beyer rightly concludes that even if the early Christians were familiar with a Qumran-type *mᵉbaqqēr*, "[The Christian] community, based on the great commission to preach the gospel and to live according to it in the most inward of all societies, was something new and distinctive, so that for the fulfillment of its mission new offices had to be created, or to develop out of the matter itself."[27] Although Reicke admits that there are some analogies between the *mᵉbaqqēr* and the Christian *episkopos*, he also affirms that there is "little reason to assume that the church got its episcopal office from the Essenes and their *mebaqqer*."[28]

Summary

As with the office of elder, it is best to affirm an almost entirely new office when considering the origin of the Christian overseer. The paucity of evidence alone prohibits any clear correlation.[29]

---

25. Jeremias, *Jerusalem in the Time of Jesus*, 261.

26. Thiering, "*Mebaqqer* and *Episkopos*," 74. Campbell also believes that the Christian *episkopos* "originated informally in the earliest Jewish period of Christianity [i.e., from the *mᵉbaqqēr*], rather than to have been adopted by the Pauline churches in some kind of dependence on Greek clubs and societies" (*Elders*, 158).

27. Beyer, "ἐπίσκοπος," 2:619.

28. Bo Reicke, "The Constitution of the Primitive Church in Light of Jewish Documents," in *The Scrolls and the New Testament*, ed. Krister Stenhahl (New York: Harper, 1957), 154.

29. Hans Lietzmann rightly states, "We cannot say with certainty how these titles ['bishop' and 'deacon'] arose, but it appears to be certain that they were not adapted from Jewish usage. Nor

Reflection Questions

1. What evidence is there that the early church borrowed the concept of elders from the Old Testament? From the Sanhedrin? From the synagogue? From culture?
2. Which of the above do you think provides the closest parallel?
3. Do you agree that the early church primarily borrowed the term itself rather than the function from its predecessors?
4. What evidence is there that the early church borrowed the concept of overseers from the Old Testament? From Greek societies? From the Jewish *mᵉbaqqēr*?
5. Which of the above to do think provides the closest parallel?

---

do we gain much light from the analogies which have been adduced from mundane spheres or from the religious organizations of the pagan world" (*The Beginnings of the Christian Church*, trans. Bertram Lee Woolf [London: Lutterworth, 1949], 145). Also see Harvey, "Elders," 318.

Do the Terms "Elder" and "Overseer" Represent the Same Office?

The focus of this question is the relationship between the Greek terms *pres-buteros* ("elder") and *episkopos* ("overseer").[1] Many scholars of the nineteenth century assumed the two terms to be synonymous. J. B. Lightfoot, for example, confidently states, "It is a fact now generally recognised by theologians of all shades of opinion, that in the language of the New Testament the same officer in the Church is called indifferently 'bishop' (*episkopos*) and 'elder' or 'presbyter' (*presbuteros*)."[2] This position was also common among the early fathers. In the early fifth century, Jerome commented, "Indeed with the ancients these names were synonymous, one alluding to the office, the other to the age of the clergy."[3] In more recent times, however, the majority

---

The material for this question is simplified and adapted from my earlier work, *The Elder and Overseer: One Office in the Early Church* (New York: Peter Lang, 2003), 1–21, 142–57. It is also found in Benjamin L. Merkle, "Hierarchy in the Church? Instruction from the Pastoral Epistles Concerning Elders and Overseers," *The Southern Baptist Journal of Theology* 7.3 (2003): 32–43; and the *Journal for Baptist Theology and Ministry* 2.1 (2004): 45–62.

1. Most modern English Bible translations avoid translating the Greek *episkopos* as "bishop" because of the later connotations the word took on.
2. J. B. Lightfoot, *St. Paul's Epistle to the Philippians* (London: Macmillan, 1881), 95. Similarly, Edwin Hatch writes, "The admissions of both medieval and modern writers of almost all schools of theological opinion have practically removed this from the list of disputed questions" (*The Organization of the Early Christian Churches*, The 1880 Bampton Lectures [New York: Lenox Hill, 1881; reprint, 1972], 39n. 31).
3. Jerome, *Letter* 69.3, in *The Principle Works of St. Jerome*, trans. W. H. Fremantle with the assistance of G. Lewis and W. G. Martley, Nicene and Post-Nicene Fathers, 2nd series (Grand Rapids: Eerdmans, 1952), 6:143. Lightfoot further notes, "But, though more full than other writers, [Jerome] is hardly more explicit. Of his predecessors the Ambrosian Hilary had discerned the same truth. Of his contemporaries and successors, Chrysostom, Pelagius, Theodore of Mopsuestia, Theodoret, all acknowledge it. Thus in every one of the extant commentaries on

view has shifted. Many have challenged this former consensus and are offering alternative positions.

Challenges to the Traditional View

What are the reasons that have caused the traditional view to be challenged? There are at least seven reasons. First, in the Pastoral Epistles "overseer" is always in the singular, whereas "the elders" is always in the plural (except in 1 Tim. 5:19). The use of the singular "overseer" in 1 Timothy 3:2 is especially noticeable against the plural "deacons" used in 1 Timothy 3:8. Second, in both 1 Timothy 3:2 and Titus 1:7, "the overseer" (*ton episkopon*) contains the definite article (i.e., "the"), which perhaps indicates the elevation of one overseer above the elders.[4] Third, teaching is the responsibility of all overseers (1 Tim. 3:2; Titus 1:9), but apparently only some of the elders have this responsibility (1 Tim. 5:17). Fourth, where the overseer and deacons are mentioned, the elders are not; and where the elders are mentioned, the overseer and deacons are not. This usage shows that the terms are not really used interchangeably since they are not used in the same contexts. Fifth, one would not expect two distinct terms to refer to the same office. Sixth, the development of the monarchical bishop in the second century suggests an incipient form already can be found in the New Testament (especially the Pastoral Epistles). While few would argue that the overseer in the Pastoral Epistles is to be equated with the monarchical bishop, many do identify the beginning development of such a system. Seventh, because the Pastoral Epistles are addressed to individuals and not churches, some argue that Timothy and Titus are intended to portray prototypes of the monarchical bishop.

Based on these (and other) reasons, scholars have proposed a number of alternate views concerning the relationship between "elder" and "overseer." There are at least four recent positions that have garnered some support.

---

the epistles containing the crucial passages, whether Greek or Latin, before the close of the fifth century, this identity is affirmed" (*Philippians*, 99).

4. For example, Hans von Campenhausen states, "In the Pastoral Epistles the 'bishop' is always spoken of in the singular. The simplest explanation of this fact is that monarchical episcopacy is by now the prevailing system, and that the one bishop has already become the head of the presbyterate" (*Ecclesiastical Authority and Spiritual Power in the Church of the First Three Centuries*, trans. J. A. Baker [Stanford: Stanford University Press, 1969], 107).

1. "Elder" is never a title of an office but is only a designation for age or honor. Although the overseers would routinely be chosen from among the elders, the elders as such were simply those who were respected as the older members of the community.[5]

2. Overseers are a special type of elder. That is, they are elders who also perform the special functions of preaching and teaching (1 Tim. 5:17). While "elder" is the title of an officeholder, those who held this office were limited in their duties. Thus, this position maintains that the overseers are a subset of specialized elders who have the added responsibilities of preaching and teaching. There is still a plurality of overseers in each church, ruling out the idea of a monarchical bishop.[6]

3. The overseer is above, but still identified with, the elders. Each church had one overseer who was the president of the elders. The overseer, however, is still identified with the council of the elders, being selected from their ranks to preside over them and the church.[7]

4. The overseer is above, but not identified with, the elders. The overseer is the monarchical bishop, with sole, supreme authority.[8]

Evidence for the Traditional View

All of the above positions deny that the terms translated "elder" and "overseer" are virtual synonyms in the New Testament. This view, however, is best able to account for all the New Testament data.[9] Although the view that the

---

5. Those who hold this view include Joachim Jeremias and R. A. Campbell. See Joachim Jeremias, "ΠΡΕΣΒΥΤΕΡΙΟΝ außerchristlich bezeugt," *ZNW* 48 (1957): 127–32; and R. Alastair Campbell, *The Elders: Seniority Within Earliest Christianity*, Studies of the New Testament and Its World (Edinburgh: T and T Clark, 1994).

6. Those who hold this view include J. N. D. Kelly and Gordon Fee. See J. N. D. Kelly, *A Commentary on the Pastoral Epistles*, BNTC (London: Adam and Charles Black, 1963), 230; and Gordon Fee, *1 and 2 Timothy, Titus*, NIBCNT (Peabody, MA: Hendrickson, 1984), 174.

7. Those who hold this view include Walter Lock, C. K. Barrett, and Luke T. Johnson. See Walter Lock, *A Critical and Exegetical Commentary on the Pastoral Epistles*, ICC (Edinburgh: T and T Clark, 1924), xx; C. K. Barrett, *Pastoral Epistles in the New English Bible* (Oxford: Clarendon, 1963), 32; and Luke T. Johnson, *Letters to Paul's Delegates: 1 Timothy, 2 Timothy, Titus* (Valley Forge, PA: Trinity Press International, 1996), 145–46.

8. Those who hold this view include Ernst Käsemann, Hans von Campenhausen, and A. T. Hanson. See Ernst Käsemann, "Ministry and Community in the New Testament," in *Essays on New Testament Themes*, SBT 41, trans. W. J. Montague (Philadelphia: Fortress, 1964), 87; Campenhausen, *Ecclesiastical Authority*, 107; and A. T. Hanson, *The Pastoral Epistles*, New Century Bible Commentary (Grand Rapids: Eerdmans; London: Marshall, Morgan and Scott, 1982), 31–34).

9. Those who hold this view include Lightfoot, *Philippians*, 95–99; Herman Ridderbos, *Paul: An*

terms refer to the same office is held by a number of scholars, pastors, and teachers, it is often assumed rather than proven. What evidence is there to suggest that the terms represent the same office?

"Elder" and "Overseer" Are Used Interchangeably

The first reason to view the elder and overseer as representing the same office is that the terms are used interchangeably. There are three texts that clearly demonstrate this usage (Acts 20:17, 28; Titus 1:5, 7; 1 Peter 5:1–2). Upon returning from his third missionary journey, Paul's ship harbored at Miletus for a few days. Knowing that he might not return to the region again, Paul decided to contact the leaders of the church at Ephesus. Luke informs us that Paul "sent to Ephesus and called the elders (*presbuterous*) of the church to come to him" (Acts 20:17). After the elders arrive, Paul gives them a sort of "farewell speech." He exhorts them, "Pay careful attention to yourselves and to all the flock, in which the Holy Spirit has made you overseers (*episkopous*), to care for the church of God" (v. 28). Thus, in verse 17 Paul summons the "elders," but in verse 28 we read that the Holy Spirit made them "overseers." This usage demonstrates that the biblical writer did not make a distinction between the two terms.

Perhaps the most convincing passage that demonstrates that the terms for elder and overseer are interchangeable is Titus 1:5–7. In verse 5, Paul writes to Titus, "This is why I left you in Crete, so that you might put what remained into order, and appoint elders (*presbuterous*) in every town as I directed you." When Paul gives the qualifications in verse 7, however, he replaces "elder" with "overseer." He writes, "For an overseer (*episkopon*), as God's steward, must be . . ." Some maintain that a distinction between the two terms must be made because "elders" is a plural noun and "overseer" is a singular noun. A number of responses can be offered to explain this change. First, "for" (*gar*) connects verse 7 to the previous verses, indicating that the same office is in view. The elders are to be blameless *for* as overseers they are God's stewards. Second, it is more natural to list the requirements in the singular

---

Outline of His Theology, trans. John R. de Witt (Grand Rapids: Eerdmans, 1975), 457; Ellis, *Pauline Theology*, 103; D. A. Carson and Douglas J. Moo, *An Introduction to the New Testament*, 2nd ed. (Grand Rapids: Zondervan, 1992), 564; George W. Knight, *The Pastoral Epistles*, NIGTC (Grand Rapids: Eerdmans; Carlisle, U.K.: Paternoster, 1992), 175–77; David Mappes, "The New Testament Elder, Overseer, and Pastor," *BSac* 154 (1997): 164–69; and William D. Mounce, *Pastoral Epistles*, WBC (Nashville: Nelson, 2000), 46:161–63.

since every elder/overseer must individually meet the qualifications. In this case, the singular form is a generic singular. Third, the switch to the singular actually takes place in verse 6 with the use of "anyone." Fourth, it is not uncommon for Paul to alternate between singular and plural generic nouns (cf. 1 Tim. 2:8 with 2:12; 2:9 with 2:11; 2:15; 5:1 with 5:3–4; 5:17 with 5:19). Fifth, because the churches in Crete were relatively young churches, it is not likely that these churches were dealing with the developed concept of a two-stage ecclesiology, where a single overseer held a distinct position above the elders.

A similar usage is found in 1 Peter 5:1–2 where Peter writes, "I exhort the elders (*presbuterous*) among you, as a fellow elder . . . shepherd the flock of God that is among you, serving as overseers (*episkopountes*)" (my translation). Although this example is not as definitive since the verb form ("serving as overseers") is used (and not the noun "overseers"), it still emphasizes that the duty or function of the elders was to oversee the congregation. It would be strange if the elders were not the same people as those who were called "overseers" since they both were to perform the same duties.

Elders Are Never Given Separate Qualifications

A second reason that supports the view that the terms refer to the same office is that Paul never mentions the qualifications for elders. If elder and overseer are two separate offices, then it would seem reasonable to expect Paul to give the necessary qualifications for each office. In both 1 Timothy 3:1–7 and Titus 1:7–9, Paul gives the qualifications for anyone who aspires "to the office of overseer" (1 Tim. 3:1). But in both 1 Timothy (5:17–25) and Titus (1:5), elders also are mentioned. If the offices are distinct, then what are the qualifications for someone to become an elder? This omission is especially telling because in 1 Timothy 5:22–25, Paul warns Timothy not to appoint someone to the office of elder too hastily since that position is to be filled only by qualified individuals (cf. 1 Tim. 4:14; 2 Tim. 1:6). If elder is a distinct office from overseer, we would expect the qualifications to be clearly stated for such an important position. What guidelines is Timothy to use in determining the moral and spiritual readiness of such a person? Is Timothy left to find his own way? No, Paul has already given Timothy the qualifications needed for someone to become an overseer (or elder) in the church. Although such arguments from silence are never conclusive, one wonders whether Paul would have ignored the requirements given the importance he attributes to the office.

Elders and Overseers Have the Same Function

A third reason for equating the two terms is that both elders and overseers have the same function—ruling/leading and teaching. For example, 1 Timothy 3:4–5 states that an overseer must "rule/manage" (*proistēmi*) his own house before he is fit to "take care of" the church (cf. Rom. 12:8; 1 Thess. 5:12). Likewise, 1 Timothy 5:17 speaks of elders who "rule" (*proistēmi*) well, indicating that all elders are involved in ruling or leading the church. In Acts 20:28, Paul charges the Ephesian elders to "oversee" and "shepherd" the church of God. Thus, both elders and overseers are given the task of ruling/leading the church.

In a similar manner, both are also given the duty of teaching the congregation. In 1 Timothy 3:2, every overseer must be "able to teach" in order to be qualified, and in Titus 1:9 an overseer must "be able to give instruction in sound doctrine and also to rebuke those who contradict." Likewise, elders who rule well should be considered worthy of double honor, "especially those who labor in preaching and teaching" (1 Tim. 5:17). It is probably best to interpret this text as teaching that all elders teach but that some work harder at it than others.[10] Because elders and overseers are given the same tasks of ruling/leading and teaching, they should be viewed as representing the same office.

Elders and Overseers Are Never Listed as Separate Offices

A final reason for equating the elder and overseer is that nowhere in the New Testament are the three offices (elder, overseer, and deacon) mentioned together. This suggests that the three-tiered ecclesiastical system that later developed in many churches is foreign to the New Testament. Not until the second century—in the epistles of Ignatius—do we see a distinction between the overseer (i.e., the monarchical bishop) and the elders (i.e., presbytery). As such, Ignatius provides us with the first example of a three-tiered system with a bishop, a presbytery, and deacons. He exhorts his readers, "Be eager to do everything in godly harmony, the bishop presiding in the place of

---

10. David Mappes rightly comments, "While all elder-overseer-pastors must be able to teach (1 Tim. 3:2) and exhort and refute with sound doctrine (Titus 1:9), they may not all have the spiritual gifts of teaching and exhorting (Rom. 12:7)" (Mappes, "New Testament Elder," 174).

God and the presbyters in the place of the council of the apostles and the deacons, who are most dear to me, having been entrusted with the service of Jesus Christ" (*To the Magnesians* 6:1).[11] For Ignatius, the overseer is clearly distinct from the council of elders and is the sole head of the city-church. This later development, however, is not found in other writings of the postapostolic era. For example, 1 Clement (44:4–5) and the Didache, both probably written at the end of the first century, use the terms for elder and overseer interchangeably.[12]

Summary

If the two terms represent the same office, then why was it necessary to employ both terms? The reason could be explained by the general use of the terms: elder is more a description of character, whereas overseer is more a description of function.[13] It appears that originally various congregations preferred one term over the other. The Jewish congregations apparently favored the term *presbuteros*, while the Gentile congregations favored the term *episkopos*. Over time, however, these two terms came to be used in the same congregations and could be used interchangeably since they referred to the leaders of the congregation. It is likely that both terms remained due to the important connotations each term carried. The term *presbuteros* conveyed

---

11. This quotation from Ignatius is from J. B. Lightfoot, J. R. Harmer, and Michael W. Holmes, eds., *The Apostolic Fathers: Greek Text and English Translations of Their Writings*, 2nd ed. (Grand Rapids: Baker, 1992). Also see Ignatius's letters: *To the Ephesians* 2:2; 4:1; *To the Magnesians* 2:1; 13:1; *To the Trallians* 2:2–3; 7:2; *To the Philadelphians* 4:1; 7:1; *To the Smyrnaeans* 8:1; 12:2; and *To Polycarp* 6:1.

12. Eric G. Jay also maintains that "for [Clement] the word [*episkopos*] is clearly a synonym for [*presbuteros*]. He gives no hint in the letter of a claim to a higher status. . . . His letter gives us no reason to suppose that either in Rome or in Corinth in the last decade of the first century the presbyters as a corporate body did not exercise [*episkopē*], the oversight of the affairs of their churches in general, with responsibility for discipline, instruction, and the administration of the sacraments. Monepiscopacy . . . was not established there on the eve of the second century" ("From Presbyter-Bishops to Bishops and Presbyters," *SecCent* 1 [1981]: 136; also see Barbara Ellen Bowe, *A Church in Crisis: Ecclesiology and Paraenesis in Clement of Rome*, HDR 23 [Minneapolis: Fortress, 1988], 149). Jay also asserts that the monepiscopacy is not found in the Didache, Polycarp, and Hermas ("Presbyter-Bishops," 128, 142–43).

13. Philip Schaff states that "the terms PRESBYTER (or Elder) and BISHOP (or Overseer, Superintendent) denote in the New Testament one and the same office, with this difference . . . that the one signifies the dignity, the other the duty" (*History of the Christian Church*, vol. 1, *Apostolic Christianity*, 3rd rev. ed. [Peabody, MA: Hendrickson, 1996; originally published in 1858], 491–92). C. K. Barrett states, "It is broadly speaking true that the one designation describes ministers from a sociological, the other from a theological angle" (*A Critical and Exegetical Commentary on the Acts*, ICC [Edinburgh: T and T Clark, 1998], 2:975).

the idea of a wise, mature leader who was honored and respected by those of the community. The term *episkopos* spoke more to the work of the individual whose duty it was to "oversee" and protect those under his care.

Reflection Questions

1. The traditional view states that the Greek terms for "elder" and "overseer" represent the same office. What are some reasons that have caused this view to be challenged?
2. Do you find any of these reasons compelling?
3. Examine Acts 20:17–28; Titus 1:5–7; and 1 Peter 5:1–2. How do these verses demonstrate that "elder" and "overseer" refer to the same office?
4. What are the main functions of elders or overseers, and how do these functions demonstrate that the two terms refer to the same office?
5. If the two terms represent the same office, then why are both terms used in the New Testament?

Does 1 Timothy 5:17 Make a Distinction Between Two Types of Elders?

The presbyterian model of church government formally acknowledges only two church offices—elder and deacon. Yet, a distinction is made between "teaching elders" and "ruling elders." Thus, within one *office* there are two *orders*. For example, the *Book of Church Order of the Presbyterian Church in the United States* declares, "Within the class of Elder are two orders of Teaching Elders and Ruling Elders. The Elders jointly have the government and spiritual oversight of the Church, including teaching. Only those elders who are specially gifted, called and trained by God to preach may serve as Teaching Elders."[1] The support for this twofold office is based on 1 Timothy 5:17, which states, "Let the elders who rule well be considered worthy of double honor, especially those who labor in preaching and teaching." Taylor explains, "All elders rule, but some elders also have special responsibilities in preaching and teaching. This is why, in some presbyterian circles, lay elders are called 'ruling elders' and ministers are referred to as 'teaching elders.'"[2]

Those who support presbyterianism are right in maintaining that there are only two church offices for today. They correctly reject the notion that only the elders who had the extra responsibilities of preaching and teaching were designated with the title "overseer." As we demonstrated in the previous question, the titles "elder" and "overseer" describe individuals who hold the same office. But is presbyterianism justified in creating two distinct types

---

1. Presbyterian Church in the U.S. General Assembly, *Book of Church Order of the Presbyterian Church in the United States*, rev. ed. (Richmond: Board of Christian Education, 1963).
2. L. Roy Taylor, "Presbyterianism," in *Who Runs the Church? 4 Views on Church Government*, ed. Paul E. Engle and Steven B. Cowan (Grand Rapids: Zondervan, 2004), 81.

of elders? Have they not, in fact, created another office by making such a distinction? Let us first consider the differences that presbyterianism makes between the two types of elders.

Teaching Elders Versus Ruling Elders

In 1 Timothy 5:17, Paul singles out some elders in the church who, because of their hard work, are worthy of double honor. It is clear that Paul makes some sort of distinction between two types of elders—those who rule well (by their preaching and teaching) and those who rule. This small chasm, however, has become a great gulf according to the distinctions that are made by some. For example, in most churches with a presbyterian style of government, the teaching elder must be (1) seminary trained, (2) thoroughly examined by the presbytery, and (3) ordained. He alone is allowed to perform the ordinances of baptism and the Lord's Supper. He also can conduct weddings and funerals and is charged with the task of preaching and teaching. He is not a member of the church where he ministers but is a member of the presbytery. As minister, he is not given a designated term or limited by term limits. He is usually paid and often dresses distinctly.

What about the ruling elder? Seminary training is not needed by the ruling elder and neither is an examination by the presbytery nor ordination. He cannot baptize or conduct the Lord's Supper. He is not allowed to officiate weddings or funerals and does not usually teach or preach. He is a member of the church where he serves, but his service is usually defined by or limited to terms. He is not normally paid and wears no unique clothing.

The Meaning of 1 Timothy 5:17

Is this the distinction that Paul had in mind? It seems very unlikely. What type of distinction is Paul making? We cannot be absolutely certain because of the lack of information we are given in this text, but there are three interpretations that can be offered that make no formal distinction between "teaching elders" and "ruling elders." Paul could be making a distinction related to (1) time, (2) talent, or (3) type of teaching.

First, it is possible that Paul is making a distinction between those who were currently spending much time in preaching and teaching and those who were not. Perhaps some were too busy with their "secular" professions or with their families and, as a result, they could not be as committed to the gospel ministry as others. According to Paul, all overseers/elders needed to be "able to teach" (1 Tim. 3:2), but perhaps only some had enough time to do much or any actual teaching. Mounce explains, "While asserting that all elders are able to teach, Paul could have based the division on those currently teaching and those who were not. Perhaps . . . [some] overseers would have had to vary the amount of time spent specifically on teaching because of other responsibilities, and this admonition would address those actively teaching."[3]

Second, it is possible to take 1 Timothy 5:17 as making a distinction between talent and gifts. While all the elders need to be "able to teach," apparently some were more gifted in teaching and preaching than others. Among those who hold the same office, there are likely to be some who are more gifted in particular areas. Consequently, they were often called upon to lead the church through exercising their gifts of teaching. "The division could be based on those who were able to teach and those who were especially gifted to teach, dividing the elders on the basis of ability and giftedness and assuming that the more gifted did more of the corporate instruction."[4] Mappes comments, "While all elder-overseer-pastors must be able to teach (1 Tim. 3:2) and exhort and refute with sound doctrine (Titus 1:9), they may not all have the spiritual gifts of teaching and exhorting (Rom. 12:7)."[5]

A third, but less likely option, is that the distinction made in 1 Timothy 5:17 primarily involves the type of preaching or teaching performed. That is, those who teach the church corporately are singled out for special respect and

3. William D. Mounce, *Pastoral Epistles*, WBC (Nashville: Nelson, 2000), 46:308. Similarly, Samuel E. Waldron notes, "The contrast is not between no teaching and teaching. It is between some teaching and a greater degree of teaching" ("Plural-Elder Congregationalism," in *Who Runs the Church?* 216). This is the position of J. N. D. Kelly, *A Commentary on the Pastoral Epistles*, BNTC (London: Adam and Charles Black, 1963), 124–25; and Jerome D. Quinn and William C. Wacker, who write, "The point here is that some (and they are relatively few, one would surmise, because of the doubling of the honorarium) have obviously devoted all their time to this service and have done it well" (*The First and Second Letters to Timothy*, ECC [Grand Rapids: Eerdmans, 2000], 459–60).

4. Mounce, *Pastoral Epistles*, 308. This is the position of C. K. Barrett, *Pastoral Epistles in the New English Bible* (Oxford: Clarendon, 1963), 79; and George W. Knight, who writes, "Although all elders are to be able to teach (1 Tim. 3:2) and thus to instruct the people of God and to communicate with those who oppose biblical teaching (Titus 1:9ff.), the 1 Tim. 5:17 passage recognizes that among the elders, all of whom are to be able to teach, there are those so gifted by God with the ability to teach the Word that they are called by God to give their life in such a calling or occupation and deserve therefore to be remunerated for such a calling and occupation" ("Two Offices [Elders/Bishops and Deacons] and Two Orders of Elders [Preaching/Teaching Elders and Ruling Elders]: A New Testament Study," *Presbyterion* 11 [1985]: 6).

5. David Mappes, "The New Testament Elder, Overseer, and Pastor," *BSac* 154 (1997): 174.

financial support. While some elders teach in the private or "small group" settings, others are given the more crucial task of instructing the entire gathered church during the worship service. As such, the phrase "elders who rule well" "could apply to gifted teachers who were currently leading in other ways (while still allowing for one-on-one teaching, both with the opponents and the other members of the church), and 'laboring hard at preaching and teaching' could apply to those currently teaching the church as a whole."[6]

It is also possible to translate the Greek word *malista* ("especially") as "namely" or "that is."[7] In this case, Paul is not making a distinction between those who rule well and those who, in addition to ruling well, also preach and teach. Rather, those who rule well are precisely those who teach and preach (i.e., Paul is stating that the elders rule well *by* their teaching and preaching). This interpretation seems to fit Paul's stress on the importance of teaching, and a threefold division of elders is hard to imagine (i.e., those who rule, those who rule well, and those who rule well and also preach and teach).

Yet, even with this interpretation, a distinction can be made between two types of elders. If ruling well is defined by "working hard at preaching and teaching," then a distinction can still be made between those who rule well (i.e., preach and teach) and those who do not rule well (i.e., do not preach and teach). For example, Knight states that it is likely that Paul "is speaking of a subgroup of the 'overseers' that consists of those who are *especially* gifted by God to teach, as opposed to other overseers, who must all 'be *able* to teach.'"[8] But it is also possible that Paul is speaking generally of all the elders and is not intending to distinguish a subgroup. Regardless of how this difficult verse is interpreted, it in no way demands one to see two offices involved. At most, the text indicates a distinction of function within one particular office. Furthermore, the distinction that Paul makes should not be exaggerated so that, in essence, a new office is created.

Summary

The distinction that is sometimes made between teaching elders and ruling elders cannot be adequately supported from Scripture. Although Paul

---

6. Mounce, *Pastoral Epistles*, 308.
7. See T. C. Skeat, who convincingly argues that *malista* is often best translated as "namely" ("'Especially the Parchments': A Note on 2 Timothy IV. 13," *JTS* 30 [1979]: 173–77).
8. George W. Knight, *The Pastoral Epistles*, NIGTC (Grand Rapids: Eerdmans; Carlisle, U.K.: Paternoster, 1992), 233.

singles out some of the elders in the Ephesian church, it is going too far to create a separate office or even to make a formal distinction between two groups of elders. In 1 Timothy 5:17, Paul is simply acknowledging that some elders, because they have more time, talent, or training, deserve to be compensated for their work in the church.

Reflection Questions

1. Why does the presbyterian model of church government make a distinction between teaching elders and ruling elders?
2. What are some of the duties the teaching elder might perform?
3. What are some of the duties the ruling elder might perform?
4. Do you think 1 Timothy 5:17 teaches that there are two distinct types of elders?
5. If 1 Timothy 5:17 is not teaching two distinct types of elders, then what kind of distinction might Paul be making?

What Is the Role of an Elder?

In the contemporary church, elders, or pastors, are busier than ever. With so many programs, committees, and events, it is often hard to find time to meet the needs of the congregation. Some view the pastor as the CEO, while others view him as an employee. Still others view the pastor as their personal therapist who has the answers to all their problems. With so many responsibilities vying for a pastor's time, what should take precedence? In other words, what is the main duty or role of an elder? There are at least four primary duties of an elder that should not be ignored. The elder is called to be (1) a leader, (2) a shepherd, (3) a teacher, and (4) an equipper.

Elder as Leader

First of all, an elder is called to lead the church. He is not just a leader in the church, but he is called, with the other elders, to lead the church. Paul writes that an elder "must manage his own household well," and then adds the reason, "for if someone does not know how to manage his own household, how will he care for God's church?" (1 Tim. 3:4–5). The analogy Paul makes is between the role of the husband and the role of the elder. If an elder cannot manage (rule/lead/care for) his own family, then how can he be expected to take on the additional responsibilities and challenges of leading the church? Later, Paul writes, "Let the elders who rule well be considered worthy of double honor" (1 Tim. 5:17). It is evident, then, that one of the main functions of an elder is to lead the church (cf. Rom. 12:8).

Similarly, the author of Hebrews instructs the congregation, "Obey your leaders and submit to them" (Heb. 13:17; cf. 1 Thess. 5:12). The leaders, probably the elders, thus have a certain authority. Authority in the church is not equally divided among the members. And yet nowhere are the leaders told to force the congregation to submit to them. That is because leadership in the church must be humble leadership that leads by example. A pastor should not ask people to do something he himself is not willing to do. Peter encourages the elders to lead the people in a way that is not domineering, "being examples to the flock" (1 Peter 5:3). The author of Hebrews writes, "Remember your leaders, those who spoke to you the word of God. Consider the outcome of their way of life, and imitate their faith" (Heb. 13:7).

Biblical leadership is humble, servant leadership. Jesus gave the perfect example of humility when He washed the feet of His disciples (John 13:1–20). Jesus explained this symbolic act to His disciples: "Do you understand what I have done to you? You call me Teacher and Lord, and you are right, for so I am. If I then, your Lord and Teacher, have washed your feet, you also ought to wash one another's feet. For I have given you an example, that you also should do just as I have done to you" (John 13:12–15). What does a humble leader look like? First of all, a humble leader does not demand respect. He realizes that his position in the church is a gift from God and that the church itself is God's church. A humble leader also is teachable. He admits that he does not have all the answers but is willing to listen and learn from others. Furthermore, he is willing to work with others because he realizes the importance of teamwork and accountability. A humble leader is also a servant. When James and John asked if they could sit at Jesus' right and left side in heaven, Jesus said to His disciples, "You know that those who are considered rulers of the Gentiles lord it over them, and their great ones exercise authority over them. But it shall not be so among you. But whoever would be great among you must be your servant, and whoever would be first among you must be slave of all" (Mark 10:42–44). Finally, and most importantly, a humble leader does all to the glory of God (1 Cor. 10:31).

Elder as Shepherd

As we already demonstrated, the title "pastor" (see Eph. 4:11) is simply another term used to describe an elder or overseer (see question 6), and "pastor" has the same meaning as "shepherd." Because the people of God are referred to figuratively as "sheep," those who tend to their needs and exercise leadership over them are figuratively called "shepherds." Peter exhorts the elders to "shepherd the flock of God that is among you" (1 Peter 5:2). Thus, the elders lead the people of God as a shepherd leads a flock of sheep. This is a significant analogy. Church leaders are not cowboys who drive the sheep. Rather, they are caring shepherds who lead and protect the sheep. Furthermore, the shepherd's primary task is not to run an organization but to care for people's souls. A pastor is not primarily a motivator, administrator, or program facilitator, but a shepherd.

In the Old Testament, the Lord rebuked the leaders of Israel for not being good shepherds. The basic charge against these leaders was that they looked after their own interests and ignored the needs of the sheep. We read in Ezekiel, "Ah, shepherds of Israel who have been feeding yourselves! Should not shepherds feed the sheep? You eat the fat, you clothe yourselves with the wool, you slaughter the fat ones, but you do not feed the sheep. The weak you have not strengthened, the sick you have not healed, the injured you have not bound up, the strayed you have not brought back, the lost you have not sought, and with force and harshness you have ruled them" (Ezek. 34:2–4).

Jesus, of course, is the perfect Shepherd. He is the Good Shepherd who "lays down his life for the sheep" (John 10:11; cf. John 15:13). He is the one who always feeds His sheep. He strengthens them, heals them, binds their wounds, and brings back those who are straying. Peter therefore describes Jesus as "the Shepherd and Overseer" of our souls (1 Peter 2:25). He is the "chief Shepherd" (1 Peter 5:4) who is the perfect example for those who are undershepherds.

The shepherd must be willing to protect the sheep. Paul warns the Ephesian elders in his farewell speech, "Pay careful attention to yourselves and to all the flock, in which the Holy Spirit has made you overseers, to care for the church of God, which he obtained with his own blood. I know that after my departure fierce wolves will come in among you, not sparing the flock" (Acts 20:28–29). A good shepherd will pay close attention to the flock and protect from wolves that would seek to harm them spiritually.

Often, however, sheep get injured and need assistance. It is therefore important for the elders to attend to the needs of those in the congregation. They need to visit not only those who are spiritually sick or weak but also those who are physically sick. James raises the question, "Is anyone among you sick?" His answer for this problem is, "Let him call for the elders of the church, and let them pray over him, anointing him with oil in the name of the Lord" (James 5:14). Isaiah gives us a picture of a good shepherd as he explains how the Lord God shepherds His people: "He will tend his flock like a shepherd; he will gather the lambs in his arms; he will carry them in his bosom, and gently lead those that are with young" (Isa. 40:11). In giving the needed qualifications for an elder, Paul states that he must be able to manage his own household well or else he will not be able to "care for" God's church (1 Tim. 3:4–5). The Greek word translated "care for" (*epimeleomai*) is found only two other times in the New Testament, both in the parable of the Good Samaritan. We are told that the Good Samaritan had compassion on the injured Jew, cleaning and binding his wounds. He then set the dying man on his animal and brought him to the inn and "took care of him" (Luke 10:34). The Samaritan then commands the innkeeper, "Take care of him" (Luke 10:35). It is this type of care that the shepherds of God's church are called to display in their lives and in their ministries.

Shepherding carries with it a great responsibility before God. The sheep are placed under the care of the shepherd. The sheep have the responsibility to follow the shepherd, but the shepherd has to be diligent in keeping watch over the sheep. The author of Hebrews exhorts his readers, "Obey your leaders and submit to them, for they are keeping watch over your souls, as those who will have to give an account" (Heb. 13:17). Thus, the reason the members of the congregation are to follow the leadership of the elders is because they are given the task of watching over their souls—a responsibility for which they will be held accountable.

Elder as Teacher

It is clear from the New Testament that an elder is primarily a teacher. The elders' calling to lead the church through their teaching distinguishes them from the deacons. One of the unique qualifications for an elder is that he must be "able to teach" (1 Tim. 3:2). Two chapters later Paul mentions that those who rule well are worthy of double honor, that is, those who work hard at "preaching and teaching" (1 Tim. 5:17). In Titus, Paul describes this role in more detail. He explains that an elder "must hold firm to the trustworthy word as taught, so that he may be able to give instruction in sound doctrine and also to rebuke those who contradict it" (Titus 1:9). Paul indicates that the goal of teaching is not only to encourage believers by giving them biblical instruction but also to firmly rebuke those who oppose the truth of the gospel. The teaching role is also inseparably connected to the function of the pastor when Paul states that God has gifted the church with "pastors and teachers" or pastor-teachers (Eph. 4:11).

There are other texts that associate the role of church leaders with teaching. Although elders or overseers are not specifically mentioned in the following examples, it is likely that those who were doing the teaching were in fact elders. Paul reminds the church in Galatia that the "one who is taught the word must share all good things with the one who teaches" (Gal. 6:6).

Two things should be observed from this verse. First, that which was being taught was the Word. This emphasis on the Word of God was evident from the beginning of the church. We read that the first believers in Jerusalem "devoted themselves to the apostles' teaching" (Acts 2:42). Second, some were so dedicated to the task of teaching that they required financial support. Though not named elders, these people were performing the function of elders among those in the congregation. In 1 Thessalonians 5:12, Paul exhorts the congregation "to respect those who labor among you and are over you in the Lord and admonish you." These leaders who are to be respected are described as those who "labor," "are over," and "admonish" the Thessalonian Christians. Most likely, those who had such leadership to lead and teach (i.e., admonish) the congregation were the elders. Likewise, in Hebrews 13:7, the leaders are defined as "those who spoke . . . the word of God" to the church. This text is most likely referring to the teaching ministry of the elders.

Paul also stresses the importance of the teaching ministry to his associate Timothy. Although it is incorrect to view Timothy as the "pastor" of the church at Ephesus because he carried more authority as Paul's apostolic delegate (see question 13), it is clear that his role overlapped with that of the elders. Paul reminds his protégé Timothy, "Devote yourself to the public reading of Scripture, to exhortation, to teaching" (1 Tim. 4:13). The reading and subsequent exposition of the Bible was at the heart and center of the worship service. For Timothy to neglect this task would be a colossal failure on his part. In 2 Timothy, Paul's last written letter in the Bible, Paul realizes that his death is imminent, and he senses the urgency to once again encourage Timothy, his son in the faith. With the utmost solemnity and seriousness, Paul writes, "I charge you in the presence of God and of Christ Jesus, who is to judge the living and the dead, and by his appearing and his kingdom: preach the word; be ready in season and out of season; reprove, rebuke, and exhort, with complete patience and teaching" (2 Tim. 4:1–2). The importance of solid, gospel teaching in the church is vital to the church's existence. The Word must be preached, and it is the task of elders to preach that Word.

Elder as Equipper

The role of the elder as teacher is important, not just for the health of the church in the present, but also for the growth of the church in the future. As a result, it is not enough for the elders simply to be teachers; they also must be purposefully equipping the next generation of elders to minister alongside them or to plant new churches in the community. Too often I have witnessed pastors who preach and teach year after year but, when all is said and done, they have effectively trained and equipped nobody to take their place. It is a sign of an unhealthy church if there is no one in the congregation who can step in the gap and fill the pulpit whenever the pastor is gone. Biblical eldership includes training others to do the task of preaching and teaching.

Again, Paul's words to Timothy are instructive. He tells Timothy, "What you have heard from me in the presence of many witnesses entrust to faithful men who will be able to teach others also" (2 Tim. 2:2). As Paul's faithful co-worker, Timothy was entrusted with the task of passing on the pure gospel as preached by Paul. He had been equipped by Paul and was now to become an equipper himself. He was to entrust what he had learned to "faithful men," which is probably another way of describing the elders of the church. But this task of equipping does not stop with the elders. They also are to become equippers "who will be able to teach others also." The task of raising up new leaders in the church does not belong primarily to Bible colleges or seminaries. It is the task of the elders to identify those young (or not so young) men who will be faithful to carry on the gospel message. Unfortunately, pastors are either too busy or too insecure to mentor and disciple other gifted men in the church. Thus, this role of the elder is perhaps the most neglected and therefore one that must be emphasized in the local church.

Summary

The office of elder is an important office because of the role the elders perform. Their primary task is not merely to run the church but to care for the spiritual lives of the congregation. As leaders, shepherds, teachers, and equippers, elders have the immense responsibility and privilege of helping God's people become more holy and more Christlike.

Reflection Questions

1. What are some incorrect ways to view an elder or pastor?
2. What are some practical ways elders might carry out their role as leaders, shepherds, teachers, and equippers?
3. What do you think is the most important role of an elder? Why?
4. What are some ways you can improve your role as an elder?
5. What is your church doing to develop new leaders?

How Much Authority Should the Elders Have?

The New Testament does not tell us precisely how much authority the elders of the local congregation should have. We have to take relevant texts from the New Testament and attempt to synthesize the principles that are taught in each text. As a result, we must be cautious of conclusions that are too rigid or dogmatic. The principles we gather from Scripture should be followed, but the outworking of these principles can be appropriated in different ways.

Elders Have Authority

In the first place, we must note that the Bible is clear that elders have authority. Paul writes to the congregation in Thessalonica, "We ask you, brothers, to respect those who labor among you and are over you in the Lord and admonish you" (1 Thess. 5:12). This text demonstrates that in the earliest stage of the church, there were some who were set apart as leaders and, as such, were to be respected because of their important work in the church. Paul makes a distinction between the "brothers" and those they are to respect. Apparently not every believer was to be honored and respected in the same way. Some, because of their gifts and function in the community, were to be considered worthy of special recognition. This text is similar to 1 Timothy 5:17, where Paul states, "Let the elders who rule well be considered worthy of double honor, especially those who labor in preaching and teaching." Just as elders have authority in their homes, so also they have authority in the church (1 Tim. 3:4–5).

Another text that demonstrates the authority of the elders is found at the end of the book of Hebrews. The author urges the congregation, "Obey your leaders and submit to them, for they are keeping watch over your souls, as those who will have to give an account" (Heb. 13:17). Although elders are not mentioned here, it is safe to assume that the "leaders" who possessed this type of authority were indeed elders.[1] The word translated "obey" (*peithō*) also can mean "to be persuaded." The normal word for "obey" or "to subject oneself" is *hypotassō*, which is a stronger word. Although the verb *peithō* demands obedience, it is "the obedience that is won through persuasive conversation."[2] The second command, "submit" (*hypeikō*), is found only here in the New Testament and means "to submit to one's authority." Similarly, Paul encourages the Corinthian believers to submit (*hypotassō*) to the household of Stephanas, as well as other fellow workers (1 Cor. 16:15–16; cf. 1 Peter 5:5). But those who lead the church must be servant leaders. Schreiner notes, "Paul does not say that the leaders are to compel the congregation to submit. He urges the congregation to submit voluntarily and gladly to leadership. The congregation takes it upon itself to follow the leadership. Paul does not instruct leaders to compel the congregation to submit."[3]

The very functions or duties of the elders communicate that their office carries with it a certain amount of authority. As teachers, they are charged with the task of authoritatively proclaiming God's Word. They are not merely offering suggestions or voicing their own opinions but are declaring, "Thus says the Lord." Consequently, the congregation has the duty to obey, not because they are the words of the preacher but the words of God, insomuch as the preacher accurately and faithfully conveys the gospel message.

As shepherds, the elders are given the task of leading God's people (Acts 20:28; Eph. 4:11; 1 Peter 5:2). If some are leading as shepherds, the assumption is that others are following their leadership. Of course, with the authority given to the shepherd also comes added responsibility. He must guide, watch over, and protect those in his flock. He is even called to go after wandering sheep and bring them back into the fold. Elders are accountable before God for their role as shepherds (Heb. 13:17). In the same way, the sheep are accountable before God to obey and follow the shepherds so that they can fulfill their responsibilities with joy (Heb. 13:17).

---

1. Wayne Grudem affirms this position: "Since the New Testament gives no indication of any other officers in the church with this kind of authority, it is reasonable to conclude that the congregation is to submit to and obey its elders" (*Systematic Theology: An Introduction to Biblical Doctrine* [Leicester: InterVarsity Press; Grand Rapids: Eerdmans, 1994], 915).
2. William L. Lane, *Hebrews 9–13*, WBC (Dallas: Word, 1991), 47b:554.
3. Thomas R. Schreiner, *Paul, Apostle of God's Glory in Christ* (Downers Grove, IL: InterVarsity Press, 2001), 386.

As representatives, the elders speak and act on behalf of the entire congregation. When Barnabas and Paul brought famine relief money on behalf of the church in Antioch, it was received by the elders of the Jerusalem church (Acts 11:30). Later, as Paul was journeying to Jerusalem from Greece, he briefly harbored at Miletus. There he called for the elders of the Ephesian church to come so that he might encourage them (Acts 20:17). Although his concern was for the whole church, he called the elders because they served as the leaders and representatives of the church.

The authority of the eldership comes from God and not from the congregation. Although the congregation affirms the elders' calling and authority, theirs is an authority with a divine origin. Paul tells the Ephesian elders that the Holy Spirit made them overseers (Acts 20:28). They were called and given authority by God and not by man. Yet, it was probably the Ephesian congregation that endorsed them and Paul then appointed them publicly to their office. In his letter to the Ephesians, Paul states that Christ has given gifts to the church, including pastor-teachers (Eph. 4:11). Therefore, the office of elder "does not derive its existence, or authority, from the congregation. The elder's authority comes from Christ, and the congregation's role is that of recognition of God's gifting and calling."[4]

Elders Have Limited Authority

It must be pointed out, however, that the elders' authority is not absolute. They derive their authority from the Word of God, and when they stray from that Word, they abandon their God-given authority. As an apostle of Jesus Christ, Paul possessed nearly unmatched authority. Yet, Luke tells us that the Bereans were more noble than others because they not only received the preached Word with eagerness, but they examined the Scriptures daily to see if Paul indeed spoke the truth (Acts 17:11). Paul himself states that even if he or an angel preached a gospel other than the true gospel, "let him be accursed" (Gal. 1:8). The authority that the elders possess is not so much found in their office but in the duties they perform. That is, the elders are not to be obeyed simply because they are elders. Rather, they are to be obeyed because they have the responsibility of shepherding and teaching the congregation. They shepherd because the Word calls upon elders to shepherd. They teach

---

4. James R. White, "The Congregation-Led Church: Response by James R. White," in *Perspectives on Church Government: Five Views of Church Polity,* ed. Chad Owen Brand and R. Stanton Norman (Nashville: Broadman and Holman, 2004), 205.

because the Word calls upon elders to teach. But when their shepherding and teaching stray from Scripture, their authority as shepherds and teachers is no longer binding on the congregation.

In addition, the authority of the elders did not extend beyond the local church. There is no evidence in the New Testament that elders exercised authority outside their congregation as the apostles did. As shepherds, they ministered to their flock, but once they ventured outside their community to another congregation, they no longer functioned authoritatively.

Furthermore, biblical church government is not an aristocracy or an oligarchy. As we argued earlier, the local congregation as a whole often took part in the proceedings of the church. They were involved in choosing new leaders (Acts 6:2–3), commissioning missionaries (Acts 13:3), affirming important theological decisions (Acts 15:22), and disciplining unrepentant church members (1 Cor. 5:2; 2 Cor. 2:6). In the New Testament, there seems to be a balance between the authority of the elders and the authority of the congregation as a whole. To ignore either side will create an unhealthy and dangerous imbalance.

Who Has the Final Authority: the Elders or the Congregation?

We have argued that both the elders and the congregation as a whole possess a certain amount of authority in the church. But which one has the final authority? This question assumes that Jesus Christ (and His Word) is the ultimate authority in the church. Everything should be done under His authority because He is "the head of the body, the church" (Col. 1:18). But, while we acknowledge Jesus' lordship, who makes the final decisions in the church? Again, no answer is explicitly given to us in the Bible. Historically, however, congregationalists have given final authority to the majority vote of the congregation. There is strong New Testament evidence for this conclusion. According to Jesus, the final step in correcting a sinning brother is to "tell it to the church" (Matt. 18:17). Paul encourages the Corinthian congregation to forgive the one who caused him so much trouble, for the "punishment by the majority is enough" (2 Cor. 2:6). By indicating a "majority," it is natural to assume there was a "minority" who were opposed to the punishment given. The conclusion often made is that some sort of vote was needed to determine the will of the majority. Although it may be going too far to base the practice of voting in the church on this one verse, it does seem clear that the entire church was involved in making the decision.

Thus, key decisions in the church should not be given only to the elders but should be brought before the entire congregation. Because the church is a body (and not merely a head or feet), all in the church are important and should be allowed to be a part of major decisions. In saying this, two things need to be stressed. First, the elders are the leaders in the church and therefore should be given freedom to lead. Every decision should not be brought before the church.[5] Important decisions, such as the addition of a new elder or deacon, the budget, or a change to the constitution or bylaws, are congregational matters. Most other areas of concern, however, should be left to the leadership of the elders and deacons. It is not usually beneficial for a church to let all the members vote on what color the carpet should be.

Second, if the church uses the democratic method of voting, then it *must* practice church discipline and keep a current record of its membership. If church discipline is not practiced, then those who should no longer be members of the church will be allowed to vote. Those who are living in open, unrepentant rebellion against God should be removed from the membership (1 Cor. 5:2). To give such a person the privilege of voting is unwise. Furthermore, those who do not attend the church on a regular basis (for reasons other than health) also should be removed from membership. If they are not an active part of the church community, they should not be deciding important matters related to the life of the church. If such people are not removed from membership, the church will find people who have not attended a worship service for many years attending business meetings and voting on important and controversial topics.

Voting, however, is not the only way to satisfy the needed balance between congregational authority and elder authority. It is possible, though less common, for the elders to lead by consensus. Or, to put it differently, the congregation moves forward, under the leadership of the elders, as a unified body. When certain issues need resolution, the church moves forward on the issue once the congregation as a whole is agreed. Votes are not counted but rather objections are discussed. Perhaps this is what Paige Patterson had in mind when he wrote, "The ministries of the church should derive from the action of the corporate body seeking the face of God and the leadership of the Holy Spirit and expressing that through some process, which for lack of a better

---

5. Phil A. Newton comments, "There is no evidence that the early church voted on every issue. Rather, the plural eldership competently and efficiently handled day-to-day matters" (*Elders in Congregational Life: Rediscovering the Biblical Model for Church Leadership* [Grand Rapids: Kregel, 2005], 58).

term may be called a vote. Better still is the idea that the congregation arrives by whatever means at a *spiritual consensus*."[6]

Summary

We have been trying to balance the dual notions that elders have authority and that the congregation as a whole has the final authority on critical issues. The elders are accountable not only to the Lord Jesus Christ but also accountable to each other and the entire congregation. Schreiner comments, "Too much focus on leaders could obscure the equality of all believers in Christ. Paul maintained a delicate balance between the role of leadership and the contribution of each member in the church. Leaders were important in the Pauline churches, but they did not operate in such a way that individual members' contributions were quashed; they led mainly by example and persuasion, not by coercion."[7] For a system like this to work, it requires people who are filled with the Holy Spirit and exhibit a spirit of humility in their relations with others.

Reflection Questions

1. What do 1 Thessalonians 5:12 and Hebrews 13:17 teach us about the authority of elders?
2. How is the authority of elders demonstrated by their duties of teaching, shepherding, and representing the congregation?
3. Where does the authority of elders come from, and why is that important?
4. In what way is the authority of the elders limited?
5. What kinds of decisions should be decided by the elders, and what kind should be decided by the entire congregation? Do you think voting is the best way for the church to make decisions?

---

6. Paige Patterson, "Single-Elder Congregationalism," in *Who Runs the Church? 4 Views on Church Government*, ed. Paul E. Engle and Steven B. Cowan (Grand Rapids: Zondervan, 2004), 140.

7. Schreiner, *Paul*, 385. Samuel E. Waldron rightly notes, "The Word of God has a tendency to put things together that we in our human wisdom tend to regard as contradictory. Thus, in spite of the apparently self-sufficient democracy suggested by the facts cited in connection with the Democratic principle, the Word of God appoints that the church should have a class of ruling officers" (*Who Runs the Church?* 218). Later he adds, "The *consent of both* the church and its eldership (and, thus, the unity of the church) is required for every act where the church as a whole has a voice" (ibid., 221).

Were Timothy and Titus Pastors/Elders?

We are not asking here whether or not Timothy and Titus performed pastoral or elderlike duties in their respective ministries in Ephesus and Crete. There is no doubt that they did perform many of the same duties and responsibilities that are expected of pastors or elders. For example, elders are responsible for teaching and preaching the Word of God (Eph. 4:11; 1 Thess. 5:12; 1 Tim. 3:2; 5:17; Titus 1:9), and this responsibility likewise is given to Timothy and Titus (1 Tim. 1:3; 4:11; 6:2; 2 Tim. 2:2; Titus 2:1, 7, 15; 3:1).

But it would be wrong to assume that the authority Timothy and Titus possessed is the same authority that pastors have today. The reason for this distinction is that Timothy and Titus were not merely pastors but had the additional authority of being Paul's apostolic delegates. Mounce rightly acknowledges the uniqueness of their position: "Timothy and Titus stand outside the church structure. They are not bishops or elders, and are not members of the local church. They are itinerant, apostolic delegates sent with Paul's authority to deal with local problems, just as they do in Acts. Timothy and Titus are never told to rely on their institutional position in the local church for authority; rather they rely on the authority of Paul and the gospel."[1]

---

1. William D. Mounce, *Pastoral Epistles*, WBC (Nashville: Nelson, 2000), 46:lxxxviii. For others who hold that Timothy and Titus did not hold any office in the church but were sent as Paul's apostolic delegates with temporary authority, see George W. Knight, *The Pastoral Epistles*, NIGTC (Grand Rapids: Eerdmans; Carlisle, U.K.: Paternoster, 1992), 29; J. N. D. Kelly, *A Commentary on the Pastoral Epistles*, BNTC (London: Adam and Charles Black, 1963), 13–14; and Donald Guthrie, *The Pastoral Epistles*, TNTC, rev. ed. (Leicester: InterVarsity Press; Grand Rapids: Eerdmans, 1990), 14:38–39.

Their Position Was Temporary

There are at least three reasons that compel us to make a distinction be-
tween the roles of Timothy and Titus and the role of the elder or overseer.
First, both Timothy and Titus held temporary positions. Timothy was one of
Paul's most faithful and trusted missionary companions. He joined Paul on
his second missionary journey and became a nearly constant companion of
the apostle. Very early in their relationship, Paul found that he could trust
Timothy with the task of finishing what he himself could not. For example,
Paul left Timothy behind in Berea when the apostle was forced to flee the
city (Acts 17:14). Later, Timothy became Paul's emissary to Thessalonica to
help strengthen the church's faith (1 Thess. 3:2–3). Then, Paul sent Timothy,
along with Erastus, to Macedonia while Paul himself remained in Asia (Acts
19:22). Paul also chose Timothy to travel to Corinth so that he could remind
the Corinthians of Paul's ways in Christ (1 Cor. 4:17). During his first Roman
imprisonment, Paul made plans to send Timothy to Philippi, although there
is no clear indication elsewhere in Scripture that he actually traveled there
during this time (Phil. 2:19). Finally, in 1 Timothy we read that Paul urged
Timothy to remain at Ephesus in order to combat the false teaching that had
infiltrated the church (1 Tim. 1:3–4). Timothy was sent as Paul's apostolic
delegate to protect the church from false teachings and to give the church
proper guidelines for who should lead the church and how the church should
function. His role was temporary. Once the church was healthy enough to
function without him, he would return to Paul and continue his traveling
ministry with the apostle. At the end of 2 Timothy, Paul instructs his beloved
friend, "Do your best to come to me soon" (4:9). Timothy's task at Ephesus
was specific, and once his task was completed, he would move to another
ministry under the leadership and authority of Paul.

The same is true for Titus who was also one of Paul's trusted associates.
He was born to Greek parents and became an early traveling companion of
Paul (Gal. 2:1, 3). Although never mentioned in the book of Acts, he accompanied Paul and Barnabas to the church in Jerusalem during the so-called
"Jerusalem Council" (Acts 15). Titus became instrumental in helping Paul
deal with the problems in the Corinthian church. Following his first canoni-
cal letter to the Corinthians, Paul made an emergency visit to Corinth, but he
was not well received. As a result, he wrote a harsh letter to the Corinthians
and sent Titus to deliver it (2 Cor. 12:18). Titus apparently returned to Paul
with good news; and when Paul later penned 2 Corinthians, he again sent

his "partner and fellow worker" as the messenger (2 Cor. 8:23). Several years later, after being released from his first Roman imprisonment, Paul made a visit to the island of Crete. For some unknown reason, however, Paul was forced to leave Crete prematurely. Because Titus was accompanying Paul at this time, Paul left Titus behind in Crete in order to fulfill the ministry Paul himself could not do. Titus's work, however, did not end in Crete. When his work in Crete was finished, or at least when things were stable, Paul wanted Titus to meet him at Nicopolis (Titus 3:12). Finally, according to 2 Timothy 4:10, Titus went to Dalmatia. As with Timothy, Titus's role in the churches in Crete was temporary. As Paul's apostolic delegate, he was left behind to establish the churches. Once they were sufficiently established, Titus moved on to another ministry under the leadership of Paul.

Their Position Was Authoritative

A second reason Timothy and Titus should not be regarded merely as pastors or elders is that it was their task to appoint elders in the churches. The authority to appoint elders is more authority than any one elder possesses. In Acts, Paul and Barnabas appointed elders in many churches in Asia Minor. As an apostle, Paul had the authority to publicly appoint these leaders to a recognized office. Timothy and Titus were also able to appoint elders, not because they themselves were elders, but because they had the greater authority of being Paul's apostolic delegates. For instance, Paul warns Timothy, "Do not be hasty in the laying on of hands, nor take part in the sins of others" (1 Tim. 5:22). As one with authority over the church, Timothy must guard against laying his hands on (i.e., appointing to the office of elder) anyone who is not truly qualified. By too hastily appointing an elder who is not fit for the office, Timothy himself takes part in the sins of others. Paul therefore warns his protégé to use his special authority with extreme care.

Paul also gave Titus the task of appointing elders in Crete. Paul writes, "This is why I left you in Crete, so that you might put what remained into order, and appoint elders in every town as I directed you" (Titus 1:5). According to Acts 14:23, it was Paul's custom to appoint elders in the churches he established. Paul's quick and unexpected departure from Crete forced him to assign this important responsibility to Titus. Titus was not an elder but was to appoint elders. His authority over the churches was temporary because no elders existed. Once elders were appointed and the church was firmly established, Titus would be free to leave the direction of the church in the hands of the elders. It is therefore incorrect to view Timothy and Titus as "senior pastors" who had the authority to hire and fire. They were temporarily assigned to help struggling churches raise up leaders so that they would no longer be needed and could continue their work elsewhere.

Their Position Was Unique

The third reason Timothy and Titus should not be viewed as elders is that a single leadership position with the authority they possessed is not found in the New Testament. It is clear that they possessed authority that is higher than that of the elders. Normally a group of elders collectively led each church. But in the case of the churches in Ephesus and Crete, Timothy and Titus stand above the congregation, carrying with them the commission and authority of the apostle Paul.

The unique authority of Timothy and Titus may not have been readily accepted and heeded by others—especially those who were promoting false teachings. So Paul's letters to his delegates serve as a concrete recommendation and validation of their ministry. In the two letters to Timothy and the single letter to Titus, Paul identifies his associates by name as the recipients of the letters (1 Tim. 1:2; 2 Tim. 1:2; Titus 1:4). And yet, Paul also writes these three letters to the congregations that Timothy and Titus were assisting. This fact is clearly seen in the conclusion of each letter as Paul greets not only his delegates but also the entire congregations (1 Tim. 6:21; 2 Tim. 4:22; Titus 3:15). By addressing these letters to Timothy and Titus, Paul not only instructed his coworkers and the congregation as a whole, but he also gave Timothy and Titus validation and authority to carry out the work of their ministry. Any who disagreed with Timothy and Titus would have been seen as going against Paul himself.

Summary

Based on the reasons considered above, it is best to view Timothy and Titus *not* primarily as pastors or elders, but as Paul's apostolic delegates. As delegates under Paul's authority, they were sent to their respective places of ministry to help establish the churches in the gospel as well as to protect the churches from false gospels. They had a specific task to accomplish and when that task was complete, they would move on to another ministry. Because they were sent by Paul and functioned as an extension of Paul's own ministry, they carried with them an authority that surpassed that of an elder or overseer. They were not elders but were given the unique task of appointing elders so that the church would be healthy and could function without them. Thus, although many of the commands given to Timothy and Titus are applicable for pastors, it is wrong to equate the ministries of Timothy and Titus with the modern-day elder or pastor.

Reflection Questions

1. What type of position did Timothy and Titus hold in their respective churches?
2. How is the authority of their position different from that of a pastor/elder?
3. How do we know the positions of Timothy and Titus were temporary?
4. What made their positions unique?
5. If Timothy and Titus should not be considered pastors/elders, then what dangers might we encounter if we try to equate their authority with the authority of a modern pastor?

Section B
Questions Related to Qualifications

What Are the Situational and Family Qualifications for an Elder?

When reading the qualifications for an elder or overseer, one is immediately struck by the relative simplicity of the qualifications. In fact, the qualifications for an elder are the basic characteristics that are expected of all Christians. The only exceptions are that an elder must not be a recent convert and must be able to teach. The focus of the qualifications is on who a person is more than what a person does. The chart on the following page is a comparison of the qualifications found in 1 Timothy 3 with those in Titus 1. The qualifications in Titus 1 are rearranged to match the order given in 1 Timothy 3. Those qualifications found only in one list are italicized.

For the most part, the qualifications given seem to be listed in random order. The one exception is that both lists begin with the qualifications of being "above reproach" and "the husband of one wife" (1 Tim. 3:2; Titus 1:6).[1] We will examine the qualifications under the subdivisions of situational qualifications and family qualifications. The next question will discuss the moral qualifications of an elder.

Situational Qualifications

These qualifications relate to one's situation in life. They are not really moral or spiritual qualifications but rather reveal one's desire and ability to serve. They also relate to the time of one's conversion and how non-Christians view the genuineness of that conversion.

---

1. The adjectives translated "above reproach" are slightly different in the Greek but are virtual synonyms.

1 Timothy 3	Titus 1
above reproach	above reproach
the husband of one wife	the husband of one wife
sober-minded	
self-controlled	self-controlled
respectable	
hospitable	hospitable
able to teach	hold firm to the trustworthy word as taught—give instruction in sound doctrine and also rebuke those who contradict it
not a drunkard	not a drunkard
not violent	not violent
gentle	
not quarrelsome	
not a lover of money	not greedy for gain
manage his own household well, keeping his children submissive	his children are believers and not open to the charge of debauchery or insubordination
not a recent convert	
well thought of by outsiders	
	not arrogant
	not quick-tempered
	a lover of good
	upright
	holy
	disciplined

Desire to Serve (1 Tim. 3:1)

Although not formally a qualification, Paul mentions that it is a good thing ("a noble task") for someone to aspire to the office of overseer. "Noble" is translated from the Greek word *kalos*, which means "good," "excellent," or "worthwhile." Although it is possible some may desire this office from impure motives such as greed or pride, Paul wants to make clear that those who are chosen to serve should want to serve. Churches often nominate people to service and then have to twist their arms to get them to reluctantly accept the position. These people may serve faithfully, but they seldom really experience joy and fulfillment in their service. It is better to select those people who are eager to serve. Indeed, it is best to select those people who are already joyfully serving in some capacity, although they may have no formal office in the church. Those who desire to serve God as elders desire a good thing. But desire alone is never enough. This desire must be accompanied by moral character and spiritual capability.

Able to Teach (1 Tim. 3:2; Titus 1:9)

This is the only qualification that directly relates to an elder's duties in the church (although 1 Tim. 3:4–5 speak of managing and caring for the church). Elders must be able to communicate God's Word in a way that is accurate and understandable. In Titus, Paul expands on what he wrote in 1 Timothy. He adds that an overseer "must hold firm to the trustworthy word as taught, so that he may be able to give instruction in sound doctrine and also to rebuke those who contradict it" (Titus 1:9). An elder must not only be "able to teach," but he must also teach sound doctrine and correct those who are in error. He cannot merely have a cursory knowledge of the Bible but must be immersed in the teachings of Scripture so that he can both exhort in sound doctrine and rebuke those who reject sound doctrine.

If all elders must be "able to teach," does that mean that all elders must teach or preach publicly? Such an interpretation is probably more restrictive than what Paul has in mind. Certainly, all elders should be involved in some kind of teaching. It would seem odd for Paul to require that all elders be able to teach if some of them are not involved in any type of teaching ministry. All elders must be able to teach and should be using their teaching abilities or gifts actively in the church. But the type of teaching should not be limited to preaching on Sunday mornings or at other times when the entire congregation is gathered. Some elders may not be gifted in teaching or preaching to large groups but may have an incredible gift to teach or disciple in a small group setting. Grudem correctly writes, "Paul never says that all the elders are to be able to teach publicly or to preach sermons to the congregation, and it would be reasonable to think that an 'apt teacher' could be someone who is able to explain God's Word privately. So perhaps not all elders are called to do public teaching—perhaps not all have gifts for teaching in that specific way. What is clear here is that Paul wants to guarantee that elders have a mature and sound understanding of Scripture and can explain it to others."[2]

Not a Recent Convert (1 Tim. 3:6)

In 1 Timothy, Paul writes that an elder must not be a new believer. He then gives the reason for this qualification: "or he may become puffed up with conceit and fall into the condemnation of the devil" (1 Tim. 3:6). When a recent convert takes on an important and respected leadership role without the deep maturity that comes with time, he may become filled with pride and end up ruining his ministry and defaming the name of God. A new convert does not truly understand his own weaknesses and the temptations that might ensnare him. As a result, he is more vulnerable to pride, which will lead to his destruction (Prov. 16:18). Time is therefore needed to let the new believer mature in his faith and gain the respect of others through faithful service in lesser roles. The difficulty is that Paul does not specify what constitutes a "recent convert." Was he referring to six months, one year, or ten years? Perhaps the answer to this question depends on the congregation or historical circumstances involved. In some churches, it might be unwise to let a person who has been a Christian for only five years become an elder. In other churches, however, it may be unwise to wait that long.

This conclusion is supported by the historical circumstances that surrounded the churches at Ephesus and Crete. The church at Ephesus was a somewhat well-established church when Paul wrote 1 Timothy. By that time, the church had been in existence for about fifteen years and already had established leaders. In this circumstance, Paul could write that elders should not be recent converts because in that church there would have been others who were more mature in their faith and could handle the respect and responsibilities given to such officeholders. Paul's letter to Titus, however,

---

2. Wayne Grudem, *Systematic Theology: An Introduction to Biblical Doctrine* (Leicester: Inter-Varsity Press; Grand Rapids: Eerdmans, 1994), 915–16n. 19.

does not contain the restriction concerning new converts. Did Paul simply forget to add this qualification, or was it purposefully ignored? It is plausible to think that Paul ignored the restriction about new converts because the situation in Crete was different than that in Ephesus. The church in Crete was much younger, making nearly all the potential candidates for eldership "recent converts." In this case, if new believers were not appointed as elders, there would be no elders. Consequently, it seems this qualification is not absolute but depends somewhat on the situational context of the congregation involved.

Well Thought of by Outsiders (1 Tim. 3:7)

"Outsiders," or non-Christians, often seem to be better judges of character than those in the church. Neighbors, coworkers, or relatives may actually spend much more time with the person than his fellow church members. An elder must maintain a good reputation before a world of watching unbelievers. If the church allows a person who has a bad reputation with non-Christians to become an elder, non-Christians will scoff and mock the church for being hypocritical. A man who is unfaithful to his family, dishonest in his business, or rude to his neighbors will bring shame on himself and on the church. Paul warns that those who have a sinful or unfavorable reputation with outsiders can "fall into disgrace, into a snare of the devil" (1 Tim. 3:7). The world is waiting to point a finger and criticize and disgrace the church. Consequently, the devil will use one's bad reputation to ensnare the person deeper into sin. Thus, an elder must have a good reputation with non-Christians.

Family Qualifications

The second area of qualifications relates to the family life of the candidate. He must be faithful to his wife and manage his children well before he can be considered fit to lead the church of God.

Husband of One Wife (1 Tim. 3:2; Titus 1:6)

This qualification appears at the forefront of both lists, directly after the general qualification of being "above reproach." This placement suggests the importance of marital and sexual faithfulness and also highlights that this may have been a problem in the Ephesian and Cretean churches. The best interpretation of this difficult phrase is to understand it as referring to the faithfulness of a husband toward his wife (see question 16). He must be a "one-woman man." That is, there must be no other woman in his life to whom he relates emotionally or physically. It is important for men to put a hedge of protection around their lives so that they do not get into a position where they became emotionally or physically connected with another woman. As a general rule, it is best if a man is never alone with a woman who is not his wife. Unfortunately, many men have disqualified themselves from ministry because of unwise decisions regarding their contact with other women. The Bible is full of warnings about sexual unfaithfulness, but these warnings often go unheeded.

Manage His Own Household Well (1 Tim. 3:4–5; Titus 1:6)

The second family qualification relates to the man's role as father. Paul writes, "He must manage his own household well, with all dignity keeping his children submissive" (1 Tim. 3:4). An elder must have respectful, obedient children. He must not be heavy-handed and authoritarian with his children but must deal with them "with all dignity." A godly father does not seek to crush the spirit of his children, forcing them into submission by harsh discipline. Rather, he relates to them with dignity and seeks to nurture their hearts. Paul writes, "Fathers, do not provoke your children to anger, but bring them up in the discipline and instruction of the Lord" (Eph. 6:4).

Paul then gives the reason why this qualification is important: "for if someone does not know how to manage his own household, how will he care for God's church?" (1 Tim. 3:5). Paul makes an important parallel between the family and the church. If a man is not able to lead his family so that his children are generally respectful and obedient, then he is not fit to lead the church, the family of God. The leadership of his family becomes tangible proof that he is either fit or unfit to lead in God's church. In addition, by neglecting his family—even for the sake of "the ministry"—a man can become disqualified to serve as an elder. Family life must take precedence over the ministry: God first, family second, ministry third.

In Paul's letter to Titus, he states that an elder's children must be "believers and not open to the charge of debauchery or insubordination" (Titus 1:6). The word translated "believers" is better translated "faithful" (see question 17). This interpretation is confirmed by the fact that 1 Timothy 3 does not mention the need for elders' children to be believers. Furthermore, the following phrase in Titus 1 clarifies what Paul meant by "faithful" when he states that they must not be open to the charge of debauchery or insubordination. Thus, a man's children become a reflection of the dedication and commitment he has of training them in the ways of the Lord.

Is There a Minimum Age for an Elder?

Neither the Old Testament nor the New Testament specifies the minimum age of an elder. In Jewish culture, a man became an elder based on his moral authority derived from his age, heredity, experience, knowledge, or wealth. It was not an official position that was given to him by someone higher in authority but was a title of honor and respect that he received from the people of his community. Of course, one's age was a prominent factor in whether a man was worthy to be counted among the "elders." In its basic meaning, "elder" refers to someone who has entered old age. It would be wrong, however, to conclude that all elders were technically considered to have entered old age (usually considered to be sixty).

In the early Christian church, those who were given certain leadership positions also were known as "elders." Because the term *presbuteros* ("elder") is often translated "older man" (1 Tim. 5:1; Titus 2:2), many assume that only old men can serve as elders. Yet, an elder in the Christian church does not have to be a senior citizen. We are told that an elder must not be a new convert (1 Tim. 3:6), but nowhere does Paul specify that an elder must be a certain age. In contrast, when listing the qualifications for a widow to receive financial support from the church, Paul indicates that she must be sixty years of age (1 Tim. 5:9).

When Paul wrote 1 and 2 Timothy, Timothy was probably about thirty-five years old. He was approximately twenty years old when he joined Paul's ministry team during his second missionary trip, which was about fifteen years before the letters to him were written. We know that Timothy was still considered young when Paul wrote to him because he says, "Let no one despise you for your youth" (1 Tim. 4:12). Later Paul warns Timothy to "flee youthful passions" (2 Tim. 2:22). If Timothy, who held a position as Paul's apostolic delegate with the authority to appoint elders, was still considered "young," then it would seem unwise to limit the office of elder to those who are considered "old." The key issues are: (1) Is the person spiritually mature, meeting the specified qualifications; and (2) Will the congregation respect his leadership? In some younger congregations, a man thirty years old might be well respected, whereas in an older congregation, a man forty years old might be considered quite young. Age alone does not guarantee spirituality.

Those who are selected must be mature, wise, and respected by those they will serve.

Summary

The situational qualifications for an elder include a desire to serve, an ability to teach, longevity as a believer, and respectability from outsiders. The family qualifications include being faithful to his wife and managing his household well. Although there is no formal age requirement for an elder, he must not be a recent convert, he must be spiritually mature, and he should be respected by the congregation.

Reflection Questions

1. As you read through the qualifications for elders/overseers in 1 Timothy 3:1–7 and Titus 1:5–9, what qualifications do you find the most surprising? Which are the most challenging?
2. Why is it important for an elder to have a desire to serve (1 Tim. 3:1)?
3. What does it mean that an elder must "be able to teach" (1 Tim. 3:2; cf. Titus 1:9)?
4. Why is it important that an elder is not a recent convert? (1 Tim. 3:6)?
5. What do you think should be the minimum age for an elder at your church?

What Are the Moral Qualifications for an Elder?

In the previous question we discussed an elder's situational and family qualifications. Now we will discuss a potential elder's moral qualifications. We will consider first the positive characteristics an elder is to emulate and then the negative characteristics an elder is to avoid.

Positive Characteristics

Above Reproach (1 Tim. 3:2; Titus 1:6)

The general or overarching qualification of an elder is that he must be "above reproach." This requirement does not call for perfection but for godliness. To be above reproach means to be free from any blemishes of character or conduct. His relationship with his wife and children is commendable, and morally he has no glaring weaknesses. Outsiders cannot point their finger and discredit his profession to be a faithful follower of Christ.

Sober-minded (1 Tim. 3:2)

The word translated "sober-minded" is sometimes translated as "temperate" and is often used in connection with sobriety from alcohol (wine). In the context of 1 Timothy 3, however, it is best understood as referring to mental sobriety, that is, a mind that can think clearly and spiritually about important matters. It is the ability to be self-controlled, having a balanced judgment and being able to rationally make coolheaded decisions. Elders must be mentally and emotionally stable enough to make important decisions in the midst of problems and pressures they will face in their ministry.

Self-controlled (1 Tim. 3:2; Titus 1:8)

Similar to the previous qualification, "self-controlled" refers to the need for disciplined exercise of good judgment. It speaks of being prudent, sound-minded, and discreet. Such discretion is often needed by elders who constantly have to make difficult decisions in the face of problems and disagreements.

Respectable (1 Tim. 3:2)

An elder also must have character that is respectable. It is not enough to get his respect from his office. If others are to follow and emulate him, he must prove that his life is worth following. His character therefore must be well balanced and virtuous if he is to be respected.

Hospitable (1 Tim. 3:2; Titus 1:8)

An elder's life must be open so that others can be a part of it. Being hospitable means making time not only for one's family but also for others. The theme of hospitality is an important biblical virtue (see Job 31:32; Rom. 12:13; Heb. 13:21; 1 Peter 4:9). If an elder is to get to know people and invest in their lives, he must take the time to build relationships with them. If he is to effectively shepherd the flock of God, his home must be open so that he can minister to the flock more than just on Sunday mornings.

Gentle (1 Tim. 3:3)

The word translated "gentle" also can mean "kind," "gracious," or "forbearing." In Philippians 4:5, Paul writes, "Let your gentleness be made known to all" (my translation). A gentle person is not overbearing but patient with others, especially when they have done wrong. He does not retaliate when wronged but returns love for evil.

A Lover of Good (Titus 1:8)

This characteristic is closely related to hospitality. It involves willingly helping others and seeking their good.

Upright (Titus 1:8)

The Greek word *dikaios* means "just" or "righteous." To be upright or righteous means living according to God's Word. First John 3:7 states, "Whoever practices righteousness is righteous, as he is righteous." Elders must abide by

God's righteous standard revealed in His Word. An elder who is righteous will make fair, just, and upright decisions for the church. Job is described as a man who was "blameless and upright, one who feared God and turned away from evil" (Job 1:1).

Holy (Titus 1:8)

Sometimes translated "devout," this characteristic involves being wholly devoted to God and His Word. It entails being set apart to God in order to obey His will. A holy person is dedicated to glorifying the name of God regardless of what others may think.

Disciplined (Titus 1:8)

Similar to the qualification of being "self-controlled," this characteristic involves self-discipline in every aspect of one's life, including physical desires. An undisciplined person yields easily to temptation, but a disciplined person fights against lust, anger, laziness, and other ungodly traits. Shepherding God's people is hard work, and discipline is needed to fulfill this ministry faithfully and effectively.

Negative Characteristics

Not a Drunkard (1 Tim. 3:3; Titus 1:7)

A man is disqualified for the office of elder if he is a drunkard (addicted to wine or other strong drink). Such a person lacks self-control and is undisciplined. The abuse of alcohol is a problem in most cultures and often results in ruined lives, marriages, and ministries. Notice, however, that Paul does not say that it is wrong to drink alcohol. Rather, he is referring to the excesses of drinking too much alcohol and drinking it too often. As a matter of fact, he later tells Timothy to drink a little wine for his stomach problems (1 Tim. 5:23). Although many churches require not only their leadership but all their members to abstain from all alcohol, this requirement is nowhere found in Scripture.[1] The real issue is the abuse of

---

1. John Piper warns against the dangers of adding requirements to Scripture: "By imposing a restriction which the New Testament never imposes, this . . . requirement, in principle, involves us in a legalism that has its roots in unbelief. It is a sign of a faded power and joy and heart righteousness that once was created by the power of Christ but cannot be preserved by laws" (*Brothers, We are NOT Professionals: A Plea to Pastors for Radical Ministry* [Nashville: Broadman and Holman, 2002], 158).

any substance that would bring shame on the person and reproach on the church.

Not Violent (1 Tim. 3:3; Titus 1:7)

A person who is violent, or "pugnacious," as it is sometimes translated, is one who is easily irritated and has a bad temper. Such a person is often ready to fight rather than to calmly talk through a difficult situation. A violent man not only uses verbal abuse but is ready to physically assault those who anger him. On the contrary, an elder must be self-controlled and patient, willing to turn the other cheek when wronged. He must be able to calmly and rationally deal with heated arguments and tense situations that often find their way into the church.

Not Quarrelsome (1 Tim. 3:3)

A man who is not quarrelsome is gentle and peaceful. People are constantly quarreling, even in the church. There are quarrels over doctrine, quarrels over the color of the carpet in the sanctuary, and quarrels over whether the church should sing hymns or choruses. An elder, however, must be able to deal with these tensions and not add to them. He must be a peacemaker and find a way to bring about reconciliation. If he is quarrelsome himself, he will not be able to effectively lead and may even divide the congregation. As Paul later writes, "The Lord's servant must not be quarrelsome but kind to everyone, able to teach, patiently enduring evil, correcting his opponents with gentleness" (2 Tim. 2:24–25). Paul also reminds Titus to encourage the congregation "to speak evil of no one, to avoid quarreling, to be gentle, and to show perfect courtesy toward all people" (Titus 3:2).

Not a Lover of Money (1 Tim. 3:3; Titus 1:7)

The love of money is a serious problem in the church. It was in Paul's day, and it is in ours. Paul writes, "Those who desire to be rich fall into temptation, into a snare, into many senseless and harmful desires that plunge people into ruin and destruction" (1 Tim. 6:9). The results of loving money can end in the destruction of one's soul. This is no small sin. Paul continues, "For the love of money is a root of all kinds of evils. It is through this craving that some have wandered away from the faith and pierced themselves with many pangs" (1 Tim. 6:10). The Bible is full of warnings to the rich. Jesus himself said, "It is easier for a camel to go through the eye of a needle than for a rich person to enter the kingdom of God" (Mark 10:25). Consequently, it is not difficult to understand why Paul includes this qualification in both 1 Timothy and Titus.

If a person is a lover of money, it is difficult for him also to be a lover of God. If our passions are divided, we become ineffective and distracted. Money itself is not the problem, however. It is the *love* of money. Whether we are considered rich and have plenty of money or are poor, the issue at stake is where our desires are found. It is not those who *are* rich who fall into temptation, but those who *desire* to be rich.

Paul's wording for the qualification in Titus is different than that in 1 Timothy. He states that an elder must not be "greedy for gain" (Titus 1:7). A greedy person is never content with God's provision but is constantly seeking ways to acquire more money—often in ways that are immoral and unethical. In 2 Corinthians, Paul warns of some ministers who peddle the Word of God for money (2 Cor. 2:17; cf. Titus 1:11). Likewise, Peter states that elders must shepherd the flock of God "not for shameful gain" (1 Peter 5:2).

Elders should be those who are free from the love and controlling influence of money. A pastor should not have unchecked control over the funds of a church. The elders must be accountable to one another and to the congregation as a whole. How many times have leaders fallen due to unethical practices with the church's finances? In contrast, we must heed the Word of God, which states, "Keep your life free from love of money, and be content with what you have, for he has said, 'I will never leave you nor forsake you'" (Heb. 13:5).

Not Arrogant (Titus 1:7)

An arrogant person is a self-willed person, one who is constantly insisting that things be done his way. It is the opposite of being gentle or forbearing (1 Tim. 3:3). He is inconsiderate of other people's opinions and feelings and attempts to get what he wants regardless of the cost to others. Such a person does not make a good elder because the elders must work together as a team, seeking the best for others and not for themselves. A shepherd must be gentle with the sheep and not seek to overpower them by his strong will.

Not Quick-tempered (Titus 1:7)

David tells us that God is "merciful and gracious, slow to anger and abounding in steadfast love" (Ps. 103:8). Those who lead the church are to model the characteristics of their heavenly Father and be slow to anger. A quick-tempered man, however, is not only easily angered, but he also is unable to control that anger. He quickly lashes out at others, rather than displaying the patience and self-control of Christ. Although all anger is not sin (Paul tells us, "Be angry and do not sin," Eph. 4:26; cf. Ps. 4:4), James reminds us that "the anger of man does not produce the righteousness that God requires" (James 1:20). Furthermore, "A man of wrath stirs up strife, and one given to anger causes much transgression" (Prov. 29:22). An elder must be able to deal patiently with difficult and emotionally charged situations that arise in one's personal life and in the context of the church.

Must an Elder Be Seminary Trained?

Nowhere does Scripture state that a elder must be seminary trained. As noted above, the focus of the qualifications is moral and not mental or cognitive. Of course, formal seminary training did not exist when Paul wrote his letters to Timothy and Titus. Many denominations, however, require their (teaching) elders to be seminary trained. As one who has been teaching in seminaries for about ten years now, I certainly believe it is often helpful and beneficial for a person to attend seminary, but by *requiring* a seminary degree, we are adding to the qualifications given in Scripture. Furthermore, churches often view a seminary degree as the proof that the candidate for eldership has outstanding moral qualifications. Such a view is quite dangerous. Holding a seminary degree does not make a person morally qualified to be an elder. Churches need to be concerned about the moral life of a potential elder more than the institution a person attended.

Summary

The qualifications for an elder are the basic characteristics that are expected of all believers. Biblically qualified elders are not superspiritual people but are those who are mature in their faith and live consistent, humble lives. They are not content to look spiritual on Sundays or Wednesdays; their spirituality pervades their entire lives. An elder has a healthy and pure relationship with his wife, and he is a godly leader in his home. His character has no glaring blemishes, and his godliness is even recognized by those who are not Christians. He is not perfect, but his life is characterized by integrity.

Reflection Questions

1. Why do you think Paul begins each list with the qualification that an elder must be "above reproach" (1 Tim. 3:2; Titus 1:6)?
2. Why is it important that an elder be hospitable (1 Tim. 3:2; Titus 1:8)?
3. Do you think that the qualification that an elder must not be a drunkard restricts an elder from drinking any alcohol?
4. Why is it important for an elder not to be quarrelsome and not to be a lover of money (1 Tim. 3:3; Titus 1:7)?
5. Do you think an elder must be seminary trained? Why or why not?

What Does It Mean That an Elder Must Be "the Husband of One Wife"?

Because there has been much debate and confusion over the qualification that an elder must be "the husband of one wife," we need to deal with it in more detail. In both 1 Timothy 3:2 and Titus 1:6, Paul writes that an elder must be "the husband of one wife," or more literally, a "one-woman man." There are four primary interpretations of this phrase: (1) an elder must be married; (2) an elder must not be a polygamist; (3) an elder must have only one wife his entire life; (4) an elder must be faithful to his wife.

An Elder Must Be Married

This interpretation maintains that all elders must be married. After all, it is argued, Paul says that an elder must be "the husband of one wife." If a man is not married, he is not the husband of one wife and thus fails to meet this qualification. Furthermore, there is a fear that if this qualification is not upheld, then other qualifications may be neglected or ignored as well.

But this interpretation should be rejected for the following reasons. First, the focus of the phrase is not that a man is married but that he is faithful to his "one" wife. The Greek literally reads, "one-woman man" (*mias gunaikos andra*), with emphasis placed on the first word, "one" (*mias*). Second, Paul clearly teaches that singleness has many advantages over being married. In 1 Corinthians, Paul even encourages singleness, explaining how those who are not married are able to serve the Lord with undivided attention (7:32–35). Third, Paul could have written that an elder must be a man who has a wife (which is different from saying he must be a "one-woman man"). Fourth, this qualification would eliminate Paul, Timothy, and the Lord Jesus Himself from being eligible to serve as elders. Fifth, to be consistent, we would have to require men to have more than one child since Paul indicates that a potential elder must manage his "children" (plural) well. Rather, this phrase should be understood as merely reflecting the common situation of the time because most people were married. It was simply the norm that men married, and there was no need to highlight the exception.

An Elder Must Not Be a Polygamist

This view maintains that an elder cannot be married to more than one woman at the same time. In many cultures, it is not only permissible but also a sign of blessing to have more than one wife. According to the Bible, however, Christians are to be monogamous. The dangers of polygamy can be seen in the life of Solomon. Although God granted him wisdom beyond that of any other person, Solomon unwisely married foreign women who introduced other gods to the king. As a result, Solomon was led astray and his kingdom was later divided.

Although polygamy is to be avoided, it is probably not what Paul had in mind when he specifies that an elder must be the "husband of one wife." We know this because Paul uses a similar phrase in 1 Timothy 5:9, where he gives qualifications for widows who are eligible to receive financial support from the church. Paul indicates that a widow must have been "the wife of one husband" (literally, "a one-man woman"). It is unlikely that Paul means that a widow must not have been married to more than one man at the same time. For, although polygamy (having more than one wife) was somewhat common in the Greco-Roman and Jewish culture, polyandry (having more than one husband) was strongly rejected by both the Jews and the Romans. Furthermore, "even if polygamy existed among the Jews, evidence is lacking that it was practiced by Christians, and therefore 'Christian polygamy' most likely is not in view."[1] If polygamy was rare, if it existed at all among Christians, it does not seem likely that it would be singled out in all three lists (1 Tim. 3:2; 3:12; Titus 1:6) and put at the head of both lists dealing with elders. Consequently, it is unlikely that the phrase "husband of one wife" was intended to address polygamy.

---

1. William D. Mounce, *Pastoral Epistles*, WBC (Nashville: Nelson, 2000), 46:171.

An Elder Must Have Only One Wife His Entire Life

Another possible interpretation is that men who are eligible to become elders are not permitted to remarry under any circumstance. If his wife dies or divorces him, an elder is to remain unmarried. If he remarries, he is no longer qualified to be an elder because he is no longer "the husband of one wife." This view has several strengths. First, it takes the phrase "husband of one wife" seriously and offers a plausible interpretation. Second, this was the view of the early church, which valued celibacy after the divorce or death of a spouse. Third, the apostle Paul, while allowing remarriage in some cases, favored singleness and celibacy (1 Cor. 7:8–9, 39–40). Thus, it may be that Paul is emphasizing the need for divorced men or men whose spouses have died to remain unmarried in order to be eligible for eldership. Others may be permitted to remarry, but the high calling of being an elder requires him to remain single and celibate.

There are, however, several reasons to reject this view. First, it is doubtful that Paul is holding elders to a higher standard of morality than he requires of all believers. All of the moral and spiritual qualifications of elders are what is expected of all believers. Second, Paul seems to indicate that sometimes remarriage is a viable option. He states, "To the unmarried *and the widows* I say that it is good for them to remain single as I am. But if they cannot exercise self-control, *they should marry*" (1 Cor. 7:8–9, emphasis added). Later he writes, "A wife is bound to her husband as long as he lives. But if her husband dies, she is free to be married to whom she wishes, only in the Lord" (1 Cor. 7:39). These verses permit remarriage if a spouse has died. Paul also uses the principle of a spouse's freedom (after the other spouse has died) to illustrate the believer's freedom from the law (Rom. 7:1–3). Third, it is wrong to treat divorce and remarriage as the unpardonable sin. If a former murderer is able to be forgiven and later serve as a spiritual leader (like the apostle Paul who was guilty of murder [Acts 9:1; 22:4; 26:10]), then it would seem rather arbitrary that a person who remarries cannot serve in such a capacity. Of course, if Scripture indicates that a remarried man cannot serve as elder, we must obey. It is unlikely, however, that this was Paul's intent.

Fourth, in 1 Timothy 5:14, Paul states that it is better for younger widows to remarry than to become idle gossips. Earlier, Paul indicates that if a widow is to be officially enrolled to receive financial assistance, she must be the "wife of one husband" (1 Tim. 5:9). It seems unlikely that by encouraging younger widows to remarry, Paul is effectively disqualifying them from ever being able to receive assistance from the church if they were widowed again. The reason they would become disqualified is because after they remarried, according to some, they would no longer be the "wife of one husband."[2] But we must assume that those who remarried and were later widowed again would still be considered the "woman of one man" and would still qualify to be enrolled for financial aid from the church. As a result, the phrase "wife of one husband" most likely does not mean that a woman only has one husband her entire lifetime, but that she was faithful to her husband while he was alive. Similarly, the "husband of one wife" should not be taken to mean that an elder can never remarry but that he must be faithful to his wife.

The more difficult issue is whether a man who has been divorced and then remarries is still qualified to serve as an elder. In Jewish, Roman, and Greek culture, it was relatively easy for a man to divorce his wife. Is Paul's intent to prohibit such men who divorce their wives and remarry from serving as elders (or deacons)? In 1 Corinthians 7, Paul addresses the issue of an unbelieving spouse deserting a believing spouse. He states that "if the unbelieving partner separates, let it be so. In such cases the brother or sister is not enslaved" (1 Cor. 7:15). The question is whether this verse gives permission for the believer to remarry if the unbeliever decides to end the marriage. When Paul addresses the situation of both spouses being believers, he states that "the wife should not separate from her husband (but if she does, she should remain unmarried or else be reconciled to her husband), and the husband should not divorce his wife" (1 Cor. 7:10–11). Does Paul's comment here also apply to the situation of an unbeliever divorcing a believing spouse? Although it is difficult to make a dogmatic decision, it seems best to treat the two situations differently. Paul could have stated that the believer who is divorced by an unbeliever also should not remarry. Instead, he states something different. He writes, "In such cases the brother or sister is not enslaved." This phrase seems to indicate that the believing spouse is free to remarry.

---

2. Mounce writes, "It seems doubtful that Paul would encourage the remarriage of 'younger widows' if this meant that they could never later be enrolled if they were again widowed. For such widows, it could be presumed that remarriage would not be inconsistent with being a 'one-man' woman, and hence the phrase in 1 Tim. 5:9 would not be a call for a single marriage" (*Pastoral Epistles*, 173; also see George W. Knight, *The Pastoral Epistles*, NIGTC [Grand Rapids: Eerdmans; Carlisle, U.K.: Paternoster, 1992], 158).

An Elder Must Be Faithful to His Wife

The final interpretation, and the one favored by this author, is that an elder must be faithful to his wife in a monogamous relationship. This view also would include the prohibition of polygamy, promiscuity, and homosexuality. A potential elder must be a "one-woman man," meaning he must honor, love, and be devoted to his wife and her alone. This view allows for the possibility of an elder being remarried after the death of his wife or after a divorce, although the phrase in question does not directly address that situation. The emphasis of the qualifications given in 1 Timothy and Titus stress the present situation of a man's moral and spiritual character. The real issue is not so much where he has come from but who he is now by God's grace. If a man is currently faithful to his wife, being above reproach, and has proven himself in that relationship, then it is possible for him to become an elder. The situation of a divorced man must be treated seriously, however. If he was the "innocent" party in the divorce and was not unfaithful, some time is still needed for him to prove himself in his new marriage. The same is true if he was divorced before he became a Christian (whether he was unfaithful in the relationship or not). But if a professing believer was unfaithful to his wife and was later divorced, then extreme caution must be exercised. The sin of unfaithfulness and divorce, like all sins, can be forgiven, and the person can become renewed. Thus, after a period of many years in his new marriage, it may be possible, though perhaps not advisable, for a divorced man to become an elder.

Summary

The qualification that an elder (or deacon) must be the "husband of one wife" has been variously interpreted. Some take it to mean that an elder must be married, while others insist it is a prohibition against polygamy. Still others argue that the phrase implies that an elder can never remarry under any circumstance. It is best, however, to view this requirement as referring to a husband's faithfulness to his wife.

Reflection Questions

1. Do you think Paul is stressing the importance of this qualification by placing it toward the front of each list?

2. Do you think Paul is teaching that all elders must be married? Why or why not?
3. How does 1 Timothy 5:9 shed light on the meaning of "husband of one wife"?
4. What are some of the strengths of the view that teaches an elder cannot remarry? What are some of the weaknesses?
5. What does it mean for a husband to be faithful to his wife?

Must an Elder Be Married and Must His Children Be Believers?

Must an Elder Be Married with Children?

There are many Christians today who are convinced that a man cannot be an elder unless he is married. The reason this view is held by many is obvious—it is what the Bible says, or at least appears to say. Paul writes that an overseer (elder/pastor) "must be . . . the husband of one wife" (1 Tim. 3:2; cf. Titus 1:6).[1] If Paul, under the inspiration of the Holy Spirit, states that an elder *must* be the husband of one wife, then the case is settled. The other qualifications, it is argued, are not negotiable. An elder *must* be above reproach, sober-minded, self-controlled, respectable, hospitable, and able to teach (1 Tim. 3:2). In the same way, if a man is not married, then he is not the "husband of one wife" and thus fails to meet this qualification. As a result, he is not qualified to serve as an elder.

The above interpretation is incorrect for a number of reasons (also see question 16): (1) the focus on the Greek text is not that a man is married but that he is faithful to his "one" wife; (2) Paul clearly teaches that singleness has many advantages over being married (1 Cor. 7:32–35); (3) Paul could have written that an elder must be a man who has a wife (which is different from saying he must be a "one-woman man"); (4) this qualification would eliminate Paul, Timothy, and the Lord Jesus Himself from being eligible to serve as elders; (5) it was simply the norm that men married, and there was no need to highlight the exception.

Another reason why it is wrong to take the phrase "husband of one wife" to mean that an elder must be married is that this interpretation forces us

---

1. The same argument can be made for deacons since Paul likewise states, "Let deacons each be the husband of one wife" (1 Tim. 3:12).

to read the other qualifications too woodenly. If we insist that all elders are married, then to be consistent we would have to require them to have more than one child. After all, Paul indicates that a potential elder "must manage his own household well . . . keeping his children submissive" (1 Tim. 3:4). Paul does not say he must keep his child (singular) submissive but that he must keep his children (plural) submissive. The point, of course, is not that a man must have more than one child but that whether he has one child or many children, he leads them well and they are submissive to him. George Knight rightly comments, "It is exceedingly doubtful that Paul intended that these words and the words about 'children' (plural, vv. 4, 12) be understood as mandating that only a married man with at least two children could be an officer in the church. Probably he wrote in terms of the common situation, i.e., of being married and having children, and then spoke of what should be the case when this most common situation exists in an officer's life."[2]

Again, if we press Paul's words beyond his original intention, we could argue not only that a potential elder must have at least two children but also that his children still live at home with him. Paul's reason for mentioning children is because a man's home life and his relationship with his children are the testing grounds for his ability to lead the church. Paul states, "For if someone does not know how to manage his own household, how will he care for God's church?" (1 Tim. 3:5). Thus, we might (wrongly) infer that if a man's children are grown up and no longer live at home, this qualification cannot be met. The point, however, is not that his children must be living at home, but if his children are living at home, he must manage them well and they must be respectful and obedient. Likewise, Paul's intent in stating that a man must be the "husband of one wife" is not that a man must be married, but that if he is married, he must be faithful to his wife. Thus, this phrase should be understood as merely reflecting the common situation of the time since most people were married.

Must an Elder's Children Be Believers?

In the qualifications for elders given in Titus 1, Paul states that an elder's children must be "believers (*pista*) and not open to the charge of debauchery

---

2. George W. Knight, *The Pastoral Epistles*, NIGTC (Grand Rapids: Eerdmans; Carlisle, U.K.: Paternoster, 1992), 157. William D. Mounce agrees, "This is not a requirement that an overseer have children, but if he does have children, they should be faithful" (*Pastoral Epistles*, WBC [Nashville: Nelson, 2000], 46:388).

or insubordination" (Titus 1:6). Does this text indicate that for a man to be qualified as an elder, all of his children must be professing believers? This interpretation is favored by some commentators and supported by many Bible translations (ESV, NIV, NASB, NRSV, RSV, NLT). A few versions, however, translate the verse to mean that a man's children must be "faithful" (HCSB, NKJV, KJV). For example, the Holman Christian Standard Bible states that an elder must be the husband of one wife "having faithful children not accused of wildness or rebellion." There are at least four reasons why this translation is to be favored.

First, the interpretation that an elder's children must be "faithful" and not necessarily "believing" reflects a possible use of the Greek term *pistos*. If the meaning is "faithful," however, we are not told the content of this faithfulness. Are the children to be faithful to God, to their families, to their church, or to their responsibilities? Although such an omission might argue against the interpretation of "faithful," the context does not leave the question totally ambiguous. In the following phrase, Paul states that an elder's children must not be "open to the charge of debauchery or insubordination." This phrase qualifies the type of faithfulness that Paul has in mind. Paul is referring to the behavior of the child ("faithful"), not the status of the child ("believing"). Furthermore, *pistos* can have the meaning of "trustworthy," "dependable," or "reliable."[3] For example, in 2 Timothy 2:2, Paul instructs Timothy to entrust the gospel message to "faithful men." The idea here is not so much that the men are believers since that is assumed. Rather, Timothy is to pass on the true gospel to men who have proven themselves obedient and trustworthy in their conduct. Thus, the content of a child's faithfulness primarily involves living a moral life and being obedient to his parents.

Second, the comparison with 1 Timothy 3:4 favors the meaning of "faithful" as opposed to "believing." Paul writes to Timothy that an elder "must manage his own household well, with all dignity keeping his children submissive." Notice that Paul does not say here that an elder's children must be believers. He simply states that a potential elder must keep his children submissive. Again, the focus is not on the children's status, but on their behavior. The children do not have to be Christians, but they must be obedient and re-

---

3. BDAG, 820–21; TDNT 6:175, 204. Paul often stresses the quality of "faithfulness" in his coworkers. He refers to Timothy (1 Cor. 4:17), Tychicus (Eph. 6:21; Col. 4:7), Epaphras (Col. 1:7), and Onesimus (Col. 4:9) as being "faithful" in the ministry. Also see Matt. 24:45; 25:21, 23; 1 Cor. 4:2; Heb. 3:5; 1 Peter 5:12.

spectful. It seems unlikely that Paul would require elders' children in Crete to be believers but have a lower standard in Ephesus, requiring them only to be faithful or obedient. This apparent distinction seems even more unlikely in light of the fact that Ephesus was the more established church. The churches in Crete were still very young compared to the more mature church in Ephesus. Would Paul place a more restrictive requirement on the less mature church? In other qualifications we find just the opposite. When writing to the church at Ephesus (1 Tim. 3:6), Paul says that an elder must not be a recent convert, but he fails to mention this requirement to the churches in Crete. It is better to see the requirement in Titus 1:6 as virtually parallel to that found in 1 Timothy 3:4—an elder's children must be faithful and submissive.

Third, the view that all of an elder's children must be professing Christians raises a series of difficult questions. What if a child is not old enough to understand the gospel and make a credible profession of faith? Is that father temporarily disqualified to serve as an elder? Does he have to wait until his child professes faith in Christ? Or should all the children of believers be considered Christians unless they renounce the faith? What if an elder has seven believing children but his eighth child forsakes the faith? This view is probably much more complicated than Paul was intending. It is more likely Paul meant that the children of elders must be faithful but was not requiring that they be professing Christians.

Fourth, it seems unlikely that Paul would require something that a father cannot control. This argument is not based on anything in the immediate context of the requirement in Titus 1:6 but is a larger theological and practical argument. The Bible teaches that salvation is of the Lord and that those who believe in Jesus are those who have been predestined, called, and justified (Rom. 8:30). Even if a father brings up his children "in the discipline and instruction of the Lord" (Eph. 6:4), there is no guarantee that his children will become Christians. Some may quote Proverbs 22:6, which states, "Train up a child in the way he should go; even when is old he will not depart from it." It is simply poor hermeneutics, however, to interpret the proverbs as promises from God. Rather, the proverbs are given to provide us with wisdom in life. Each proverb should be viewed not as a promise but as a general principle. That is, generally speaking, when children are trained correctly, they will not depart from that training but will remain faithful to what they have been taught. But this does not mean that such will always be the case. There have been many good parents who have faithfully raised their children in the discipline and instruction of the Lord, only to see them reject their parents' teaching and go down their own path. Consequently, it seems unlikely that Paul would place a requirement on candidates for eldership that is simply beyond their control. Alexander Strauch rightly comments, "Those who interpret this qualification to mean that an elder must have believing, Christian children place an impossible burden upon the father. Even the best Christian fathers cannot guarantee that their children will believe. Salvation is a supernatural act of God. God, not good parents (although they are certainly used of God), ultimately brings salvation (John 1:12, 13)."[4]

Summary

The qualifications that an elder must be the "husband of one wife" and have children who are "submissive" should not be taken to mean that all elders must be married or, in addition to being married, also have children. Instead, these requirements merely reflect the common situation during the first century when most men were married and had children. It is therefore unnecessary to insist that an elder be married and/or have children. In addition, while an elder's children must be obedient and submissive, the biblical qualifications do not include that his children must be believers. The Greek word sometimes translated "believing" in Titus 1:6 also can mean "faithful"—the latter meaning being confirmed by the parallel text in 1 Timothy 3:4. Requiring an elder's children to be believers also raises many difficult questions and places a requirement on a father that he cannot control.

Reflection Questions

1. Do you think Paul is teaching that all elders must be married? Why or why not?
2. If elders are not required to have children, then why does Paul mention this in his list?
3. Should a man be appointed as an elder if his children are not Christians?
4. How does 1 Timothy 3:4 help clarify the above question?
5. Do you think godly parents who raise their children well are guaranteed that their children will become believers (cf. Prov. 22:6)?

---

4. Alexander Strauch, *Biblical Eldership: An Urgent Call to Restore Biblical Church Leadership*, 3rd ed., rev. and expanded (Littleton, CO: Lewis and Roth, 1995), 229.

What Are the Reasons for Affirming That Women Can Be Elders?

The question of whether a woman can hold the office of elder is hotly debated. Often, proponents on either side of the debate not only criticize the arguments held by those who have opposing views but also challenge their commitment to Scripture. We must realize that there are Bible-believing Christians on both sides of the debate. What is important, however, is that we listen honestly to Scripture and try to put aside our biases. The following represents some of the arguments used by those who affirm that women can (and should) be elders/pastors. Although I do not affirm this view, I will try to fairly represent the arguments. These arguments will then be answered by the opposing view in the next two questions.

The Testimony of Galatians 3:28

One of the strongest (and perhaps most repeated) arguments in favor of allowing women to be elders is found in Galatians 3:28, where Paul states, "There is neither Jew nor Greek, there is neither slave nor free, *there is neither male nor female*, for you are all one in Christ Jesus" (emphasis added). This verse affirms the equality of males and females in the sight of God. Consequently, because God does not view us any differently, it would be wrong for us to still make distinctions based on gender. According to this verse, all gender distinctions are of the old order. In Christ, however, God's original intent of having male and female ruling as equals is restored. This equality is also confirmed by Ephesians 5:21, which teaches mutual submission: "Submit to one another out of reverence for Christ" (NIV). Therefore, to still insist on gender distinctions is to ignore the fullness of God's restoration that is given to us in Jesus Christ. Consequently, Galatians 3:28 must be

Books

Can woman teach

Biblical manhood & womanhood

the grid through which all other texts concerning the role of women must be read.[1]

Women Possess All Spiritual Gifts

Because women possess all spiritual gifts, it would be wrong to prohibit some from serving as elders and thus disallowing them to use their God-given gifts. For example, we know that in the New Testament women had the gift of prophecy. In 1 Corinthians 11, Paul maintains that women must wear head coverings while praying or prophesying. He writes, "Every wife [or woman] who prays or prophesies with her head uncovered dishonors her head" (1 Cor. 11:5). Paul makes the assumption that some women prayed and prophesied in church. He simply writes to remind them to cover their heads before they do so. In addition, Acts 21:9 mentions that Philip the evangelist had four unmarried daughters "who prophesied." This pattern seems to fit with the prophecy from Joel 2 that Peter quoted on the Day of Pentecost: "And in the last days it shall be, God declares, that I will pour out my Spirit on all flesh, and your sons and your daughters shall prophesy" (Acts 2:17).

There are many other instances in the New Testament of women functioning in leadership roles. Luke tells us that both Priscilla and Aquila taught Apollos, "[explaining] to him the way of God more accurately" (Acts 18:26). Women are called Paul's "fellow workers" (Rom. 16:3; Phil. 4:2–3) and "workers" (Rom. 16:12). Furthermore, it has been strongly argued by many that women functioned as deacons in the New Testament churches. In Romans 16:1, Paul commends to the church Phoebe, "a deacon of the church at Cenchreae" (NRSV). In listing the qualifications for deacons, Paul notes that "women [deacons] likewise must be . . ." (1 Tim. 3:11 NRSV). Although the term "deacons" is not in the original Greek, other grammatical considerations indicate that it is understood (see question 38). Finally, it is likely that women were even apostles. At the end of Romans, Paul mentions Junia (clearly a female name), who was well known "among the apostles" (Rom. 16:7 NRSV). If women possessed the gift of prophecy, were among Paul's co-

---

1. The central role of Gal. 3:28 for the egalitarian view can be seen in Alvera Michelsen, "Egalitarian View: There Is Neither Male nor Female in Christ," in *Women in Ministry: Four Views*, ed. Bonnidell Clouse and Robert G. Clouse (Downers Grove, IL: InterVarsity Press, 1989), 204–5; Ronald Allen and Beverly Allen, *Liberated Traditionalism: Men and Women in Balance* (Portland, OR: Multnomah, 1985), 134; Mary Hayter, *The New Eve in Christ* (Grand Rapids: Eerdmans, 1987), 134; and Paul K. Jewett, *Man as Male and Female: A Study in Sexual Relationships from a Theological Point of View* (Grand Rapids: Eerdmans, 1975), 142.

workers, and were deacons and even apostles, it seems reasonable to conclude that women were also elders in the early church.

The Historical Situation Behind 1 Timothy 2:11–12

Those who deny that women can be elders usually appeal to 1 Timothy 2:11–12 as the key text for their position. There Paul writes, "Let a woman learn quietly with all submissiveness. I do not permit a woman to teach or to exercise authority over a man; rather she is to remain quiet." Although at first glace Paul appears to be restricting women from teaching and having authority over men in the church, egalitarians claim that before we blindly apply this verse, we must understand the historical situation behind it. That is, we must seek to understand why Paul made such a prohibition. The reason favored by most egalitarians is that during the New Testament era, women were inadequately educated. Consequently, in 1 Timothy 2:12, Paul is merely restricting *uneducated* women or women who were advocating false doctrine (due to their lack of education) from teaching. Thus, Paul's prohibition does not apply to us since women in general are no longer among the "uneducated" of society. This interpretation explains why Paul uses Eve as an analogy in the following context: "Adam was not deceived, but the woman was deceived and became a transgressor" (1 Tim. 2:14). Affirming this position, Keener maintains that Eve was deceived because "she was not present when God gave the commandment, and thus was dependent on Adam for the teaching. In other words, she was inadequately educated—like the women in the Ephesian church."[2] Likewise Grenz comments, "Perhaps Paul is suggesting that Eve's later creation provides a clue to why she was deceived. She was not present in the Garden when God gave Adam the command; thereby Eve serves as an analogy to the Ephesian women who are inadequately educated."[3] Therefore, since women were uneducated, many had embraced false doctrine and were spreading heresy by their teaching. As a result, Paul gives a blanket response to this problem and cuts women off from teaching altogether. The assumption is that once women are educated or not teaching false doctrine, then they would be permitted to teach in the church.

A similar argument can be made in regard to Paul's second prohibition

---

2. Craig S. Keener, *Paul, Women, and Wives: Marriage and Women's Ministry in the Letters of Paul* (Peabody, MA: Hendrickson, 1992), 116.
3. Stanley J. Grenz with Denise Muir Kjesbo, *Women in the Church: A Biblical Theology of Women in Ministry* (Downers Grove, IL: InterVarsity Press, 1995), 138.

in 1 Timothy 2:12. In addition to forbidding women to teach, he also forbids them "to exercise authority over a man." Many scholars maintain that the word translated "exercise authority" is better translated "to domineer." In this case, Paul is not forbidding women from exercising any authority in positions of leadership but is merely stating that it is improper for a woman to domineer men in an ungodly manner, attempting to usurp more authority than is proper.

Consistency in the Use of Paul's Arguments from Creation

Those who restrict women from eldership often cite Paul's arguments from creation in 1 Timothy 2:13–14 as the main defense for their position. It is maintained that Paul's prohibition in 1 Timothy 2:11–12 cannot be culturally limited since Paul does not argue from culture but from creation. He argues from the order of creation ("For Adam was formed first, then Eve") and from the order of accountability in creation ("Adam was not deceived, but the woman was deceived"). Based on Paul's reasoning, it is therefore concluded that women cannot "teach or have authority over men" in the context of the local church.

But can the above method of interpretation also be applied to 1 Corinthians 11:8–9, where Paul employs similar arguments from creation to bolster his position? In 1 Corinthians 11, Paul demonstrates that women need to have their heads covered while praying or prophesying. To prove his point, he argues from creation that the woman was created *from* man ("for man was not made from woman, but woman from man") and *for* man ("Neither was man created for woman, but woman for man"). The question that must be raised then is whether it is inconsistent to reject Paul's appeal for women to wear head coverings and, at the same time, affirm his command for women not to teach or have authority over men since in both contexts Paul uses virtually the same reasoning.

This apparent inconsistency is raised by Keener, when he writes, "Although many churches would use arguments [from the order of creation] to demand the subordination of women in all cultures, very few accept Paul's arguments [in 1 Cor. 11:8–9] as valid for covering women's heads in all cultures."[4] He continues,

---

4. Keener, *Paul, Women, and Wives*, 19.

The same argument Paul uses in one passage for forbidding women to teach he uses in another passage to argue that married women . . . must cover their heads in church. In the one passage, Paul does not want the women of a certain congregation to teach; in the other passage, he wants the women of a certain congregation to cover their heads. We take the argument as transculturally applicable in one case, but not so in the other. This seems very strange indeed.[5]

Keener, however, is not alone in pointing out this apparent inconsistency. In a similar vein Groothuis comments, "If Paul's creation-order rationale here [in 1 Timothy 2:12] renders universal and transcultural the prohibition of women teaching authoritatively, then why doesn't Paul's creation-order rationale for women's head coverings (1 Cor. 11:6–9) make the wearing of headgear a universal and transcultural requirement for women in church?"[6] Thus, just as women no longer need to wear head coverings while praying, so also they are not restricted by Paul's prohibition not to teach or exercise authority over men.

The Meaning of 1 Corinthians 14:33–35

In 1 Corinthians 14 Paul writes, "For God is not a God of confusion but of peace. As in all the churches of the saints, the women should keep silent in the churches. For they are not permitted to speak, but should be in submission, as the Law also says. If there is anything they desire to learn, let them ask their husbands at home. For it is shameful for a woman to speak in church" (vv. 33–35). This passage often is used as evidence to support the claim that women cannot be elders. If elders teach the congregation, and if women are to remain silent when the congregation gathers, then it naturally follows that women cannot be elders.

Such an interpretation, however, is overly simplistic. It is often noted that Paul did in fact permit women to speak in church. Just a few chapters earlier, he instructed women to wear head coverings while they pray or prophesy (1 Cor. 11:5). It is wrong, therefore, to interpret Paul's words apart from the greater context—both literary and historical. If the literary context demonstrates that Paul allowed women to speak—at least while

---

5. Ibid.
6. Rebecca Merrill Groothuis, *Good News for Women: A Biblical Picture of Gender Equality* (Grand Rapids: Baker, 1997), 219.

praying or prophesying—then the historical context also helps reveal the true intent of Paul's prohibition. Perhaps, as many egalitarians affirm, women were disturbing the worship service. Because women were on one side of the congregation and their husbands on the other side, similar to the arrangement of the synagogue, these uneducated women were interrupting the church service by asking their husbands—who were sitting some distance away—questions about the sermon. Or perhaps they were asking men other than their husbands. Or maybe they were simply "chattering" loudly or even promoting false teachings. Regardless of which position is correct, the key is that women were not allowing the worship service to continue without disruption. As a result, Paul urges the congregation to be orderly since God is a God of peace, not confusion. He then tells the women to be silent and learn from their husbands at home (instead of asking disrupting questions during the worship service). Thus, by their actions, the women were bringing shame on the church.

Another, although much less popular approach, is to claim that Paul did not pen the words in the text. Gordon Fee, for example, claims that the words could not have been written by Paul but must have been added later by a scribe. Fee writes, "Although these two verses [1 Cor. 14:34–35] are found in all known manuscripts . . . the two text-critical criteria of transcriptional and intrinsic probability combine to cast considerable doubt on their authenticity."[7] Fee later concludes, "On the whole, therefore, the case against these verses is so strong, and finding a viable solution to their meaning so difficult, that it seems best to view them as an interpolation [i.e., a later scribal addition]."[8]

Summary

In Christ there is neither male nor female (Gal. 3:28). All verses related to the role of women must be interpreted in light of this truth. The New Testament gives us evidence that this radical equality was already breaking through during the early church. Women had the gift of prophecy, were among Paul's coworkers, and were deacons, and even apostles. When prohibitions are given that limit the role of women in the church, we must consider the historical context in which the prohibitions were given. In the context

---

7. Gordon D. Fee, *The First Epistle to the Corinthians*, NICNT (Grand Rapids: Eerdmans, 1987), 699.
8. Ibid., 705.

of the churches at Ephesus and Corinth, uneducated women were teaching false doctrine and were being disruptive. Paul's prohibitions should not be understood as universal truths but as culturally conditioned statements. In a different context, such as today, women are educated and thus Paul's prohibitions no longer apply. Thus, women should be allowed to be elders who both teach and have authority over men.

Reflection Questions

1. What does Galatians 3:28 teach about whether women should be elders?
2. What are some of the ways women functioned in leadership roles in the New Testament?
3. How does the historical situation in Ephesus affect your understanding of 1 Timothy 2:11–12?
4. Do you think Paul's arguments from creation in 1 Corinthians 11:8–9 help us better understand his similar arguments in 1 Timothy 2:13–14?
5. Why did Paul instruct women not to speak in church in 1 Corinthians 14:33–35 but allow them to pray or prophesy in 1 Corinthians 11:5?

What Are the Reasons for Affirming That Women Cannot Be Elders? (Part 1)

In response to the previous question, we will now offer a point-by-point reply to the reasons for claiming that women can be elders. This response will be divided into two parts. Part 1 will cover the first three reasons, and part 2 will cover the last two reasons and then offer a summary.

The Testimony of Galatians 3:28

Although Galatians 3:28 speaks of the equality of men and women before God, it does not follow that such equality dissolves all role distinctions between men and women now. The context of Galatians 3:28 reveals that Paul is explaining that in Christ all people have equal access to the promises of Abraham and the salvation those promises bring. Whether Jew or Greek, slave or free, male or female, "if you are Christ's, then you are Abraham's offspring" (Gal. 3:29). Paul is not suggesting that all role distinctions have been permanently eliminated. Rather, his point is that all Christians, regardless of race, social status, or gender, have direct access to God as sons and daughters. Becoming an heir with Christ to the promises of Abraham is based solely on faith.

It must be stressed that the issue before us is not equality of person. Men and women are equally loved and valued by God. Both are created in God's image (Gen. 1:27), and both share the commission to be fruitful and take dominion over the earth (Gen. 1:28). Men and women are equal in redemption

---

Some of the material for this question is adapted from my earlier work, "Paul's Arguments from Creation in 1 Corinthians 11:8–9 and 1 Timothy 2:13–14: An Apparent Inconsistency Answered," *JETS* 49.3 (2006): 527–48.

and in their standing before God. It does not follow, however, that equality in person also means equality in role. This truth is best illustrated by the triune Godhead. God is a trinity. The Father is God. The Son is God. The Spirit is God. All are equally God. But all members of the Trinity do not have the same function or role. We read in 1 Corinthians 11:3 that "the head of Christ is God." In their relationship, the Son willingly submits to the will of the Father. As a result, God the Father is the head of Christ. Later we read, "When all things are subjected to him [Christ], then the Son himself will also be subjected to him [the Father]" (1 Cor. 15:28). The Son's being subjected to the Father does not make Him less than the Father but emphasizes the hierarchical relationship that exists in the Godhead. Although equal in substance to the Father, Christ submits Himself to the Father and obeys His will. This does not mean, however, that the Father is higher or greater than the Son. Both are equally God. In the same way, men and women have different roles but are equal in God's sight. Simply because a wife is to submit to her husband does not mean she is inferior to him any more than Christ is inferior to the Father because He submits himself to the Father.

Women Possess All Spiritual Gifts

Women are wonderfully gifted by God. No one denies this fact. The question is whether it is God's intent for women to serve as elders and teachers in the church. We know that some women had the gift of prophecy in the early church (Acts 21:9; 1 Cor. 11:5); but in 1 Timothy 2:12, Paul writes, "I do not permit a woman to teach or to exercise authority over a man." If women were prophesying in church—something that Paul does not prohibit—then, as the argument goes, his statement in 1 Timothy 2:12 cannot be taken as absolute. This type of reasoning, however, is not convincing because it assumes that prophesying and teaching were the same thing. Wayne Grudem has convincingly demonstrated that prophecy was a spontaneous utterance and thus distinct from teaching or preaching.[1] Towner rightly notes, "It should be pointed out that teaching, the activity prohibited here [in 1 Tim. 2:12], and

---

1. See Wayne Grudem, *The Gift of Prophecy in 1 Corinthians* (Lanham, MD: University Press of America, 1982); idem, *The Gift of Prophecy in the New Testament and Today*, rev. ed. (Wheaton: Crossway, 2000); idem, "Prophecy—Yes, but Teaching—No: Paul's Consistent Advocacy of Women's Participation Without Governing Authority," *JETS* 30 (1987): 1–23; contra Anthony C. Thiselton who maintains that prophecy "should not be restricted to the uttering of some supposedly 'spontaneous' oracular utterance," but "denotes the public proclamation of gospel truth as applied pastorally and contextually to the hearers" (*The First Epistle to the Corinthians*, NIGTC [Grand Rapids: Eerdmans; Carlisle, U.K.: Paternoster, 2000], 826).

prophecy, an activity which (to judge from 1 Cor. 11.4) Paul allowed women to take part in, were probably not equivalent."[2]

The example of Priscilla teaching Apollos as proof that women can teach men is also based on flawed reasoning. First, the text does not say that Priscilla alone taught Apollos but that her husband, Aquila, was also with her (Acts 18:26). Second, the analogy fails because this teaching did not take place in the context of the congregational worship service. Paul's prohibition in 1 Timothy 2 is given in the context of several passages dealing with conduct and procedure when the assembly of believers is gathered for corporate worship.[3] Based on the context, Paul's prohibition of women teaching and having authority over men applies primarily in the context of the congregational worship service. Furthermore, examples of women as Paul's fellow workers and laborers do not prove women can be pastors, for no one denies that women were involved in ministry, only whether they functioned as pastors or elders.

It also is debatable whether Romans 16:1 and 1 Timothy 3:11 actually refer to the office of deacon (see question 39). But even if they do, that only proves that women can be deacons, not elders. It is also questionable whether Junia was an apostle, for the text can mean that she was "well known *among* the apostles" or "well known *to* the apostles" (Rom. 16:7). The later interpretation, which does not recognize Junia as an apostle, has recently been defended by Daniel Wallace and Michael Burer.[4] After carefully examining the particular Greek phrase (*episēmoi* + the preposition *en*) in biblical Greek, patristic Greek, papyri, inscriptions, and classical and Hellenistic texts, they convincingly conclude that the normal way to communicate the exclusive meaning (i.e., "*to* the apostles") was employed by Paul.[5]

---

2. Philip H. Towner, *The Goal of Our Instruction: The Structure of Theology and Ethics in the Pastoral Epistles*, JSNTSup 34 (Sheffield: Sheffield Academic Press, 1989), 215.

3. So George W. Knight, *The Pastoral Epistles*, NIGTC (Grand Rapids: Eerdmans; Carlisle, U.K.: Paternoster, 1992), 128; Thomas R. Schreiner, "An Interpretation of 1 Timothy 2:9–15: A Dialogue with Scholarship," in *Women in the Church: A Fresh Analysis of 1 Timothy 2:9–15*," ed. Andreas Köstenberger, Thomas R. Schreiner, and H. Scott Baldwin (Grand Rapids: Baker, 1995), 113; contra J. M. Holmes, *Text in a Whirlwind: A Critique of Four Exegetical Devices at 1 Timothy 2.9–15*, JSNTSup 196 (Sheffield: Sheffield Academic Press, 2000), 96–97.

4. See Daniel B. Wallace and Michael H. Burer, "Was Junia Really an Apostle?" *NTS* 47 (2001): 76–91.

5. The exclusive view (i.e., "to/by the apostles") has previously been held by John Murray, *The Epistle to the Romans*, NICNT (Grand Rapids: Eerdmans, 1968), 2:229–30; Charles Hodge, *A Commentary on Romans*, Geneva Series of Commentaries (1835; Carlisle, PA: Banner of Truth Trust, 1989), 449; and R. C. H. Lenski, *The Interpretation of St. Paul's Epistle to the Romans* (Minneapolis: Augsburg, 1961), 906–7.

The Historical Situation Behind 1 Timothy 2:11–12

Apparently some women were causing commotion in the church at Ephesus by their elaborate dress and their desire to teach. Paul, therefore, writes to Timothy and exhorts women to dress modestly and prohibits them from teaching and having authority over men. In 1 Timothy 2:13, Paul gives the first reason why he does not permit women to teach or have authority over men in the context of the local church. He states, "For Adam was formed first, then Eve." In this text, Paul uses an argument from the order of creation in the creation account in Genesis (esp. Gen. 2:7, 22). Why does Paul use the Genesis text to make his case? The fact that Adam was created before Eve signifies that he is the one with authority in their relationship. In his second reason for prohibiting women from teaching or having authority over men, Paul makes an allusion to Eve being deceived by the serpent in the Garden (Gen. 3:6, 13): "and Adam was not deceived, but the woman was deceived and became a transgressor" (1 Tim. 2:14). Egalitarians often claim that Eve's deception was caused by a lack of knowledge (and thus a lack of "education"). But does this interpretation of 1 Timothy 2:13–14 fit with the Genesis account? Is the lack of education among the women of Ephesus really the problem that lies at the heart of Paul's prohibition? There are at least seven reasons why such a view must be rejected.

First, Eve's being dependent on Adam for teaching is not the same as being inadequately taught. If Adam told his wife the commandment from God, then was not Eve educated as much as Adam? Based on the Genesis account, we know that Eve had been instructed by Adam. The serpent tempts Eve by saying, "Did God actually say, 'You shall not eat of any tree in the garden'?" (Gen. 3:1). Eve then responds with the words she had been taught by Adam, "We may eat of the fruit of the trees in the garden, but God said, 'You shall not eat of the fruit of the tree that is in the midst of the garden, neither shall you touch it, lest you die'" (Gen. 3:2–3). It is clear that Eve received God's command from Adam and therefore was just as "educated" as he was. The issue was not lack of knowledge but lack of faith in God's promises. Thus, Eve's deception was not based on her inferior knowledge or education but on her willingness to let the words of the serpent hold more sway over her decisions than the Word of God. Consequently, the explanation for Eve's deception cannot be based on what Eve did or did not know.[6] Therefore, the deception

6. Wayne Grudem notes, "Deficient education cannot be the meaning because the prohibition was so simple. How many years of education does one need in order to understand the meaning of,

does not lie in the fact that Eve did not know better, but that although she knew better, she was tricked into eating anyway.

Second, if Paul's point is that Eve sinned with less knowledge than Adam, then Adam is guilty of the greater sin, which is not the point that Paul is trying to make.[7] Paul is explaining why the Ephesian women were not to teach the men. If Paul is trying to demonstrate that women should not teach men, then how does it help his argument to show that Adam committed the greater sin? It would seem to prove just the opposite.

Third, there is no proof in 1 or 2 Timothy that women were actually teaching false doctrine, for Paul never identifies a woman as a false teacher. He mentions only Hymenaeus (1 Tim. 1:20; 2 Tim. 2:17–18), Alexander (1 Tim. 1:20), and Philetus (2 Tim. 2:17–18). Although women are mentioned as being led astray by the false teachers (1 Tim. 5:13; 2 Tim. 3:6–7), they are never referred to as being the teachers themselves. Thus, the position that women were teaching false doctrine is highly speculative. Furthermore, nowhere in the Genesis account is it suggested that Eve taught Adam. It is not convincing to argue that just as Eve taught Adam to eat the fruit, bringing sin to mankind, so too the uneducated women at Ephesus were teaching the men false doctrine, bringing sin to the church. The focus in both Genesis and Paul is not that Eve taught Adam but that Eve was deceived.

Fourth, if Paul meant to say that women are not permitted to teach since they are uneducated, then why not say that in those words? Paul simply could have written, "I do not permit a woman to teach or have authority over men but to learn in quietness for uneducated women are more likely to be deceived and teach false doctrine." Instead, Paul bases his reasoning on the order of creation. Keener writes, "Presumably, Paul wants [women] to learn so that they could *teach*."[8] If Paul wanted to say what Keener claims, he did a terrible job of communicating his intentions.

'but the tree of the knowledge of good and evil you shall not eat, for in the day that you eat of it you shall surely die'?" (*Evangelical Feminism and Biblical Truth: An Analysis of More than One Hundred Disputed Questions* [Sisters, OR: Multnomah, 2004], 295).

7. We are not denying that Adam, as the representative head of all mankind, was guilty of the greater sin (cf. Rom. 5:15–21), but are merely pointing out that Paul is not arguing in this passage that Adam was more guilty since he knew something more than Eve.

8. Craig S. Keener, *Paul, Women, and Wives: Marriage and Women's Ministry in the Letters of Paul* (Peabody, MA: Hendrickson, 1992), 112. Rebecca Merrill Groothuis likewise states, "In other words, the point of the illustration is that, in order to avoid deception and serious error, those who lack instruction in God's Word (as did Eve and the Ephesian women) should defer to the expertise of those who are more thoroughly instructed (as were Adam and the male leaders in

Fifth, there must have been some "educated" women in Ephesus at the time Paul wrote 1 Timothy. We know from Acts 18:26 that Priscilla was well educated, and she was very likely in Ephesus at that time since she is mentioned as being there when Paul writes 2 Timothy (2 Tim. 4:19). Steve Baugh has convincingly demonstrated that it is misleading to maintain that women were considered "uneducated" because they did not normally achieve high levels of formal education. Based on his extensive research, Baugh notes, "Few people in antiquity advanced in their formal education beyond today's elementary school levels, including men like Socrates, Sophocles, and Herodotus."[9] In addition, many of the more affluent women participated in private lectures. One reason for this was that upper-class women often needed to be literate in order to manage large households. Based on the description of the manner in which some women were dressing with elaborate hairdos, gold, pearls, and expensive clothing (1 Tim. 2:9; cf. 1 Tim. 6:17–18), at least some of the women in the Ephesian congregation were considered upper-class and most likely some would have been considered "educated." Would Paul make such a sweeping statement barring all women from teaching if some were indeed well qualified?[10] Furthermore, in his discussion concerning head coverings in 1 Corinthians 11, Paul does not simply give in and placate the dictates of culture. He does not say that women cannot pray and prophesy at all, but that they should do so in a way that maintains a cultural distinction between men and women. But why doesn't Paul use this line of reasoning in 1 Timothy 2? Why doesn't he tell the women to teach and have authority only if they do it without teaching false doctrine? Why does he seem to completely limit the public role of women in 1 Timothy 2 but refuses to do so in 1 Corinthians 11? Paul will let culture dictate certain elements in

---

the Ephesian church). Thus, Paul's intent in referring to Adam and Eve is not to say that women in general should submit to the spiritual authority of men, but that women—and, in principle, men as well—who do not have adequate spiritual understanding should defer to and learn from those who do" (*Good News for Women: A Biblical Picture of Gender Equality* [Grand Rapids: Baker, 1997], 222).

9. S. M. Baugh, "A Foreign World: Ephesus in the First Century," in *Women in the Church*, 46.

10. Schreiner states, "A prohibition against women alone seems to be reasonable only if *all* the women in Ephesus were duped by the false teaching" ("An Interpretation of 1 Timothy 2:9–15," 112). Grudem adds, "Even if *some* women were teaching false doctrine at Ephesus, why would that lead Paul to prohibit *all* women from teaching? It would not be fair or consistent to do so" (*Evangelical Feminism*, 287). Furthermore, when Paul gives the qualifications for male teachers in 1 Timothy 3, he does not even mention the need for proper education.

his teaching when they are superficial—like the wearing of head coverings. He realizes that some things are not as important as others, and he will accommodate when possible. But is it likely that Paul would restrict women from teaching or having authority simply because that culture says women should not do such things, or because some women were uneducated or were teaching false doctrine? Paul will restrict freedoms or add certain qualifications when they are "irrelevant," but it does not seem to be Paul's style to give such a far-reaching command in order to accommodate or deal with a problem or abuse.

Sixth, if Paul's prohibition is meant to address only women who were uneducated or teaching false doctrine, what about men who would fall into this same category? Are we to assume that they are permitted to teach heresy since they are not mentioned? Keener concludes that Paul's principle "is that those who do not understand the Scriptures and are not able to teach them accurately should not be permitted to teach others."[11] If Paul's real concern is that no one teaches false doctrine, then why does Paul limit his application to women? After all, it was the men who were guilty of teaching false doctrine (cf. 1 Tim. 1:20; 2 Tim. 2:17–18).

Seventh, Paul's argument is based directly on creation. In other words, Paul's appeal to the creation of Adam before Eve demonstrates the different roles that God had established based on creation. The order of creation becomes the reason Paul prohibits women from teaching men. Therefore, the Genesis account gives the reasons for why a woman is not to teach or have authority over a man. It is based on creation and therefore transcends cultures. Some insist, however, that the context favors interpreting the prohibition for women not to teach or have authority over men as determined by the culture of the time. For example, Groothuis claims, "It is inconsistent to regard the dress code in 1 Timothy 2:9 as culturally relative and, therefore, temporary, but the restrictions on women's ministry in 2:12 as universal and permanent."[12] But this argument fails to take note of the context of Paul's teaching since Paul clearly gives us the principle underlying his prohibitions when he says, "Women should adorn themselves in respectable apparel" (1 Tim. 2:9). Before he gives the culturally relative prohibitions, he first gives the universal principle behind them: women are to dress modestly and discreetly. Therefore, although the prohibitions of wearing braided hair, gold,

11. Keener, *Paul, Women, and Wives*, 120.
12. Groothuis, *Good News for Women*, 214.

pearls, and expensive clothing are culturally relative, the previously stated principle is not. Paul is not saying that tending to one's hair, wearing jewelry, or wearing expensive clothes is wrong. Rather, he is saying that modesty and discreetness should be maintained when giving consideration to how one appears in public. It is misleading, then, to claim that the dress code in 1 Timothy 2 is culturally relative without acknowledging that Paul does give us a transcultural principle. Furthermore, there are other examples where we find culturally relative issues mixed with transcultural principles. To simply appeal to the context where a culturally relative issue exists and then claim that the whole context must be dealing with such issues is not good exegesis. Finally, it is not likely that the word *authentein* in 1 Timothy 2:12 means "to domineer" or "to usurp authority." Baldwin has demonstrated that the phrase is best translated positively, meaning "to exercise authority."[13] Consequently, it cannot be argued that Paul is merely forbidding women from domineering men in an ungodly manner; rather he is forbidding women from exercising any authority in positions of leadership in the church.

Reflection Questions

1. What is Paul's theological reason for stating that "there is neither male nor female" in Jesus Christ (Gal. 3:28)?
2. How does the Trinity help us understand the distinction between one's role and one's worth?
3. Do you think women possess all spiritual gifts? If so, is it necessary that all church offices be open to them so that they can fully exercise those gifts?
4. If the historical situation in Ephesus is the reason behind Paul's prohibitions in 1 Timothy 2:11–12, then why does Paul base his argument on creation (1 Tim. 2:13)?
5. How would you respond to the view that Paul prohibited women from teaching and having authority over men because the women of Ephesus were not properly educated or they were abusing their authority by trying to domineer men?

---

13. See H. Scott Baldwin, "A Difficult Word: αὐθεντέω in 1 Timothy 2:12," in *Women in the Church*, 65–80.

What Are the Reasons for Affirming That Women Cannot Be Elders? (Part 2)

Consistency in the Use of Paul's Arguments from Creation

The main text for not allowing women to be elders is 1 Timothy 2:12, where Paul states that women are not to teach or have authority over men. It is argued that this verse cannot be limited in its application to the context of the Ephesian church because Paul bases his statement not on culture but on creation (1 Tim. 2:13–14). But as we have seen above (question 18), some point out an (apparent) inconsistency because in 1 Corinthians 11:5 Paul teaches that women must cover their heads while praying or prophesying— a teaching that is also based on creation (1 Cor. 11:8–9). Thus, while both statements made by Paul are based on creation, the same people who insist that 1 Timothy 2:12 must be upheld in the context of the modern church are quick to dismiss 1 Corinthians 11:5. The following comments are a reply to this apparent inconsistency.

From the evidence found in 1 Corinthians, it appears that the Corinthians were basing their Christianity on an erroneous view of spirituality caused by an embrace of over-realized eschatology.[1] This teaching affirms that the king-

---

Some of the material for this question is adapted from my earlier work, "Paul's Arguments from Creation in 1 Corinthians 11:8–9 and 1 Timothy 2:13–14: An Apparent Inconsistency Answered," *JETS* 49.3 (2006): 527–48.

1. See Anthony C. Thiselton, "Realized Eschatology at Corinth," *NTS* 24 (1978): 510–26; Philip H. Towner, *The Goal of Our Instruction: The Structure of Theology and Ethics in the Pastoral Epistles*, JSNTSup 34 (Sheffield: Sheffield Academic Press, 1989), 33–36; Fee, *First Epistle to the Corinthians*, 498; idem, "Praying and Prophesying in the Assemblies: 1 Corinthians 11:2–16," in *Discovering Biblical Equality: Complementarity Without Hierarchy*, ed. Ronald W. Pierce, Rebecca Merrill Groothuis, and Gordon D. Fee (Downers Grove, IL: InterVarsity Press, 2004), 158–59; and Jason David BeDuhn, "'Because of the Angels': Unveiling Paul's Anthropology in 1 Corinthians 11," *JBL* 118 (1999): 317–18.

dom of God has come in all its fullness and therefore rejects the notion that the kingdom has "not yet" fully arrived. As a result, the real issue at stake in 1 Corinthians 11 is something more than head coverings. The more important issue is the Corinthians' desire to eliminate creational gender and role distinctions.[2] Because of their over-realized eschatology, some women wanted to minimize or erase the distinction between genders and be like the angels now (Matt. 22:30). Thus, they were seeking to assert their newfound freedom by disregarding a common cultural custom (i.e., head coverings for women while worshiping), something their society would consider disgraceful.[3] The Corinthians' position would have been strengthened by misapplying Paul's teaching that men and women were equal in Christ (cf. Gal. 3:28). Therefore, Paul's main concern is not head coverings, since that was merely a cultural outworking of an unchanging truth—God created men and women differently and this distinction is not eliminated when we become Christians.

In defending the current need for gender and role distinctions, and thus head coverings, Paul offers three arguments. He argues from creation (1 Cor. 11:7b–9), from nature (vv. 14–15), and from practice (v. 16). The most significant argument, and the one with which we are most concerned, is his argument from creation.

In 1 Corinthians 11:7–9 Paul writes, "For a man ought not to cover his head, since he is the image and glory of God, but woman is the glory of man. For man was not made from woman, but woman from man. Neither was man created for woman, but woman for man." Paul first gives us the reason why a man should not wear a head covering: he is the image and glory of God (v. 7). Seeking to explain this statement, Paul then alludes in verse 8 to the creation account in Genesis 2:21–23, where it is recorded that Eve was created after Adam. In 1 Corinthians 11:9 Paul gives further evidence that a woman is the glory of man by alluding to Genesis 2:18. This text clearly indicates that Eve was created to be Adam's helpmate. What is absolutely crucial in understanding the use of Paul's arguments from creation in 1 Corinthians 11:8–9 is that

---

2. Thomas R. Schreiner summarizes, "The fundamental principle is that the sexes, although equal, are also different." He continues, "Now, in the first century, failure to wear a covering sent a signal to the congregation that a woman was rejecting the authority of male leadership. Paul was concerned about head coverings only because of the message they sent to people in that culture" ("Head Coverings, Prophecies, and the Trinity: 1 Corinthians 11:2–16," in *Recovering Biblical Manhood and Womanhood: A Response to Evangelical Feminism*, ed. John Piper and Wayne Grudem [Wheaton, IL: Crossway, 1991], 138).

3. For a survey of women's head coverings in antiquity, see Craig S. Keener, *Paul, Women, and Wives: Marriage and Women's Ministry in the Letters of Paul* (Peabody, MA: Hendrickson, 1992), 22–31.

he is not directly using these verses to make the case that head coverings are needed for women when they pray or prophesy. In other words, Paul does not say, "A woman must have her head covered when she prays or prophesies. For man does not come from the woman but the woman from man, and man was not created for the woman but the woman for the man." Rather, Paul uses the creation account in Genesis to affirm his previous statement that "woman is the glory of man." Even in verse 7, when Paul explains why a man must not cover his head ("since he is the image and glory of God"), the focus is not so much that a head covering is in itself wrong but on the disgrace or shame it brings. Thus, it is misleading and inaccurate to claim that Paul uses an argument from creation to affirm the need for women to wear head coverings. Instead, Paul appeals to creation to demonstrate the differences between men and women that God established from the beginning—and violating these distinctions brings shame instead of glory. By covering his head, the man brings shame on Christ (since man is the image and glory of God), and by not covering her head, the woman brings shame on man (since woman is the glory of man).

The position that Paul's main concern in this passage is gender and role distinctions is supported by a number of clues found in the context of this passage. First, the fact that Paul introduces his arguments the way he does makes little sense if head coverings are Paul's main concern. In verse 3, Paul begins by saying, "But I want you to understand that Christ is the head of every man, and the man is the head of a woman, and God is the head of Christ" (NASB). That something more important is at stake seems obvious because Paul explains the functional relationship between man and Christ, woman and man, and Christ and God. In their relationship, the man has authority over the woman just as Christ has authority over the man and God the Father has authority over Christ. Based on the understanding that "head" refers to "authority over," it seems likely that the underlying problem involves not only gender distinctions but also role distinctions.[4] Functionally, the wife is under the authority of her husband and therefore needs to demonstrate her submissiveness by wearing a head covering.

---

4. For the argument that "head" should be understood as "authority over," see Wayne A. Grudem, "Does *Kephalē* Mean 'Source' or 'Authority Over' in Greek Literature? A Survey of 2,336 Examples," *TJ* 6 (1985): 38–59; idem, "Appendix 1: The Meaning of *Kephalē* ('Head'): A Response to Recent Studies," in *Recovering Biblical Manhood and Womanhood*, 425–68; idem, "The Meaning of κεφαλή ('Head'): An Evaluation of New Evidence, Real and Alleged," *JETS* 44 (2001): 25–65 (also in idem, *Evangelical Feminism and Biblical Truth: An Analysis of More than One Hundred Disputed Questions* [Sisters, OR: Multnomah, 2004], 552–99).

Second, Paul's comparison of a woman who prays or prophesies without a head covering to a woman with a man's haircut also signifies that the main issue at stake is gender and role distinctions and not merely the wearing of a piece of cloth on one's head. In 1 Corinthians 11:6, Paul explains, "For if a woman does not cover her head, let her also have her hair cut off; but if it is disgraceful for a woman to have her hair cut off or her head shaved, let her cover her head" (NASB). Just as it is wrong for a woman to blur the gender distinctions by wearing a man's hairstyle, so too it is wrong for a woman to blur such distinctions by not covering her head while praying or prophesying. Paul presses this analogy by saying that if a woman wants to disgrace both herself and her husband by having a man's hairstyle, then she might as well go all the way and shave off all her hair.

Third, Paul's argument from nature in verses 14 and 15 likewise suggests that God's creational gender and role distinctives are in view. In these verses we read, "Does not nature itself teach you that if a man wears long hair it is a disgrace for him, but if a woman has long hair, it is her glory? For her hair is given to her for a covering." In speaking of "nature," Paul is not referring to culture or "social conventions" but to God's design in creation (cf. Rom. 1:26–27). God created women to have longer hair than men, and thus nature teaches us that it is not fitting for a man to have long hair and so appear like a woman. Paul's argument from nature, then, does not directly prove that women must wear head coverings but that the differences between men and women are part of God's creational design. Since the distinctions between men and women are part of God's plan, however, it is imperative for the Corinthian women to wear head coverings.

Fourth, in verse 16 Paul states, "We have no other practice, nor have the churches of God" (NASB). According to Paul, the wearing of head coverings was not limited to the church at Corinth but was a custom in all the churches in the Greco-Roman world. Such a universally accepted custom suggests the presence of an underlying principle governing the need for such a practice.

Finally, it is important to notice the passive nature of a head covering. By its very function, a head covering was a sign or symbol that pointed to a greater reality.[5] In verse 10 Paul calls the head covering a "symbol of authority." It had no meaning in itself but was a concrete expression of an intangible

---

5. Grudem rightly comments, "All interpreters agree that head covering was a symbol for something else, and that Paul was concerned about it because of what that symbol meant" (*Evangelical Feminism*, 333).

truth. Thus, Paul is not concerned about head coverings *per se*. Rather, he is concerned with the meaning that wearing a head covering conveys.

Paul's argument, then, is that women must wear head coverings when praying or prophesying because of a more important underlying issue—God created men and women differently, and we must not seek to eliminate such distinctions.[6] It has been shown that Paul's arguments from creation in 1 Corinthians 11:8–9 are not directly given to mandate that women wear head coverings. Rather, his arguments from creation are given to prove, or better, explain, how man is the image and glory of God and how the woman is the glory of man. That is, Paul uses the argument from creation to demonstrate that the gender and role differences between men and women are based on God's design in creation. Thus, Christian women are not required to wear head coverings today when praying because the symbol of a woman's head being covered is different today than it was during the time of Paul. As a result, Paul's argument from creation is only indirectly linked to the need for head coverings. The transcultural truth that undergirded Paul's admonition, however, still applies for us today. Women are created differently than men, and this distinction must be maintained in the church and in the family. In contrast, Paul's arguments from creation in 1 Timothy 2:13–14 directly follow the prohibition for women not to teach or have authority over men. As a result, verses 13 and 14 are best taken as the grounds for that prohibition and thus are transcultural. Therefore, the command for women not to teach or have authority over men should be upheld in the church today.

The Meaning of 1 Corinthians 14:33–35

Those claiming that women can and should be elders are correct in noting that Paul's statement in 1 Corinthians 14:33–35 cannot be absolute. As already noted, Paul clearly teaches that women could pray and prophesy during the worship service (1 Cor. 11:5). But the position that Paul's prohibition was given because women were somehow disturbing the church service remains unconvincing. Rather, there is a stronger argument for the position that Paul's prohibition is related to the immediate context of judging the content of the prophecies given during the worship service. In the previ-

---

6. Schreiner summarizes: "Thus, we can conclude that Paul wants women to wear head coverings while praying or prophesying because to do otherwise would be to confuse the sexes and give the shameful impression that women are behaving like men." He later adds that "head coverings reflect the role relationship intended between man and woman" ("Head Coverings," 131).

ous verses, Paul states that while prophecies are given "let the others weigh what is said" (1 Cor. 14:29). He later adds, "The spirits of prophets are subject to prophets" (1 Cor. 14:32). It is in this context—during the judging of the prophecies—that women are to remain silent. This principle is consistent with what Paul says in 1 Timothy 2:11–12 because judging the prophets would be considered exercising authority over men.

The principle that women cannot stand in judgment concerning the content of the prophecies given but must remain silent is not based on culture. Paul states that the principle is transcultural and is the practice of "all the churches of the saints" (1 Cor. 14:33). The principle is not so much silence but submission (1 Cor. 14:34). Furthermore, Paul appeals to Scripture (the "Law") to defend the practice (1 Cor. 14:34). By basing his argument in Scripture, Paul's reasoning seems to run contrary to the notion that he is merely giving a temporary command based on a local circumstance. Rather, he is giving an implication of what it means for women to be submissive in the context of the worship service.

Summary

In the last two questions we have been offering a response to the view that women should be permitted to be elders. Besides the responses given above, other reasons can be given in support of male-only eldership. First, Jesus Himself was male. This fact was not simply a random choice but a theological necessity. Jesus was the "last Adam" or the "second man" who, like Adam, acted as a representative on behalf of others (Rom. 5:12–21; 1 Cor. 15:45, 47). As the King of Israel, He had to be the firstborn son of the Davidic lineage and, as the Lord of the universe, His headship required that He be male (Gen. 2:20–23; 1 Cor. 11:3).

Second, when Jesus chose twelve leaders, or "apostles," who would accompany Him, He purposefully chose twelve men. Some critics claim that Jesus was merely accommodating to the culture of His time since it would have been culturally inappropriate for Him to choose any women. But this assumption cannot be defended because Jesus often acted in ways that were countercultural. If Jesus' work of redemption abolishes all gender distinctions, then it would have been fitting for Jesus to choose some women as apostles to signify this intended outcome. Even if He chose just one woman to be an apostle, Jesus could have shown to the world that He would someday eliminate all gender distinction. Instead, after spending the night in prayer with His heavenly Father (Luke 6:12), Jesus appointed twelve males to lead the church after His resurrection and ascension. Later, when the apostles needed to replace Judas as the twelfth apostle, the only two who were considered for the position were males (Acts 1:23). The early church also followed the example of Jesus in appointing seven men to establish an official body of servants who could assist the apostles by caring for the church's widows (Acts 6:1–6).

Third, throughout the New Testament, male leadership in the family is clearly established. Paul, for example, repeatedly affirms male headship in the marriage relationship.

> Wives, submit to your own husbands, as to the Lord. For the husband is the head of the wife even as Christ is the head of the church, his body, and is himself its Savior. Now as the church submits to Christ, so also wives should submit in everything to their husbands. (Eph. 5:22–24)

Similarly he states, "Wives, submit to your husbands, as is fitting in the Lord" (Col. 3:18). Later, Paul urges older women to "train the young women to love their husbands and children, to be self-controlled, pure, working at home, kind, and submissive to their own husbands" (Titus 2:4–5).

Peter equally affirms male headship. He writes,

> Likewise, wives, be subject to your own husbands. . . . Do not let your adorning be external—the braiding of hair, the wearing of gold, or the putting on of clothing—but let your adorning be the hidden person of the heart with the imperishable beauty of a gentle and quiet spirit, which in God's sight is very precious. For this is how the holy women who hoped in God used to adorn themselves, by submitting to their husbands, as Sarah obeyed Abraham, calling him lord. And you are her children, if you do good and do not fear anything that is frightening. (1 Peter 3:1, 3–6)

The entire New Testament presents a unified voice that teaches male headship in marriage and the family. This principle also was extended to the wider church family. Indeed, Paul calls the church "the household of God" (1 Tim. 3:15). In listing the qualifications for an elder, Paul simply assumes that the position is intended only for men. He indicates that an elder must be "the husband of one wife" (1 Tim. 3:2; Titus 1:6) and "must manage his own household well" (1 Tim. 3:4). There is no hint in the context that women are eligible to serve as elders. For these reasons, it is best that eldership in the church be limited to males.

Reflection Questions

1. How did the Corinthians' eschatology affect their view of men and women?
2. What evidence is there to support the notion that gender and role distinctions are the underlying issues in Paul's discussion about head coverings in 1 Corinthians 11:2–16?
3. What do you think is the best explanation for why Paul prohibits women from speaking in 1 Corinthians 14:33–35?
4. What is the underlying principle for this prohibition (cf. 1 Cor. 14:33)?
5. Do you think the fact that Jesus' disciples were all male and that male leadership in the family is taught in the Bible supports all male leadership in the church?

Section C
Questions Related to the Plurality of Elders

Should Each Church Have a Plurality of Elders?

The concept of shared leadership is a common theme in the Bible. In the Old Testament, leadership was shared by the elders of Israel. In the New Testament, Jesus chose twelve apostles to lead the church. In addition, the early church appointed seven men to assist the apostles by caring for the church's widows (Acts 6:1–6). This pattern of plurality was continued with the establishment of the Christian eldership.

Evidence for Plurality from Acts

The first mention of Christian elders appears in Acts 11:30, which tells us the church in Antioch sent Barnabas and Paul to the elders in Jerusalem with money to aid in the famine relief. Later, in Acts 15, the elders are referenced along with the apostles in the context of the Jerusalem Council. Similar to the apostles, the elders formed a collective body of leadership.

On Paul's first missionary journey, he and Barnabas preached the gospel in Asia Minor, especially in the cities of Antioch, Iconium, Lystra, and Derbe. On their return trip, Luke records that they "appointed elders for them in every church" (Acts 14:23). In this verse we are specifically told that a plurality of elders were appointed in every church. Although the church was recently established, Paul and Barnabas believed it was important for each church to possess more than one spiritual leader. Even though Luke mentions Barnabas and Paul appointing "elders" only in Acts 14:23, it is likely that this was Paul's customary procedure. Ramsay comments, "It is clear, therefore, that Paul everywhere instituted Elders in his new Churches; and on our hypothesis as to the accurate and methodical expression of the historian [i.e., Luke], we are bound to infer that this first case is intended to be typical of the way of appointment followed in all later cases. When Paul directed Titus [Titus 1:5] to appoint Elders in each Cretan city, he was doubtless thinking of the same method which he followed here."[1] Likewise, Lightfoot writes, "On their very first missionary journey the Apostles Paul and Barnabas are described as appointing presbyters in every church. The same rule was doubtless carried out in all the brotherhoods founded later; but it is mentioned here and here only, because the mode of procedure on this occasion would suffice as a type of the Apostles' dealings elsewhere under similar circumstances."[2]

At the end of his third missionary journey, Paul summoned "the elders of the church to come to him" (Acts 20:17). Together, these elders were exhorted to "shepherd the church of God" (Acts 20:28 NASB). Many conclude that because the church of Ephesus is referred to in the singular (i.e., not to the churches of Ephesus), there was only one body of believers in Ephesus, which was governed by a plurality of leaders. Strauch, for example, comments, "The natural reading of the passage, then, indicates that there is one church in Ephesus and one body of elders to oversee it."[3] Some, however, have argued that the church at Ephesus could have had a circle of house churches similar to Rome or Corinth. For instance, although Carson states, "A plurality of elders, if not mandated, appears to have been common, and perhaps the norm," he then adds,

> On the other hand, only "church" (*ekklēsia* in the sing.) is used for the congregation of all believers in one city, never "churches"; one reads of churches in Galatia, but of the church in Antioch or Jerusalem or Ephesus. Thus it is possible, though not certain, that a single elder may have exercised authority in relation to one house group—a house group that in some cases constituted part of the citywide church—so that the individual elder would nevertheless be one of many in the citywide "church" taken as a whole.[4]

Although the situation that Carson describes was certainly possible, the New Testament never indicates that a single congregation was ruled by one elder, so it seems unwise to base our practices on such speculation.

---

1. William M. Ramsay, *St. Paul the Traveller and the Roman Citizen*, 2nd ed. (New York: G. P. Putnam's Sons; London: Hodder and Stoughton, 1896), 121.
2. J. B. Lightfoot, *St. Paul's Epistle to the Philippians* (London: Macmillan, 1881), 193.
3. Alexander Strauch, *Biblical Eldership: An Urgent Call to Restore Biblical Church Leadership*, 3rd ed., rev. and expanded (Littleton, CO: Lewis and Roth, 1995), 143.
4. D. A. Carson, "Church, Authority in the," *EDT*, ed. Walter E. Elwell (Grand Rapids: Baker, 1984), 229.

Evidence for Plurality from the Rest of the New Testament

Luke's record fits well with Paul's own account that each church was led by a plurality of elders. Paul writes to young Timothy, "Let the elders who rule well be considered worthy of double honor, especially those who labor in preaching and teaching" (1 Tim. 5:17). When Paul writes to the church at Philippi, he specifically greets the "overseers and deacons" (Phil. 1:1). Although the term for elder is not used in this context, we have already demonstrated that the Greek terms for elder and overseer referred to the same group of people (see question 9). Later, Paul directed Titus to "appoint elders in every town" (Titus 1:5). At the end of his ministry, Paul still believed in the necessity of establishing a body of elders in the local church.

The practice of having a plurality of elders is consistently found in the non-Pauline writings of the New Testament as well. James, the Lord's brother, raises the question, "Is anyone among you sick?" His answer is, "Let him call for the elders of the church, and let them pray over him, anointing him with oil in the name of the Lord" (James 5:14). Again, we should note that the sick person is to call for the "elders" (plural) of the "church" (singular). Finally, the apostle Peter exhorts the "elders" among the believers scattered throughout Pontus, Galatia, Cappadocia, Asia, and Bithynia (1 Peter 5:1).

In almost every reference in the New Testament, the term for "elders" is found in the plural. There are a few exceptions, however. In 1 Timothy 5:19, Paul states, "Do not admit a charge against an elder except on the evidence of two or three witnesses." In this verse the singular form is used, not because the church in Ephesus had only one elder, but because the context refers to accusations brought up against an individual elder. Verse 17 clearly mentions that there was a plurality of elders in the Ephesian church. The other two occurrences of the singular form occur in the latter two epistles of John, where John describes himself as "the elder" (2 John 1; 3 John 1). In this case, the singular must be used because the title is used as a personal designation (cf. 1 Peter 5:1, where Peter calls himself a "fellow elder").

There are also other terms used to describe the plurality of leaders in the church. Paul urges the Corinthians to "be subject" to the household of Stephanas "and to every fellow worker and laborer" (1 Cor. 16:15–16). In his first letter to the church at Thessalonica, Paul exhorts the believers "to respect those who labor among you and are over you in the Lord and admonish you" (1 Thess. 5:12). Although "elders" are not mentioned, it is clear that those to whom Paul is referring were the spiritual leaders of the congregation, performing elderlike functions. Finally, the author of Hebrews also indicates that the church to which he writes was led by a plurality of shepherds. In Hebrews 13:7, the author states, "Remember your leaders, those who spoke to you the word of God. Consider the outcome of their way of life, and imitate their faith." He then exhorts the congregation, writing, "Obey your leaders and submit to them, for they are keeping watch over your souls, as those who will have to give an account" (Heb. 13:17). In the closing of his letter, he adds, "Greet all your leaders and all the saints" (Heb. 13:24). In each case, the author refers to a plurality of leaders.

Summary

The New Testament evidence indicates that every church had a plurality of elders. There is no example in the New Testament of one elder or pastor leading a congregation as the sole or primary leader. There were a plurality of elders at the churches in Jerusalem (Acts 11:30), Antioch of Pisidia, Lystra, Iconium, and Derbe (Acts 14:23), Ephesus (Acts 20:17; 1 Tim. 5:17); Philippi (Phil. 1:1), the cities of Crete (Titus 1:5), the churches in the dispersion to which James wrote (James 5:14), the churches in the Roman provinces of Pontus, Galatia, Cappadocia, Asia, and Bithynia (1 Peter 5:1), and possibly the church(es) to which Hebrews was written (Heb. 13:7, 17, 24). Based on this evidence, Grudem notes, "First, no passage suggests that any church, no matter how small, had only one elder. The consistent New Testament pattern is a plurality of elders 'in every church' (Acts 14:23) and 'in every town' (Titus 1:5). Second, we do not see a diversity of forms of government in the New Testament church, but a unified and consistent pattern in which every church had elders governing it and keeping watch over it (Acts 20:28; Heb. 13:17; 1 Peter 5:2–3)."[5] Strauch similarly states, "On the local church level, the New Testament plainly witnesses to a consistent pattern of shared pastoral leadership. Therefore, leadership by a plurality of elders is a sound biblical practice."[6] Marshall likewise comments, "The picture that emerges from relevant passages (Phil. 1.1; Acts 20.17, 28; 14.23; 16.4) suggests a plurality of leaders in a church."[7]

---

5. Wayne Grudem, *Systematic Theology: An Introduction to Biblical Doctrine* (Leicester: InterVarsity Press; Grand Rapids: Eerdmans, 1994), 913.
6. Strauch, *Biblical Eldership*, 37.
7. I. Howard Marshall, *A Critical and Exegetical Commentary on the Pastoral Epistles*, in collaboration with Philip H. Towner, ICC (Edinburgh: T and T Clark, 1999), 153.

It is often difficult, however, to apply this biblical teaching in our current context. Many would argue that even if it can be shown that New Testament churches had a plurality of elders, it does not necessarily mean that churches today must follow that paradigm. Something *described* in the Bible is different than something *prescribed*. The first *explains* what happened in history; the second *exhorts* us to do something. Yet, once we leave the biblical model of biblical eldership, we leave the sure footing of apostolic precedent and begin wandering in the wilderness of pragmatism.

Reflection Questions

1. What New Testament verses demonstrate that the early churches had a plurality of elders?
2. How do we account for the few verses that speak of the "elder" in the singular (see 1 Tim. 5:19; 1 Peter 5:1; 2 John 1; 3 John 1)?
3. In Acts 14:23 we read that Paul appointed elders in the churches of Asia Minor (i.e., Antioch, Iconium, Lystra, and Derbe). Even though we don't read of Paul appointing elders in other churches, what evidence is there in Acts that other churches had elders?
4. If every congregation in the first-century church had a plurality of elders, do you think our churches ought to do the same?
5. Why do you think it is helpful to have a plurality of elders?

How Many Elders Should Each Congregation Have?

The Bible never identifies a specific number of elders that should lead each local congregation. In the previous question, we argued that a plurality—at least two elders—was the pattern of the earliest congregations. Apart from having a plurality, we are left to use godly wisdom and common sense. Before we present various methods of determining the number of elders for a congregation, a few introductory comments are in order.

First, it is important that every elder has a strong desire to serve in that capacity. Paul informs us that it is a noble task if someone aspires to the office of elder (1 Tim. 3:1). Likewise, Peter informs us that elders should shepherd God's flock, not from compulsion, but willingly (1 Peter 5:2). One should not agree to serve as an elder out of guilt, because he was nominated, or because he received the most votes. To be effective, an elder must love and enjoy the hard work of being a shepherd. Second, we must remember that eldership is a calling. Paul tells the elders of the Ephesian church, "Pay careful attention to yourselves and to all the flock, *in which the Holy Spirit has made you overseers*" (Acts 20:28, emphasis added). Paul may have appointed and installed these men to their office, but ultimately it was God who raised them up to serve in His church. Likewise, we read in Paul's letter to the Ephesian church that the ascended Christ "gave some to be . . . pastors and teachers" (Eph. 4:11 NKJV). Pastors, or elders, are a gift from Christ to His church. Therefore, from one perspective, a church should appoint as many elders as God gives to a local congregation. Third, being an elder does not have to be a full-time or even a paid position. An elder can have a "secular" job and still be effective in shepherding people in the congregation. What is required is diligence, faithfulness, and a calling from God. Fourth, every candidate must meet the qualifications before he is eligible to serve as elder. *How many* elders is not as important as *who* the elders are. There are three main approaches to determining the number of elders a church should have.

Fixed-number System

In a fixed-number system, a specific number of elders is determined. For example, a church that has five hundred members may decide that they will be led by ten (and only ten) elders. The advantage to this system is that the church can set an ideal number of elders so that the board can function efficiently. This system often is used by large churches. As a church grows, if the number of elders grows with it, the elder board can become large and bogged down by its size. Therefore, in an effort to be more efficient, churches will adopt a set number of elders that is more manageable and unified.

There are definite disadvantages to this system. One disadvantage is that it often closes the door for godly, qualified men to serve. If the number of elders is fixed, and if the elders serve long terms, it may be years before anyone else in the church can become an elder. Another disadvantage is that this system does not account for a lack of qualified men to serve. If there is an opening on the elder board, the church will feel compelled to fill that opening. If the constitution requires ten elders, then those positions must be filled whether anyone is qualified to fill them or not. Finally, if the number of elders is set and then the church experiences growth, the workload for the elders can become overwhelming. Eventually, the elders will become administrators who simply make the important decisions of the church. They will be so busy that they do not have the time to fulfill their primary task—shepherding the souls of the congregation. Instead, they become disassociated from the congregation, being viewed merely as the decision makers. As a result, if this model is chosen, there should be some built-in flexibility so that the number can increase (or decrease) if needed.

Ratio System

With this system, the church determines an approximate ratio of elders to members. For example, a church may decide that one elder is needed for every fifty members. Unlike the fixed-number system, the number of elders required will increase or decrease if the number of members rises or falls. A disadvantage to this system is that as a church grows, the number of elders can become quite large. Some churches that use this system have elder boards with fifty or more elders. The advantage, of course, is that the elders are not as likely to become overworked since there are enough shepherds to tend to the sheep. Phil Newton provides some helpful advice: "Whatever number or ratio is established, quality must be emphasized over quantity. It is better to begin with a smaller group of well-qualified elders than to fill a quota with unqualified men."[1]

Open System

Some churches opt for a more open approach and do not specify the number of elders they should have or a certain ratio. If there is a perceived need for more elders, the church will pray that God will provide them with gifted and qualified men. An advantage to this approach is that it focuses more on letting God provide the right people rather than seeking to fill an empty position. Many churches are uncomfortable with this system because it is not exact enough. It does not provide a fixed number of elders or a certain ratio of elders to church members.

Summary

The Bible does not specify the number of elders for each local congregation. Apart from teaching a plurality, the Bible is silent regarding this issue. It is therefore important that each local church seek wisdom from God concerning which approach is best for them. Each system has clear advantages and also possible pitfalls. The key is that each person appointed to be an elder is properly qualified.

Reflection Questions

1. How do Acts 20:28 and Ephesians 4:11 teach that eldership is a calling from God?
2. What are the advantages of having a fixed number of elders? What are the disadvantages?
3. What are the advantages of using the ratio system to determine the number of elders? What are the disadvantages?
4. What are the advantages of using the open system of elders? What are the disadvantages?
5. What system do you think is best for your church?

---

1. Phil A. Newton, *Elders in Congregational Life: Rediscovering the Biblical Model for Church Leadership* (Grand Rapids: Kregel, 2005), 134.

What Is the Relationship Between Staff Members and Elders?

The organizational structure of many churches today bears almost no resemblance to the pattern found among the New Testament churches. Because of the professionalization of the ministry, the rise of pragmatism, and the growing size of congregations, the biblical model has been set aside for something more modern or more efficient. As a result, countless churches have embraced the corporate business model and thereby marginalized the biblical model. These churches have adopted a "staff-led" structure as opposed to an elder-led structure. In many churches, the deacons (or a council by some other name) function as the board of trustees. They are in charge of hiring and firing the senior pastor, who reports to this board. The senior pastor functions as the CEO. He is the president of the church and is responsible for giving the church vision and success. The members of the pastoral or ministerial staff function as vice presidents over various ministries (evangelism, music, youth, children, missions, etc.). The congregation comprises the shareholders who, as a body, vote to elect the various trustee members.

The result of this structure (or other nonbiblical structures) is that churches struggle to understand and implement the concept of a plurality of elders. They might ask, "Who are the elders? Is every staff member automatically an elder? Is the pastor also considered an elder?" In the following discussion, we will seek to present biblical answers to these questions.

Not All Staff Members Are Elders

Sometimes churches classify all staff members as elders since they serve the church in a full-time capacity. But simply because someone is hired by the church to perform a certain leadership function does not mean that person should be counted among the elders. Each staff member must meet the qualifications listed in the New Testament before he can serve as an elder (1 Tim. 3:1–7). Thus, for example, if a staff member is not "able to teach," he is disqualified from being an elder. Also, staff members who are not involved in shepherding the congregation—a primary task of a pastor—also should not be counted among the elders. In addition, a staff member may be too young or too inexperienced to be trusted with responsibilities of eldership. If someone is not respected by the congregation, then it would be counter-productive to install him to the office of elder. It is also not wise to use terms such as "youth pastor" for someone who is not an elder. Again, such usage confuses the biblical teaching because "elder" and "pastor" refer to the same office. Thus, to call someone who is not an elder a youth pastor is mislead-ing. The same would be true for a children's pastor, singles' pastor, or college pastor.

Not All Elders Are Staff Members

We also must note that while not all staff members should be elders, not all elders should be staff members. That is, it is unhealthy to limit those who can serve as elders to those who are employed by the church. This un-biblical distinction divides the congregation into professional clergy who do the ministry and the laity who support the ministry. Instead, it is better to leave the eldership open to anyone who is qualified to serve—whether they are on staff or not. Thus, "to exclude non-staff members from the eldership weakens the leadership group and deprives them of some of the most capable Christian servants in the church."[1] Excluding non-staff members from elder-ship also can lead to instability in leadership when a staff member accepts a position in another church. Each time a pastor leaves, the church undergoes a difficult crisis as the church is left without leadership. Consequently, it is healthy for a church to have more non-staff elders than staff elders. This helps protect the church from being overly dependent on paid staff. Ideally, there would be a minimum of three elders: one staff elder and two non-staff elders. On the other hand, the board of elders probably should not be so large that separate committees are needed to study issues or make important decisions (such as an executive committee). Not subdividing the eldership simplifies the authority structure and helps avoid unnecessary divisions.

---

1. Phil A. Newton, *Elders in Congregational Life: Rediscovering the Biblical Model for Church Leadership* (Grand Rapids: Kregel, 2005), 147.

Some Staff Members Should Be Elders

In other congregations, virtually no staff members are among the eldership. In some cases, the senior pastor is the only staff member who is an elder. This model also is not ideal because it also tends to create an unbiblical distinction between paid staff and unpaid leaders and creates a third office in the church. In addition to pastors and deacons, the third office of elder is added. But as has been demonstrated earlier, "pastor" and "elder" refer to the same office (see question 6).

Do Not Distinguish Between Staff Elders and Non-staff Elders

Having a staff-led church often leads to alienation of the congregation from their pastors/staff. The full-time paid leaders in the church are hired professionals who usually come from other churches. The congregation views it as the responsibility of the paid staff to do the work of the ministry. In order to overcome this separation and alienation, some churches have attempted to institute a "lay-elder" system. These lay elders are given some responsibility in the church but are still separate and distinct from the pastoral staff. This system represents an attempt by the pastoral staff to provide some leadership in the church that does not leave the congregation feeling isolated from the professional staff members. This particular system, however, has a number of problems. First, it still maintains a distinction between the professional and nonprofessional leaders. The professional staff still runs the church and makes most of the important decisions. Second, it introduces a distinction between "pastors" and "elders," a distinction that we have previously demonstrated is unbiblical (see questions 6 and 9). Therefore, to make a distinction between pastors who are paid staff members who run the church on a daily basis and elders who are unpaid non-staff members is to create an office that is not found in the Bible. It is not wrong, of course, to have paid and unpaid workers in the church. What is unwise, however, is to give unpaid elders less authority in the church by creating a distinct office. The titles "lay elder" or "lay pastor" confuse the biblical teaching and are better left unused.

Summary

It is not wise to simply include all staff members as elders. Every candidate for eldership must meet the qualifications given in Scripture. It also is not wise to limit elders to those who are staff members. Rather, it is best to have a balance between paid and unpaid (or staff and non-staff) elders—even allowing for more non-staff elders than staff members. This balance ensures that the church draws from those most qualified to serve and provides needed stability in leadership. It is also better to make no distinction between the elders, whether they are on staff and serve the church full-time or whether they are non-staff elders who serve the church only in their spare time.

Reflection Questions

1. What is the relationship between the pastor(s) and staff at your church?
2. Why is it best not to include all staff members among the eldership?
3. What are some reasons a church might not want all elders to be among the paid staff?
4. What are the pitfalls of having two types of elders (i.e., "staff elders" and "lay elders")?
5. What changes might your church make in this area to become more biblical?

Should There Be an Equality (Parity) Among the Elders?

If a plurality of elders is accepted as the appropriate biblical model for today, and a method of determining the number of elders is in place, another question that must be answered relates to the authority that exists among the elders. Should all the elders have the same amount of authority in the church? Or should one (or more) of the elders be given a special authority that weighs more heavily than the others? Some contend that the senior pastor should be given more authority because he is the leader of the church. He usually has more pastoral education and training and leads the church on a "full-time" basis. It is argued, therefore, that the "senior pastor" should be granted a special authority that is above the rest of the elders.

All Elders Have Equal Authority

Such a distinction, however, once again creates a separate office and does harm to the unity of the eldership. There are a number of reasons why all the elders should possess equal authority in the church. First, all the elders have to meet the same qualifications. The qualifications do not list certain degrees, and no distinction should be made between teaching elders and ruling elders (see question 10). Second, all elders share the same responsibilities—primarily teaching and shepherding. Although some may spend more time in these important tasks, all elders will be involved in them to some extent. Also, a distinction should not be made between elders who serve only part-time and those who serve full-time or between elders who are paid and elders who are unpaid. Third, giving more authority to one elder implicitly creates a separate and distinct office. If the "pastor" (the full-time, paid staff) receives more authority than the "elders" (the part-time, non-staff), the outcome is that an unbiblical distinction has been made. Strauch is correct when he states, "To call one elder 'pastor' and the rest 'elders' . . . is to act without biblical precedence." He continues, "It will, at least in practice, *create a separate, superior office over the eldership, just as was done in the early second century when the division between 'the overseer' and 'elders' occurred.*"[1] Consequently, all elders are due the same respect and honor and should be equal in value, power, and rank.

What About "First Among Equals"?

We would be mistaken, however, to claim that all elders are equal in gift-edness or leadership skills. Again, Strauch aptly comments, "Although elders act jointly as a council and share equal authority and responsibility for the leadership of the church, all are not equal in their giftedness, biblical knowl-edge, leadership ability, experience, or dedication."[2] This distinction is often referred to as "first among equals" (*primus inter pares*). Jesus Himself prac-ticed this concept. Out of the twelve disciples, Peter, James, and John were chosen to receive special attention from their Master. And out of the three, Peter often was singled out and given special leadership. Because of his gifts and calling, he was the most prominent among the apostles. Yet, Peter was an apostle just like the rest of the Twelve. He was never given a special title. He did not wear different clothes or receive a higher salary. The others were not subordinate to him or function as his attendants or servants. He was equal in rank and authority to the rest of the apostles. At the same time, however, he was a natural leader and as such became the "first among equals." This con-cept also is illustrated in the relationship of Philip and Stephen to the Seven and in the relationship between Paul and Barnabas (Acts 6:8; 8:5–8, 26–40; 13:13; 14:12).

The "first among equals" concept is also expressed in the way congrega-tions are to honor their elders. Paul writes, "Let the elders who rule well be considered worthy of double honor, especially those who labor in preaching and teaching" (1 Tim. 5:17). Thus, special honor and respect (and pay) is to be given to those who prove themselves faithful and effective in their min-istry, especially in the areas of communicating God's holy Word. We know from the qualifications listed in 1 Timothy 3 that all elders must be "able to

---

1. Alexander Strauch, *Biblical Eldership: An Urgent Call to Restore Biblical Church Leadership,* 3rd ed., rev. and expanded (Littleton, CO: Lewis and Roth, 1995), 47–48.
2. Ibid., 45.

teach" (v. 2). Some, however, may be especially gifted in preaching or teaching. Because of their training and giftedness, they may be asked to preach more often than the others. They do not need a special title in front of their name if they are employed by the church and have dedicated their lives to "full-time" ministry. After all, they are simply elders. Thus, the principle of "first among equals" allows for elders to have different functions based on giftedness without creating a separate or distinct office for one who has greater gifts than the rest of the elders.

What Are the Benefits of "First Among Equals"?

The benefits of this principle are immediately evident. First, it allows those who are especially called and gifted to dedicate more of their time to the pastoral ministry. Those elders who have other full-time employment are, of course, extremely important to the ministry and can be greatly used by God. Paul himself was a tentmaker and often worked this trade to support his ministry. But in today's society, an elder who works a full-time job often has little time or energy to devote to the church. Sometimes it is more beneficial to the life and growth of the church if an elder is employed by the church. As a result, he is able to dedicate all his energy to the study and proclamation of God's Word, to shepherding, to counseling, or to other important tasks.

A second benefit is that those who are exceptionally gifted as leaders or teachers have accountability. They are not given a higher position as full-time workers but are simply given a greater responsibility. They are allowed to exercise their gifts to the fullest without being given unmatched authority in church. Consequently, this structure provides the needed accountability for those most gifted at leading and teaching while at the same time allowing them to maximize their gifts in the church.

What Are the Challenges to "First Among Equals"?

The "first among equals" principle must be exercised with great care. It is important for the "first" among the elders to understand his role. If he seeks to take advantage of his prominence in a way that elevates himself, biblical eldership will not function properly. As the elder who is the most visible because of his teaching and preaching responsibilities, he will be able to influence the congregation in ways the other elders cannot. But, as Waldron warns, "The fact that one of the elders exercises greater influence does not give him a right to an office the other elders do not possess. To claim such an office is to usurp their authority."[3] Thus, he must consciously and deliberately seek to build up the other elders so that they will be just as respected by the congregation. Because he is one of the elders, he is accountable to the other elders and therefore must be willing to defer to them.

Those elders who are "nonprofessional" elders also face challenges. Far too often the other elders neglect their duties and turn over the care of the church to one or two elders who are on the church's payroll. They must learn to view themselves as full-fledged shepherds who are responsible for the members of the congregation. Simply because they are not "full-time" elders does not mean that they have less authority than those who are paid by the church. Being an elder also will require great sacrifice on behalf of the congregation. The task of shepherding involves much time and energy and is often burdensome (see 2 Cor. 11:28, where Paul speaks of the daily pressure he bore from the churches he planted). In addition, these elders must be willing to keep the "first among equals" accountable. This means that elders must not be afraid of confrontation.

Summary

The Bible teaches a diversity among the eldership—not a diversity of office, but a diversity of gifts, financial support, leadership, and influence. The Bible clearly teaches that God sovereignly gifts His people and that He gifts them differently (Rom. 12:3–8; 1 Cor. 12:4–31; Eph. 4:11; 1 Peter 4:10–11). We must learn to celebrate our differences and maximize our gifts for the glory of God without creating a new office or style of church leadership foreign to the New Testament.

Reflection Questions

1. What is the biblical evidence to support the teaching that all elders should have the same amount of authority?
2. How would you describe the concept of "first among equals"?

---

3. Samuel E. Waldron, "Plural-Elder Congregationalism," in *Who Runs the Church? 4 Views on Church Government*, ed. Paul E. Engle and Steven B. Cowan (Grand Rapids: Zondervan: 2004), 175. Later, he offers two helpful qualifications related to the principle of "first among equals": "First, the official authority must remain with the eldership as a whole. To put this another way, no elder should claim an office or authority not possessed by all. Second, the situation where one elder has such influence must not be seen as necessary or normative."

3. Can the concept of "first among equals" be practiced if all the elders do not have the same amount of authority?

4. What are the benefits of "first among equals"? What are the challenges?

5. How do you think this concept would work out practically in your church?

How Should the Elders Make Decisions?

Making decisions is often a difficult task. But making a group decision can sometimes be nearly impossible. For this reason, many people contend that a church that is run by a council of elders who all possess the same amount of authority is doomed to failure. Without the leadership of one, dominant elder who can by himself make the tough decisions, the council will experience frustration and have difficulty moving forward. Such reasoning, however, ignores the wisdom and advice of Scripture. For example, we read in Proverbs, "Where there is no guidance, a people falls, but in an abundance of counselors there is safety" (11:14; also see 15:22; 24:6). Furthermore, the testimony of the New Testament is that the churches were led by a plurality of leaders who were given equal authority. It is dangerous to give one man the authority to make decisions in the church. The Bible gives warnings against those who desire to be first and who think more highly of themselves than they ought (Rom. 12:3; 3 John 9). Decisions should be made by the elders as a unified body. When there is conflict or disagreement (and there will be), the following considerations will help the council move forward in a way that is honoring to God and beneficial to the church of Jesus Christ.

Pray Much

If prayer is important for the life of every Christian, then it is equally important that leaders in the church be devoted to prayer. In prayer we seek the Lord's advice and direction. In prayer we ask God for wisdom to implement His Word. In prayer we ask God for grace to love our brothers and sisters. In prayer we ask God for patience to deal with wandering sheep. In prayer we ask God for humility so that we do not think more highly of ourselves than we ought. Prayer must be at the center of an elder's life. As a board, the elders should corporately seek God's guidance for the church. They should seek to unite their hearts together for the common purpose of shepherding God's people.

Put Away Disputes and Arguments

Although there is a place for sanctified debate, outright disputes and arguments must be avoided. Again, we read in Proverbs, "The beginning of strife is like letting out water, so quit before the quarrel breaks out" (17:14). Those who involve themselves in quarrels are likened to "fools" (Prov. 20:3). When Paul gives the qualifications needed for someone to become an elder, he specifically mentions that he must not be quarrelsome (1 Tim. 3:3). It is imperative, therefore, that those selected to be elders not be men who seek disputes and arguments.

Pacify Anger

If disagreements among the elders are to be resolved, the elders must be able to control their anger and their tongues. Paul writes that elders must be "self-controlled," and "not violent but gentle" (1 Tim. 3:2–3). Because elders have the responsibility of shepherding God's people and must make difficult decisions in that process, they must learn to control their emotions and their words. According to Proverbs, "A soft answer turns away wrath, but a harsh word stirs up anger" (15:1). The way elders relate and speak to one another is a test of their character. A godly man is able to control his tongue and diffuse wrath instead of stirring it up. James encourages us to be "slow to speak" and "slow to anger" because man's anger does not lead to righteousness (James 1:19–20). Likewise, Paul instructs us, "Let no corrupting talk come out of your mouths, but only such as is good for building up" (Eph. 4:29). When elders disagree with one another, they must learn to disagree in a way that is peaceful and does not threaten their relationship with each other.

Practice Mutual Consideration and Humility

Each elder also must seek to value the advice and counsel of his fellow elders. This practice takes maturity and humility. Although each elder undoubtedly will have his own opinion or preference, each must learn to listen to the opinion and input of the others. Scripture informs us that "wisdom is with those who take advice" (Prov. 13:10 NRSV). Although it is often easier to give our input than it is to listen to the advice of others, it is necessary and prudent for elders to sometimes restrain from speaking (Prov. 10:19; 17:28). It is dangerous to select as an elder a person who is not humble or does not value the opinions of others.

Proceed by Evaluating Every Issue Biblically

Because the Bible is our basis and standard for all life and godliness, every decision related to shepherding the church should be evaluated biblically. Emotions and preferences often cloud our thinking and cause us to base our decisions on something other than what is revealed in the Bible. In addressing an issue, we might respond, "We have never done it that way before," or "But his father was my Sunday school teacher," or "The Smith family might decide to stop their giving." While the elders should be sensitive to the feelings and concerns of the congregation, ultimately their convictions based on Scripture should drive their decisions. If all the elders are firmly convinced that the Scriptures are God's infallible and sufficient Word, it will help unify the elders as they make important and difficult decisions.

Promote Consensus

Voting is often the quickest way to divide an elder board and therefore should be taken as a last measure. It is better to strive to build a consensus. If at first there is no unanimous voice among the elders, then more time (and prayer) may be needed to unify the council. Christians are encouraged to live in peace, harmony, and unity with one another (Rom. 15:5; Eph. 4:3, 13; Col. 3:14). If one (or more) of the elders is not in agreement, then it is necessary for the elders to hear the objection and seek to answer the concern. It may be a matter of clarifying an issue or accommodating the dissenting elder's concern. Most of the decisions made by the elders should be unanimous decisions so that all members of the board fully support the decision made.

Prepare to Defer

Certain issues, however, are complex, and applying the Scriptures to such issues can be challenging. The result is that sometimes a unanimous decision is not possible. Based on principle and convictions, one or more elders may not agree with the majority. If it appears that more discussion will be unfruitful and that the matter will not be resolved any time soon, it may be appropriate for the dissenting elder to defer to the wisdom of the majority.

He does not personally agree that the majority decision is the best, but for the sake of peace and unity, he is willing to defer to his fellow brothers. Such an act takes humility and trust. It takes humility because he is willing to admit that his opinion or solution may not be the best. It takes trust because he will be, in a sense, endorsing the decision made by the other elders. By deferring he is stating that he will no longer make an issue of the decision and will support the elders in implementing the decision.

Produce and Implement a Policy in the Case of an Impasse

In rare cases, an elder board may not be able to come to an agreement, and certain elders are not willing to defer to the others. Their convictions are so strong, and they believe the matter is so crucial, that it would simply be wrong for them to defer. In the case of such an impasse, it is helpful for the elders to have a policy in place for decision making. It is at this last stage that voting may be required.

Summary

Elders constantly have to make difficult decisions. The following advice is offered to help elders resolve disagreements.

1. *Pray much.* The elders should regularly pray together as they seek guidance from the Lord.
2. *Put away disputes and arguments.* The elders must learn to discuss issues without arguing and fighting.
3. *Pacify anger.* The elders must be able to control their emotions and their words.
4. *Practice mutual consideration and humility.* The elders must not value their own opinions over those of their fellow elders but must be willing to listen and value the input of others.
5. *Proceed by evaluating every issue biblically.* The Bible must be the standard by which decisions are made.
6. *Promote consensus.* It is best for the elders to make unanimous decisions so that all the elders give their full support.
7. *Prepare to defer.* In most cases where an elder does not agree with the majority, he should be willing to defer to and support the opinion of his fellow elders.
8. *Produce and implement a policy in the case of an impasse.* As a last

resort, the elders need to have a plan for deciding an issue when one or more elders are not willing to defer.

Reflection Questions

1. How does your church normally make decisions?
2. Do you think one person should be given the authority to make important decisions?
3. What elements listed in this chapter do you think are the most important? Why?
4. Why might it not be a good idea to implement voting as the primary method for the eldership to make decisions?
5. Do you think the concept of deferring is an act of humility or an act of cowardice?

What Are the Advantages of Having a Plurality of Elders?

If having a plurality of elders is God's design, there will be many benefits to be gained by following God's wisdom. Although having a plurality of elders does not guarantee the church leadership will not encounter problems or conflict, it does at least provide several safeguards against some problems and difficulties that a single-pastor church often faces. There are at least four advantages to having a plurality of elders in each local congregation.

Biblical Accountability

Biblical accountability is needed for two reasons. First, it helps protect a pastor from error. Pastors often possess a lot of authority in their churches—too much authority with too little accountability. Such authority can cause one to believe that he is more important than others, and thus he may become proud. Others may act in ways that are insensitive or unscriptural but be blinded to their faults. Each person has certain blind spots and faults or deficiencies that can distort judgment. If a pastor has little or no accountability, these tendencies can go unchecked.[1] When a church has only one pastor, or a senior pastor with unmatched power, there is usually no accountability structure built into the system—except for the congregation or the deacons to fire the pastor, which is far too common.

---

1. Wayne Grudem notes, "A common practical problem with a 'single elder' system is either an excessive concentration of power in one person or excessive demands laid upon him. In either case, the temptations to sin are very great, and a lessened degree of accountability makes yielding to temptation more likely (*Systematic Theology: An Introduction to Biblical Doctrine* [Leicester: InterVarsity Press; Grand Rapids: Eerdmans, 1994], 931). Later, he adds that a strength of the plural-elder system "is seen in the fact that the pastor does not have authority on his own over the congregation, but that authority belongs collectively to the entire group of elders (what may be called the elder board)" (ibid., 933).

A plural eldership model helps to provide the needed accountability that is lacking in most churches so that one man does not dominate the church. Phil Newton stresses, *"Plural eldership serves to prevent one man from falling prey to the temptation of dominating a congregation."*[2] Similarly Strauch writes, "Only when there is genuine accountability between equals in leadership is there any hope for breaking down the terrible abuse of pastoral authority that plagues many churches."[3] There must be others who are equal in status and authority who can face a fellow elder and confront him if he is being unreasonable or is living in sin—just as Peter was confronted by Paul (a fellow apostle) when Peter refused to eat with Gentiles (Gal. 2:11–14). A pastor needs the constant reminder that he is not above the law but is subject to the other elders. Every pastor is prone to sin and must constantly monitor his spiritual walk. Paul warns the Ephesian elders, "Pay careful attention to yourselves and to all the flock" (Acts 20:28). Later he exhorts Timothy, "Keep a close watch on yourself and on the teaching" (1 Tim. 4:16). But a pastor not only needs to keep watch over his own life; he also needs the help of others.

Second, biblical accountability is needed to help foster maturity and godliness among the elders. As the elders serve and lead together, they will often be challenged by the godly examples they see in each other. They will "stir up one another to love and good works" (Heb. 10:24). The more mature elders can help train the younger ones in how to be effective shepherds. As the proverb says, "Iron sharpens iron, and one man sharpens another" (Prov. 27:17).

Balance

A plurality of elders also provides the church with balance. No one person has all the gifts or the time necessary to provide all that a congregation needs. As a result, most pastors are not capable of adequately fulfilling all the responsibilities set before them. They may be gifted in one area but lacking in another. Some pastors are especially gifted at preaching and teaching. Others are better gifted in administration, counseling, or discipling. By having a team of elders, the deficiencies of one man are balanced by other elders who complement his weaknesses. Thus, it provides a variety of gifts

---

2. Phil A. Newton, *Elders in Congregational Life: Rediscovering the Biblical Model for Church Leadership* (Grand Rapids: Kregel, 2005), 60.

3. Alexander Strauch, *Biblical Eldership: An Urgent Call to Restore Biblical Church Leadership,* 3rd ed., rev. and expanded (Littleton, CO: Lewis and Roth, 1995), 43.

and perspectives that are often absent when one pastor ministers alone. A plurality of elders also allows each elder to focus on his specific calling and gifting instead of expending massive amounts of time and energy on areas of the ministry in which he is not particularly gifted. When the elders function as a team, they complement each other, allowing each elder to devote most of his time to the area of ministry in which he is most gifted.

Burden Sharing

A third benefit of having a plurality of elders is that the burden of the ministry is shared by others. Caring for the church is often too much for one man to handle and can lead to frustration and burnout. Speaking from his experience, Strauch comments, "If the long hours, weighty responsibilities, and problems of shepherding a congregation of people are not enough to overwhelm a person, then dealing with people's sins and listening to seemingly endless complaints and bitter conflicts can crush a person."[4] Is it any wonder that so many pastorates are short-lived? Many pastors are living and ministering under the incredible burden of shepherding God's people alone. Often there is no one to come beside the pastor and encourage him when he is weary from doing good. From his wisdom, Solomon writes, "Two are better than one, because they have a good reward for their toil. For if they fall, one will lift up his fellow. But woe to him who is alone when he falls and has not another to lift him up! Again, if two lie together, they keep warm, but how can one keep warm alone? And though a man might prevail against one who is alone, two will withstand him—a threefold cord is not quickly broken" (Eccl. 4:9–12). It is difficult for a congregation to become mature and equipped for the work of the ministry through the labor of a single pastor. If one man attempts to do all the work himself, he will begin to neglect other important areas of his life—such as his own spirituality or his own family.

A church is better able to handle cases of church discipline when there is a plurality of elders. A lone pastor will tend to shy away from such confrontation or might be viewed by others as handling the situation too severely. It is usually too much responsibility for a single pastor to carefully handle such a difficult situation. But with the wisdom that comes from a group of godly men, the situation will almost certainly be dealt with in a more God-honoring manner. During this difficult time, the elders can encourage one

---

4. Ibid., 42.

another to do what is right instead of merely settling with what is expedient. The criticisms that might be leveled against a single pastor do not fall as hard on a group of elders who can shoulder the weight together.

Better Picture of the Church

A final advantage of having a plurality of elders is that it better represents the nature of ministry and the church. When the church is led by a single pastor, this conveys the idea that only a select few can serve God in such a capacity. The gulf between the "clergy" and "laity" becomes widened and eventually uncrossable. A plurality of elders, however, demonstrates that doing the work of the ministry is not designated only for a select few. When ordinary members show themselves to be qualified and gifted to serve as elders, it opens a massive door of opportunity for others. They begin to think, "Perhaps someday I can become an elder too." This encourages them to live godly lives so that they too can serve someday as an elder. In this way, plural eldership takes the focus off the paid staff and puts it on the average person, encouraging each one to consider serving in a more committed capacity. Waldron notes that plural eldership "allows the development of younger leaders within the church by eliminating the sense that there is room for only one leader and one ministry in the church."[5]

Christ alone is the head of the church (Col. 1:18). He is the Chief Shepherd, and those whom Christ calls to lead the church are merely undershepherds. They shepherd the congregation under the authority and direction of the Word and the Spirit. But when each local church has only one pastor or senior pastor, this distinction can become blurred. Often, we hear comments like, "I attend Pastor John's church." What they mean by this statement is that they attend the church where Pastor John is the senior pastor. In a sense, it is simply a shortened way to say where they attend church. And yet, such language can lead to a faulty view of the pastoral ministry. The church does not belong to any pastor, and thus it is not really *his* church. Plural eldership, however, tends to keep the focus on Christ as the head of the church. Again, Waldron aptly comments, "A church led by a plurality of elders will have in its very system of leadership a constant reminder that the head of the church is *not* the pastor or the bishop, but *the Lord Jesus Christ.*"[6]

---

5. Samuel E. Waldron, "Plural-Elder Congregationalism," in *Who Runs the Church? 4 Views on Church Government*, ed. Paul E. Engle and Steven B. Cowan (Grand Rapids: Zondervan: 2004), 176.
6. Ibid.

Summary

Following God's design for the church is always the best way. The New Testament churches consistently had a plurality of elders, and there are many advantages that a church experiences when this pattern is upheld. One advantage is the biblical accountability the elders receive from one another. Such accountability helps protect the most prominent elder from receiving too much authority and also helps foster godliness among the elders. Another advantage is the balance that is provided when one pastor is not responsible for leading the church. Instead, a team of men provide a variety of gifts and perspectives that are often absent when only one man leads the church. A third advantage is the sharing of burdens. Leading the church is too much for one person to handle. By having a plurality of elders, the weighty task of shepherding God's people can be accomplished with greater success. Finally, when a church has multiple elders, it offers a better picture of the New Testament church since it minimizes the distinction between clergy and laity and emphasizes that the work of the ministry is not given only to a select few. It also helps keep the focus on Jesus Christ as the head of the church.

Reflection Questions

1. How might a plurality of elders help protect a pastor/elder from error?
2. How might a plurality of elders help provide balance in the church?
3. Do you think it is healthy for one man to bear the weight of pastoring a church?
4. Why does having a plurality of elders present a better picture of the church?
5. How significant are the advantages of having a plurality of elders?

Why Do So Few Churches Have a Plurality of Elders?

With all the benefits of plural eldership mentioned in the previous question, one might get the impression that most churches embrace this teaching. Unfortunately, this is not the case. This does not mean that there are not churches that embrace and practice plural eldership. Numerous churches and denominations have diligently applied the teaching of Scripture to their system of church government. In addition, there are hundreds of church leaders who are seeking to restore a more biblical form of eldership to their churches. When they read what the New Testament has to say concerning church organization and leadership, they ask themselves, "Why doesn't my church look like this?" They read of Paul appointing elders in churches and of elders mentioned in his epistles and ask, "Why doesn't my church have elders?" But the fact remains that having a plurality of elders is a foreign concept in most evangelical churches. Why is this the case? Let me offer three reasons why so few churches have a plurality of elders.

Lack of Qualified Men

In order to be qualified to be an elder, a man must meet certain qualifications (1 Tim. 3:1–7; Titus 1:6–9; 1 Peter 5:2–3). Although most of these qualifications are what is expected of all Christians, very few men actually meet the qualifications. Of course, the qualifications can be applied too rigorously so that almost no one can meet them. But godliness, not perfection, is the requirement. Yet, even when the requirements are fairly applied, there seems to be so few who are left to serve. It seems that the desire to serve as an elder has all but vanished in the church. Men are so preoccupied with advancing their careers that the church is virtually ignored and with it the spirituality required to serve as an elder. Paul says that it is a "noble task" for a man to aspire to the office of elder (1 Tim. 3:1). Spiritual laziness and a zeal for the American dream have squelched the desire of potential elders. For many, it is simply easier to hire someone from the outside to handle the "business" of the church. We have become a service-oriented society. When we need something done, we simply hire someone to do it. Unfortunately, this mentality has carried over into the church. The pastorate has become so professionalized that many congregations will not even consider hiring a person as their pastor unless he has "Dr." in front of his name. Strauch aptly states that "people are selfish and lazy by nature, particularly when it comes to spiritual matters, and are more than eager to pay others to do their work."[1] As a result, many churches that began with the hope of having a plurality of elders simply gave up and opted for the more conventional (though less biblical) model of having one pastor and a board of deacons.

Lack of Biblical Knowledge

It is a simple fact that in today's churches the average Christian has never been taught the doctrine of a plurality of elders. Most pastors don't bother themselves with such "irrelevant" issues as church government, so they never teach their people what the Bible says about it. Proper church government, however, is far from being irrelevant. Many churches have become so pragmatic that they simply employ whatever model of leadership seems to be successful in the marketplace. They claim that the Bible does not give us a specific leadership model but allows flexibility for each church to "do what is right in its own eyes." Consequently, the doctrine of biblical eldership has fallen on rocky soil and is devoured by the birds before it ever enters the heart of the church and bears fruit. "I am convinced," opines Strauch, "that the underlying reason many Christians fear the plurality of elders is that they don't really understand the New Testament concept or its rich benefits to the local Church."[2]

Fear of Change

Fear is a motivating factor in the lives of many people, and fear of change often is what holds back a church from adopting and implementing plural eldership. Pastors fear that the congregation will reject their ideas. They fear

---

1. Alexander Strauch, *Biblical Eldership: An Urgent Call to Restore Biblical Church Leadership*, 3rd ed., rev. and expanded (Littleton, CO: Lewis and Roth, 1995), 49.
2. Ibid., 38.

that the church will split if they try to change the constitution or bylaws in regard to church government. They fear that their efforts will fail and the church will be worse off than before. They fear having to do the hard work of educating the congregation about eldership. Other pastors fear that they might lose some of their power and authority in the church. Newton agrees: *"At the root of much opposition to plural eldership are pastors who fear the loss of their authority in the church."*[3]

Those in the congregation also are fearful. They fear that things might not be as comfortable as they are now. They fear that elders will take authority away from the congregation. They fear that they might lose their right to vote in business meetings. They fear that their church might be adopting the church government of a denomination different from their own. They fear that they might be expected to lead. They fear that they might be asked to no longer lead.

But often what people fear the most is simply change. They may even acknowledge that such a doctrine is found in the Bible, but they are not convinced that it is worth the trouble of actually conforming their church polity to the Scriptures. Pastors often will talk about the need for changing their church government but never take any steps to actually do anything about it. Fear has become a powerful deterrent to recovering biblical eldership. The Bible, however, tells us that "perfect love casts out fear" (1 John 4:18).

Summary

For many years churches have been looking to the corporate world for successful models of leadership. In order for the church to be successful, they say, the pastor needs to function like a CEO. He needs to be a strong leader and a visionary. He must speak to the needs of the people and at the same time tell them what they want to hear. Congregations that have followed through with this model often look more like corporations than churches. The end result often leaves many people dissatisfied and spiritually malnourished. As a result, there is a growing desire for churches to organize themselves according to the wisdom of God and not the wisdom of man. "For the foolishness of God is wiser than men, and the weakness of God is stronger than men" (1 Cor. 1:25). As churches grow in their commitment to God and to His Word, they will become more concerned with the leadership structure of

---

3. Phil A. Newton, *Elders in Congregational Life: Rediscovering the Biblical Model for Church Leadership* (Grand Rapids: Kregel, 2005), 59.

their churches. Men will desire to live godly lives to the glory of God and will be qualified to serve in His church. Pastors will become convicted and begin to teach the congregation about biblical church polity. And fear will disappear as the truth of God's Word emboldens elders and their congregations to live and minister according to God's design for the church.

Reflection Questions

1. Do you know of any churches that practice plural eldership?
2. Do you think the leadership qualifications in your church are too stringent or too lenient (according to 1 Tim. 3:2–7 and Titus 1:6–9)?
3. Have you ever been taught about plural eldership in any of the churches you have been a member of or attended?
4. How strong is the fear of change (even changing to conform to the Bible) in your church?
5. What are some other reasons that might prevent a church from embracing plural eldership?

How Does a Church Transition to a Plurality of Elders?

Transition is never easy. It requires conviction, patience, and time. Many pastors desire to see their churches move from a single-elder model to a plural-elder model but simply do not know where to begin. Below are six essential elements for leading a church in the transition to a plurality of elders.

Entreat the Lord

Prayer is the first element needed for transition. Woe to anyone who would seek to implement change in the church without first asking for the Lord's direction and blessing. We must realize that we are dependent on God's strength and wisdom to accomplish anything—especially change in the church. It is crucial that we bathe every part of the transition process in prayer. At times, especially during the selection of elders, it is necessary to call the entire congregation to seek God's guidance in prayer.

Establish Trust

Before a pastor can successfully implement change, he must be trusted by the congregation. It may take several years of faithful service before enough trust is built with the congregation for a pastor to proceed with the transition to plural eldership. The people need to know that the pastor loves them more than he loves the doctrine of plural eldership. They need to believe him when he tells them that plural eldership will help him serve them better. They need to be convinced that he is not driven by his own agenda but

I am indebted to Phil A. Newton's book *Elders in Congregational Life: Rediscovering the Biblical Model for Church Leadership* (Grand Rapids: Kregel, 2005) for many of the insights in answering this question.

is humbly seeking to obey God's Word. If the congregation does not see and feel these things first, then a pastor's labor will be in vain.

A pastor's goal is to shepherd the flock by caring for their souls. It is not to make his church perfectly in sync with his own doctrine. The church members must believe that the pastor's motives are genuine and that his desire is for the congregation to be conformed to the image of Christ. Overzealous pastors fresh from seminary often believe they can (and should) immediately attempt to install an elder-led church polity. Their efforts, however, often are met with resistance. In their frustration they conclude that the church members are unspiritual and disobedient to the will of God. Often, however, a congregation's resistance is not the result of their reluctance to obey God but a reaction to the insensitivities of a pastor. A pastor must establish trust before he can expect a successful transition.

Evaluate the Leadership Structure

It is helpful for a pastor to take time to assess the current leadership structure of the church. He should note both the title given for each position and the functions performed. Before a church can transition to something, it must properly identify what it is changing from. It might also help to compare the current system of leadership to that found in the church's constitution, bylaws, or other governing documents. Is the church following its own constitution? Does a plurality of elders fit within the church's constitution or creedal statement? Eventually, some changes might need to be made to the church's governing documents. Such change must be approached with extreme caution since these documents often are viewed as sacred.

Educate the Congregation

The next step is to convince the congregation that plural eldership is biblical. A pastor must assess the congregation's beliefs and knowledge of the Bible. Instead of immediately teaching about biblical leadership, it might be necessary to begin with the inspiration, authority, and sufficiency of Scripture. If the people are not convinced God's Word is inspired, authoritative, and sufficient for all life and godliness, they will not be persuaded it is necessary to conform their church to the teachings of Scripture.

The pastor will then need to preach about God's design for the church. It is best to do this through expository preaching. Instead of jumping from one

text to another throughout the sermon, it is better to give a thorough explanation and application of one scriptural passage in its context. "Exposition,"
comments Newton, "provides the best means for unfolding the contexts surrounding the passage and helping the congregation to understand how the
early church's structure developed in the crucible of life."[1]

Key leaders who will study the teaching in more detail should be selected.
It is important that the leaders of the church be fully convinced that the
plural-elder model is consistent with the biblical teaching concerning church
leaders. These leaders should be trained in a small group setting, where each
passage can be carefully studied. Before introducing secondary literature
(i.e., books on eldership), it is better to let them see for themselves what
the Scripture teaches. The pastor also should allow times of feedback from
the congregation. The church members need to be a part of the transition
process.

Emphasize Qualifications

Without godly, qualified men leading the church, all the talk about biblical eldership is useless. Some churches, in a rush for change, ignore or
minimize the biblical requirements set forth in Scripture. "If the church
transitions to elder leadership but then installs as elders men who lack biblical qualifications, even greater problems may result."[2] It is important that
the entire church is aware of the biblical qualifications so that they can know
what is expected in elders and thus hold the elders accountable. Knowing
the requirements also will deter men who are not qualified from seeking
eldership.

Thus, it is better to emphasize the character of elders more than the function of elders. Functions will vary depending on the church, but the character of an elder must be consistent regardless of his function. "The goal of a
church should not be to establish plural eldership at any cost, but rather to
elevate the standards of spiritual leadership in the church at any cost."[3]

Engage the Plan Slowly

Slow implementation is crucial for a smooth and (relatively) painless transition to take place. I once heard an illustration about a pastor who was con-

---

1. Newton, *Elders in Congregational Life*, 132.
2. Ibid., 133.
3. Ibid., 56.

vinced the piano in his church should be on the right side of the sanctuary instead of the left side. Having studied music and being experienced in leading worship, he was certain that the piano needed to be moved. After considering what to do, the pastor came up with a plan. The following Saturday night, he came to church and moved the piano to its proper location. "That was easy," he thought to himself. After the Sunday morning service, the pastor received an envelope from one of the deacons. The note inside informed the pastor that the board of deacons had decided to fire him. Several years later the same pastor was in the area and decided to visit his old church. When he entered the building, he was shocked to see that the piano was on the right side of the sanctuary. After the service he grabbed the current pastor and informed him that he had tried to move the piano but was fired as a result. So he asked, "How did you move the piano without getting fired?" The new pastor smiled and replied, "One inch at a time."

The point of the illustration is that change takes time. Newton, for example, suggests that a full transition to a plural eldership should take between eighteen months and three years. Time is needed to establish trust and educate the congregation. Time is needed to be sure the candidates meet the biblical requirements provided in 1 Timothy 3; Titus 1; and 1 Peter 5. Although transition is not usually easy, it is often necessary so that our churches reflect God's design.

Summary

The transition to a plurality of elders is often a long and difficult process. It is important, therefore, that the congregation, and especially the current leadership, employ the following principles with diligence.

1. *Entreat the Lord.* Seek the Lord's direction and wisdom.
2. *Establish trust.* The pastor or leadership team must first gain the trust of the congregation and only then seek to begin transition to plural eldership.
3. *Evaluate the leadership structure.* The current leadership structure of the church must be assessed.
4. *Educate the congregation.* The members of the church must be convinced that plural eldership is biblical.
5. *Emphasize qualifications.* It is more important to stress the character of elders than their function.

6. *Engage the plan slowly.* The implementation should take place slowly to ensure a smooth transition.

Reflection Questions

1. What would it take for your church to transition to plural eldership?
2. How can a pastor establish trust with his congregation?
3. What should be done if a church is not following its own constitution or bylaws?
4. In what practical ways might a pastor educate the congregation about plural eldership?
5. How long do you think it would take your church to make a transition to plural eldership?

Section D
Questions Related to the Selecting, Ordaining,
Paying, and Removing of Elders

How Should Elders Be Selected?

The selection of elders is an important but difficult issue. It is important because elders have authority and responsibility in the church and thus it is necessary that only gifted and qualified men are selected. It is difficult because we are never told precisely how to select our elders. As a result, there are a wide variety of views and practices on this issue. In the following discussion, we will examine the strengths and weaknesses of different methods of selecting elders. But first we will give some introductory comments.

Introduction

We must remember that one should not be selected for eldership unless he is qualified, and the only way to know whether one is qualified is to examine him. Whether we are convinced that the existing elders should select new elders or we think that is the responsibility of the congregation, somewhere during the selection process, potential elders must be examined. If no examination is made, then we make a mockery of the process. Those who are not qualified should not be appointed as elders. The testing of one's fitness for office is explicitly stated in the qualifications given for deacons. Paul reminds Timothy and the congregation at Ephesus that potential candidates "must also first be tested; then let them serve as deacons if they are beyond reproach" (1 Tim. 3:10 NASB). If testing is needed for potential deacons, it is certainly needed for potential elders. Indeed, Paul later warns Timothy, "The sins of some men [in the context, potential elders] are conspicuous, going before them to judgment, but the sins of others appear later" (1 Tim. 5:24). Thus, time and testing is needed to reveal the true character of a person.

Churches also should avoid having two separate standards for those who are "professional" pastors and those who are merely "lay" pastors. The Bible makes no such distinctions, and neither should we. As Strauch notes, "All pastor elders are to be fully qualified, formally examined, and publicly installed into office."[1]

Those who are selected also should have a desire to serve (1 Tim. 3:1). A desire to serve God as an elder is not something that can be contained. Such a person will seek ways to serve in the church regardless of whether he is given a title or not. As the elders see a man's aspiration to serve evidenced by his commitment to others and to God's Word, they should give this person opportunity to use and identify his gifts. The elders should help train and nurture his abilities so that he will be equipped for eldership himself someday. Consequently, before a man is appointed as an elder, he will have been serving the church in some capacity, thereby proving himself in leadership.

Selection by a Higher Authority

In some churches, the selection of a church officer is done by someone outside and above the local congregation. For example, in Roman Catholic, Anglican, Episcopal, and some Methodist churches, the congregation does not choose a particular leader; rather, the leader is appointed by a bishop (or some other church official). But as we have discussed earlier (see question 4), there are many New Testament examples of the local congregation of believers choosing, or at least affirming, church officers or delegates (Acts 1:15, 23–24; 6:2–3; 13:3; 14:27; 15:3, 22; 2 Cor. 8:19).

Selection by the Congregation

The selection of elders must be done very carefully and prayerfully. Paul warns Timothy not to appoint anyone to the office of elder too hastily, lest he be held responsible for their sin (1 Tim. 5:22). Many people in favor of a congregational approach to church government strongly affirm the right of the congregation (not merely the elders) to choose the candidates for eldership. There is biblical evidence in support of this method of choosing leaders. In Acts 6, seven men are chosen to help serve the church. The apostles tell the congregation in Jerusalem, "Select from among yourselves seven men of good standing, full of the Spirit and of wisdom, whom we may appoint to this task" (Acts 6:3 NRSV). Further evidence is found in the congregation's key role in church discipline (Matt. 18:15–17; 1 Cor. 5:2; 2 Cor. 2:6). Thus, it

---

1. Alexander Strauch, *Biblical Eldership: An Urgent Call to Restore Biblical Church Leadership*, 3rd ed., rev. and expanded (Littleton, CO: Lewis and Roth, 1995), 277.

is argued, important decisions in the church, such as the selection of leaders, should be decided by the entire congregation.

There appears to be no scriptural objection to allowing the congregation to choose its leaders. This does not mean, however, that congregations must vote in this process. In fact, if not used appropriately, voting can be rather dangerous for a church. I have experienced and heard of cases where churches selected elders at business meetings. A person stands up and nominates someone from the floor, another seconds the motion, and then that person's name is added to a list. After all the nominations are in, the members of the congregation then vote for their top candidate(s). The winners are then announced, and the new elders are installed into office. Such a method is dangerous and unbiblical.[2] The candidates are never examined for qualifications, and the whole process can become a mere popularity contest. If congregations are to be involved in the selection process, the process must be carried out to ensure that the potential candidates are morally and spiritually qualified.

Selection by the Existing Elders

Others maintain that it is better if the existing elders select the new elders. Because the elders are the spiritual leaders of the church and know the members of the congregation better than most, they are the most qualified to choose who should be an elder. In 1 Timothy 5:17, Paul indicates that elders "rule" the church ("Let the elders who rule well be considered worthy of double honor"). The term "rule" (*proistēmi*) means to "lead," "manage," or "direct" (cf. Rom. 12:8; 1 Thess. 5:12; 1 Tim. 3:4–5, 12, where the same word is used). Thus, the elders are to "lead" the church in making important decisions. It would seem unwise for the elders to be silent during the selection of the church's future leaders.

---

2. Wayne Grudem states, "When I mention a congregational vote I do not mean to suggest the idea of a competitive election such as is found in secular politics. It may simply involve a requirement that the congregation vote to ratify candidates who have been nominated by a mature group within the church (such as the present 'elders), or, on the other hand, it may involve a church-wide election, or other processes may be used. Scripture is silent regarding the actual process; therefore, God has decided to leave the matter to the wisdom of each congregation in its own setting" (*Systematic Theology: An Introduction to Biblical Doctrine* [Leicester: InterVarsity Press; Grand Rapids: Eerdmans, 1994], 922n. 32).

Summary

The best approach is not to choose one method over the over but to allow the elders to have a leadership role in the process while, at the same time, allowing the congregation to have a voice in the matter. That is, both the congregation and the elders must be involved in the selection process. The congregation should be involved because the prospective elder will serve the congregation. Thus, the congregation must have a voice in examining and approving the candidates. The elders must be involved because they are the spiritual leaders of the church. To ignore their insights and opinions would be unwise. Whether the congregation votes or not, the main issue is that the elders get the input of the members. Strauch appropriately comments, "Biblical elders want an informed, involved congregation. Biblical elders eagerly desire to listen to, consult with, and seek the wisdom of their fellow believers."[3] It is entirely possible that some people in the congregation have a greater knowledge of and closer personal relationship with a prospective elder and can offer helpful insight in evaluating the biblical qualifications. But it should be the elders primarily who investigate potential concerns, screening the candidates thoroughly. The congregation also should be given opportunity to ask potential candidates about critical matters such as their doctrinal beliefs, personal spirituality and giftedness, family life, and commitment to serving the church. Mounce aptly summarizes, "The screening process would probably have involved the whole church with special responsibility falling on the overseers since they were responsible for the general oversight of the church and rebuking error (Titus 1:9)."[4]

In one church I attended, the elders were primarily responsible for identifying and selecting potential elders. Once the elders determined that a person was qualified, they would present the candidate before the church with their recommendation. The elders would then allow one month for the congregation to voice their concerns. If an issue was brought to the attention of the elders that would disqualify the candidate, the elders would then investigate the situation. Once all the issues were adequately dealt with, the elders would appoint the candidate as an elder. In the above model, the elders led the process but also actively sought the input of the congregation.

---

3. Strauch, *Biblical Eldership*, 283.
4. William D. Mounce, *Pastoral Epistles*, WBC (Nashville: Nelson, 2000), 46:201.

Reflection Questions

1. How are elders or other leaders selected in your church?
2. Do you think that selection process could be improved?
3. Who do you think should choose the leaders?
4. How can voting by the congregation be dangerous for a church?
5. Can you envision a system in which both the existing elders and the congregation are involved in choosing potential leaders?

Should Elders Have Terms or Serve for Life?

It is clear from the testimony of the New Testament that each church was governed by a plurality of elders and that each elder met certain qualifications. What is less clear is the length of time an elder is to serve. Because the Bible is silent regarding this issue, we must use godly wisdom and consistently apply biblical principles that are closely related to this topic. The two positions are that elders should serve for a specified term and that elders should serve for life.

Should Elders Serve Terms?

Many churches maintain that the best approach to the eldership model is to have elders serve terms. The length of the term varies from one year to several years. Some churches have mandatory sabbaticals after every term or designated number of years, while other churches incorporate the idea of term limits. In this model, every "term" new elders begin to serve, while some existing elders end their service. There are several advantages to using this model.

It Allows More Men to Serve as Elders

Churches often have a number of potential leaders in their midst who are never asked to serve in the church. By having elders serve a designated term, the church is forced to seek new leaders to step up and take their place. As a result, this process helps to expand the leadership base in the church. It also provides more diversity among elders. If the same men are always the elders of the church, then it is possible for them to become closed to the needs and views of others. When new elders are allowed to rotate in, their fresh views and opinions can stimulate the existing elders to more effective service.

It Avoids Overworking the Elders

If the elders are chosen from among both the staff and those who are non-staff (those who have careers in other professions), then having terms provides non-staff elders with time off to recuperate from their hectic schedules. Demands of work, family, and church can be overwhelming at times. Many men are willing and qualified to serve as elders but simply cannot commit the time it takes to serve. Or perhaps they can commit some time but are not willing or able to commit to serve as elders "for life." Such a commitment could scare away many capable men from the valuable service they can offer the church. Because the staff elders serve the church full-time, they could remain as elders without having terms. But having terms avoids overworking elders who have other professions.

It Affords a Method of Removing Bad or Ineffective Elders

Another benefit of having terms is that it provides a method of removing men who should not be elders. Paul warned Timothy, "The sins of some men are conspicuous, going before them to judgment, but the sins of others appear later" (1 Tim. 5:24). Inevitably, a man who is not really qualified for one reason or another will be chosen to serve as an elder. At the time he is selected, everything is fine. Later, however, it becomes obvious that this person should not have been selected to serve. If this elder is called to serve for life, it might be very difficult to remove him as an elder. But if the elders serve only a specified term and are then released from their office, the elder easily can be replaced with someone who is better able to serve the church.

Should Elders Serve for Life?

Actually, a better way to phrase the question is, "Should elders serve indefinite terms?" Serving as an elder is not like a justice serving on the Supreme Court, who is given a life term. The moral and spiritual qualifications of elders are much higher than the qualifications for those serving on the highest court in America. Thus, we should not really talk about serving "for life," as though there is nothing that can be done to remove an elder who does not have a set term. Rather, in this model elders serve an indefinite term. The term can be ended if the elder becomes disqualified because he no longer meets the biblical qualifications or if he voluntarily steps down for personal or family reasons. There are several advantages to having elders serve indefinite terms.

It Removes the Distinction Between Paid and Nonpaid Elders

Earlier, we argued that "pastor," "elder," and "overseer" all refer to the same office (see questions 6 and 9). We also demonstrated that the Bible does not teach that there are two types of elders—teaching elders and ruling elders (see question 10). If this analysis of the biblical data is correct, then it is unhelpful to reintroduce distinctions in the eldership when it comes to length of service. If the paid, or staff, elders serve indefinite terms but all the nonpaid, or non-staff, elders are forced to serve specific terms, such distinction again drives a wedge between the so-called clergy and the laity. It is also unhelpful to make a distinction between the "pastor(s)" and the "elders" or to claim that someone is a pastor and also an elder. If "pastor" and "elder" refer to the same office, then making such distinctions—although it may be easier for the congregation to initially grasp—is counterproductive and actually introduces a third office into the leadership structure. By allowing all the elders to serve an indefinite term, the artificial distinction between paid and nonpaid elders is removed. It also conveys to the congregation that those men who serve as elders, although they are not church staff or compensated for their labors, are worthy of the same respect and honor as those who work full-time for the church.

It Retains Consistency Among the Elders

When new elders come and go, as they do with the model that uses terms, it often causes a disruption in the work of the elders. Much time is spent getting new elders informed about past decisions and issues related to the shepherding of the congregation. In addition, new elders may not have the same philosophy or experience as the other elders. As a result, the progress among the elders is delayed by orienting the new elders, and there is a loss of continuity and efficiency. By serving indefinite terms, however, the elders do not need to waste time in constantly reviewing old decisions and informing the new elders concerning the particulars of the ministry.

Furthermore, if the elders serve terms, this process inevitably will remove wise, mature elders who understand the needs of the church. Some elders are effective in their service and also have the desire and ability to remain as elders. If they serve under the term model, regardless of their calling and effectiveness, they are forced to rotate off the board so that someone else can serve. As mentioned earlier, the downside of the indefinite-term model is that it is difficult to remove an ineffective or disqualified elder. Consequently, churches that use this model must have a means by which the other elders and/or the congregation are able to remove an elder.

It Requires Biblical Qualifications

Both models of eldership, of course, should have the same requirements for elders. But if a church is willing to give elders an indefinite term of service, the congregation is more likely to take the qualifications more seriously. If the office begins to be viewed as insignificant because "it's only a one-year term," then it also seems likely that the requirements to hold that office are going to be viewed as insignificant. Also, the term model assumes there will be enough leaders who are equipped and qualified to serve as elders. As new elders rotate in and old elders rotate off the board, the church must constantly find men who are qualified to fill the empty positions. Phil Newton offers some practical help: "It would be inadvisable . . . to establish a rotating system of elders unless the size and maturity of the church membership ensures an adequate number of elders to maintain plurality."[1] He continues, "Filling spots with unqualified men can weaken the effectiveness of the entire elder body, especially if biblical standards are compromised simply to fill a quota."[2] With the indefinite-term model, the qualifications will be taken more seriously because those appointed to office typically will serve much longer terms than those who are limited to serve a specified number of years.

Summary

Since the Bible does not specify the length elders should serve, wisdom is needed to apply biblical principles to this issue. Having specified terms allows many men to serve, avoids overworking the elders, and affords a method of releasing ineffective or unqualified elders. Having an unspecified, or indefinite, term removes the unbiblical distinction between professional and lay elders, retains elders who are effective in their service, and encourages congregations to require that the biblical standards be met.

---

1. Phil A. Newton, *Elders in Congregational Life: Rediscovering the Biblical Model for Church Leadership* (Grand Rapids: Kregel, 2005), 151.
2. Ibid., 152.

Reflection Questions

1. What do you think is the greatest advantage to instituting terms for elders?
2. What is the greatest disadvantage?
3. What do you think is the greatest advantage to elders serving indefinite terms?
4. What is the greatest disadvantage?
5. Which system do you prefer? Why?

Should Elders Be Ordained?

In most denominations or churches, officeholders are publicly recognized when they are installed into office. The question before us, then, is how we are to understand the significance of this act and when it should be performed.

The Significance of Ordination

In order to discuss the significance of publicly recognizing an officeholder, we need to look at the different terms used in the New Testament to describe this process. We read in Acts 14:23 that Paul and Barnabas "appointed elders" in every church in various cities in Asia Minor. The Greek term translated "appointed" is *cheirotoneō*, which is a compound word taken from "hand" (*cheir*) and "to stretch" (*teinō*). In classical Greek the word meant "choose" or "elect," originally by raising the hand. In time, however, the "hand" element became a dead metaphor.[1] Thus, in biblical Greek, *cheirotoneō* simply means to appoint someone to an office or designate someone for a specific task. The only other occurrence of the verb in the New Testament is found in 2 Corinthians 8:19, where a well-known brother was "appointed by the churches" to accompany Paul on his journey. It is clear in this instance that *cheirotoneō* means to designate or appoint one to a position.[2] Nevertheless, in patristic Greek it again came to mean "ordain with the laying on of hands." Because of this later usage, some interpreters read this meaning back into the New Testament and maintain that Paul and Barnabas ordained men to the office of elder by the laying on of their hands, indicating some special

---

1. It is therefore unlikely that the verb means "having appointed by popular vote." See J. M. Ross, "The Appointment of Presbyters in Acts xiv. 23," *ExpTim* 63 (1951): 288–89; and Alexander Strauch, *Biblical Eldership: An Urgent Call to Restore Biblical Church Leadership,* 3rd ed., rev. and expanded (Littleton, CO: Lewis and Roth, 1995), 137–39.
2. For a similar use, see Philo, *De Specialibus Legibus* 1.14.78.

conference of authority or ecclesiastical power. Although the laying on of hands is often associated with the appointing of elders, the author conveys such meaning by using a different term. For example, when Luke wants to speak of the laying on of hands, he uses the verb *epitithēmi* plus the noun "hand" (*cheir*) (Acts 6:6; 8:17, 19; 9:12, 17; 13:3; 19:6; 28:8; also see 1 Tim. 5:22). Others claim that the word *cheirotoneō* means to vote in the context of Acts 14:23. Although this is a possible meaning of the verb, it is not likely based on the context. Paul and Barnabas appointed the elders of the church; they did not vote for them.

The other verb used to convey the idea of "appointing" is found in Titus 1:5, where Paul exhorts Titus to "appoint [*kathistēmi*] elders in every town." In both classical and biblical Greek, *kathistēmi* is used with the meaning of appointing someone to office. For example, Jesus asks someone, "Who *appointed* Me a judge or arbitrator over you?" (Luke 12:14 NASB, emphasis added). We also read that Joseph was shown favor by Pharaoh, "who *appointed* him ruler over Egypt and over all his household" (Acts 7:10 NRSV, emphasis added).

The laying on of hands is often associated with the appointing or commissioning of someone for a specific office or task. The seven who were chosen to serve the church in order to lighten the responsibilities of the apostles were "set before the apostles, and they prayed and laid their hands on them" (Acts 6:6). At the church in Antioch, the Lord chose Barnabas and Paul to perform a special task: "Then after fasting and praying they laid their hands on them and sent them off" (Acts 13:3). In another context, Paul exhorted Timothy not to neglect the gift that was given to him "by prophecy when the council of elders laid their hands" on him (1 Tim. 4:14).[3] It should be noted that here the entire body of elders, not just one elder or bishop, laid hands on and appointed Timothy to service. Finally, Paul warns Timothy, "Do not be hasty in the laying on of hands" (1 Tim. 5:22). Although Paul does not specify the public installation of someone to the office of elder, the context deals exclusively with elders.[4]

Prayer and fasting also is associated with the selection and appointing

---

3. Later, Paul indicates that the gift was given to Timothy through the laying on of his hands (2 Tim. 1:6), which probably indicates that Paul was part of the council of elders mentioned in 1 Tim. 4:14.

4. The laying on of hands is also found in connection with those receiving the Spirit (Acts 8:17, 19; 19:6) and those receiving healing (Acts 9:12, 17; 28:8).

of leaders. The apostles followed the example of Jesus, who prayed all night before choosing His twelve disciples, the apostles (Luke 6:12–13). After the church selected the Seven, we read that the apostles "prayed and laid their hands on them" (Acts 6:6). Similarly, when Barnabas and Paul were appointed as missionaries, the church fasted and prayed and then sent them off (Acts 13:3).

The New Testament never uses the word *ordain* (in the modern, technical sense) in connection with a Christian leader who is installed to an office.[5] Thus, it is often misleading to use the term *ordain* in our modern context if one has in mind the biblical concept of publicly appointing or installing someone to an office. Today, the word *ordain* carries with it the idea that special grace is transferred through the act of laying on of hands. Unlike the Episcopal tradition, which claims that the authority of the office comes from the bishop passed to the appointee by the laying on of hands, the authority of the office comes from God, who calls and gifts men to lead His church (Acts 20:28; 1 Cor. 12:28; Eph. 4:11). The New Testament does not teach that those chosen to lead the church are "ordained" to a sacred, priestly office, or that only so-called "ordained" clergymen possess the right to preach, baptize, conduct the Lord's Supper, or pronounce a benediction.

It is the church's duty to recognize those whom God has set apart for this important duty. Grudem comments, "If one is convinced that the local church should select elders, then it would seem appropriate that the church that elected that elder—not an external bishop—should be the group to confer the outward recognition at election by installing the person in office or ordaining the pastor."[6] Strauch warns against understanding the appointment of elders in light of the Old Testament priesthood.

> Elders and deacons are not appointed to a special priestly office or holy clerical order. Instead, they are assuming offices of leadership or service among God's people. *We should be careful not to sacralize these positions more than the writers of Scripture do.* The New Testament

---

5. R. Banks, for example, writes, "Ordination, as we know it, does not appear in the Pauline letters" ("Church Order and Government," in *Dictionary of Paul and His Letters*, ed. Gerald F. Hawthorne, Ralph P. Martin, and Daniel G. Reid [Downers Grove, IL: InterVarsity Press, 1993], 135).

6. Wayne Grudem, *Systematic Theology: An Introduction to Biblical Doctrine* (Leicester: InterVarsity Press; Grand Rapids: Eerdmans, 1994), 925.

never shrouds the installation of elders in mystery or sacred ritual. There is no holy rite to perform or special ceremony to observe. Appointment to eldership is not a holy sacrament. Appointment confers no special grace or empowerment, nor does one become a priest, cleric, or holy man at the moment of installation.[7]

The Time of Ordination

It is common for people to be given the title "pastor" without having been ordained. But if the above analysis is correct, then to rightfully be a "pastor" (or deacon) is to be "ordained" in the sense of being publicly installed into that office. The idea of separating the title from the public act of commissioning is not found in the Bible. Elders are not appointed to the office after they become elders. But by becoming elders, they are appointed to the office.

Thus, to be appointed to the office of elder implies that a man has met the biblical qualifications, has been called by God, has been approved by the congregation, and consequently has been publicly recognized as one who holds that office. It does not necessarily imply that he works full-time for the church or has been to seminary. Rather, it means that God has called and gifted a person to humbly lead the church. It is also without biblical precedent to call some church leaders "pastors" before ordination and then "reverend" or "minister" after ordination.

Summary

Elders should be "ordained" if by ordination we simply mean the public recognition of someone to a particular office and ministry. Perhaps it would be more appropriate, and biblical, however, to speak of their "appointment" or "commission." The appointment to a ministry was often accompanied by prayer and fasting and the laying on of hands. These public acts draw attention to the seriousness and importance of the appointment. In addition, elders should be appointed as soon as they take their office.

---

7. Strauch, *Biblical Eldership*, 285.

Reflection Questions

1. Before reading this section on ordination, what was your understanding concerning the significance of the term?
2. Has your understanding changed?
3. What is the significance of the laying on of hands in association with
   ordination?
4. When is the appropriate time for ordination?
5. What is the potential danger of using extrabiblical terminology (e.g.,
   "reverend") in association with ordination?

Should Elders Be Paid?

There are many questions today concerning the payment of elders. Should they be paid at all? If one is paid, should they all be paid? How much should they be paid? In seeking to answer some of these questions, we will first discuss the biblical basis for elders to be paid and then discuss why it is not necessary for all of them to be paid.

The Right of Elders to Be Paid

Besides being a missionary who traveled extensively planting churches, Paul also worked a "secular" job. Luke records that when Paul came to Corinth during his second missionary journey, he stayed with Aquila and Priscilla because they were of the same trade as the apostle (i.e., they were both tent-makers; Acts 18:3). As a general rule, Paul did not receive money from the people to whom he was currently ministering. In 1 Corinthians 9:1–18, Paul uses the example of his not accepting money from the Corinthians in order to illustrate how he willingly relinquished his rights. His ultimate goal is to demonstrate to the Corinthians that they should likewise relinquish their rights to eat certain foods so as not to offend a weaker brother (chap. 8). Thus, in 1 Corinthians 9, Paul offers several reasons why he is entitled to receive financial compensation for his labor among the Corinthians. His point, however, is that although he had the right to receive such compensation, he refused any support so that the gospel would not be hindered. In support of his right to compensation, Paul not only offers arguments from culture (1 Cor. 9:7) but also bolsters his position by quoting the Old Testament. He states,

> Do I say these things on human authority? Does not the Law say the same? For it is written in the Law of Moses, "You shall not muzzle an ox when it treads out the grain." Is it for oxen that God is concerned?

Does he not speak entirely for our sake? It was written for our sake.
(1 Cor. 9:8–10)

In this text, Paul quotes from Deuteronomy 25:4, "You shall not muzzle the ox while he is threshing" (NASB). Threshing is the process of separating the grain from the straw. Small amounts of grain could be threshed by using a stick or rod, but oxen were used for larger quantities. Because of the dry weather in Palestine, outdoor threshing floors were used. These threshing floors consisted of a large, flat rock surface usually on top of a hill so that it was exposed to the wind. Oxen were driven on this circular piece of level ground over unbound sheaves of grain so that the ripe grain was shaken out of the ears by the trampling of the animals' hooves. Another method was to harness oxen to a rough sledge on which the driver rode, guiding the oxen in circles. The sledge consisted of two heavy boards, curved upward at the front, with sharp pieces of stone or iron attached to the bottom, which served to loosen the kernels of grain. If the wind was blowing, the threshed grain would be tossed high into the air so that the lighter chaff could be blown away leaving only the grain.[1]

The oxen doing this work were not to be muzzled but were to have freedom to eat the grain below them. The obvious point of this verse is that it would be cruel to deny those doing the work the fruit of their labor. Paul is using the common rabbinical argument of lesser to the greater (*qal wahomer* or *a fortiori*). In other words, if animals that work are not to be denied reward for their labor, how much more should men be granted payment for their labor. Paul simply applies this principle to himself and his ministry among the Corinthians. Just as it is wrong to muzzle an ox while it is threshing (i.e., working), so also it is wrong not to support financially those who work in order to advance the kingdom of God. He later supports this principle by appealing to the words of the Lord: "In the same way, the Lord commanded that those who proclaim the gospel should get their living by the gospel" (1 Cor. 9:14).

Paul believed not only that he had the right to receive financial compensation for his labors, but also that hardworking elders had claim to that right. In his first letter to Timothy, he writes, "Let the elders who rule well be considered worthy of double honor, especially those who labor in preaching and

---

1. Henry Gehman, ed., *The New Westminster Dictionary of the Bible* (Philadelphia: Westminster Press, 1970), 944–45.

teaching" (1 Tim. 5:17). There are three main interpretations as to the meaning of "double honor": (1) twice the respect (respect on account of age and
respect on account of office, or respect as an elder and extra respect as one
who rules well); (2) double financial pay (twice as much as elders who do not
rule well, or twice as much as widows who are on the church dole); (3) honor
and honorarium ("twofold" honor in the sense of respect and financial pay).
Although the normal meaning of the word translated "honor" (*timē*) refers
to the respect or worth given to someone, the third interpretation is to be
preferred due to the context of the verse. In 1 Timothy 5:3, Paul commands
the church, "Honor [*timaō*] widows who are truly widows," which clearly
refers to financial support (see esp. vv. 4, 8, 16). Furthermore, Paul's quote
in 1 Timothy 5:18 of Deuteronomy 25:4 and a saying of Jesus confirm that
financial support is in view. Similar to 1 Corinthians 9, Paul's use of the Old
Testament text is to validate the principle that those who do the work ought
to reap benefits from their work. In this case, elders who spend their days
leading and teaching the church ought to be not only respected for their duties but also financially compensated.

The second scriptural proof that worthy elders should be paid is from a
saying of Jesus found in Luke 10:7 (Matt. 10:10 has a slight variation in that
it has "food" instead of "wages"). In the context of Luke 10, Jesus sends out
the seventy disciples. He commands them to go into various cities in order to
preach the kingdom of God. They are not to carry moneybags but are to stay
in the homes of those they meet. In verse 7 Luke records Jesus' command
to the seventy to "remain in the same house, eating and drinking what they
provide, for the laborer deserves his wages. Do not go from house to house."
Matthew's account occurs in the context of Jesus sending out the twelve disciples. Jesus tells His disciples, "Acquire no gold nor silver nor copper for
your belts, no bag for your journey, nor two tunics nor sandals nor a staff,
for the laborer deserves his food" (Matt. 10:9–10). Some have thought that
this saying of Jesus stems from certain Old Testament laws. For example,
Deuteronomy 24:14–15 states, "You shall not oppress a hired servant who is
poor and needy, whether he is one of your brothers or one of the sojourners
who are in your land within your towns. You shall give him his wages on
the same day, before the sun sets (for he is poor and counts on it), lest he cry
against you to the LORD, and you be guilty of sin." Similarly, in Leviticus
19:13 we read, "You shall not oppress your neighbor or rob him. The wages of
a hired servant shall not remain with you all night until the morning."

Paul uses the saying of Jesus in a similar manner in which we find it used by Jesus in Matthew and Luke. Jesus' words were spoken in the context of itinerant preachers being supported by others for the work they were performing. Likewise, Paul applies the saying to make the case that certain elders should be paid for the duties they perform for the church of God. Thus, Paul's charge to Timothy and the church at Ephesus to pay worthy elders is grounded in the command of Christ Himself.

This principle is found elsewhere in Paul's letters. In Galatians 6:6, he writes, "One who is taught the word must share all good things with the one who teaches." In this verse, Paul makes a distinction between those who give instruction and those who receive instruction. This verse suggests that there was a class of instructors or catechizers who taught the Word to such an extent that they needed to be financially supported.[2] It should be noted, however, that such teaching was at an incipient stage since Paul admonishes the "one who is taught" to share with the teacher rather than charging the congregations as a whole to recompense those who teach. Paul commands the Galatian Christians to make sure they support their teachers. Obviously, Paul recognized these teachers not only as being gifted to teach "the word" (i.e., the Christian message), but also as having the right to receive support for their labors.

The Right of Elders Not to Be Paid

In the previous section we established the biblical truth that elders who spend most of their time teaching and shepherding the congregation deserve to be paid. This does not mean, however, that all (or any) of the elders must be paid for their work or that only those who work full-time for the church can rightfully be called "elders." As an apostle and missionary, Paul certainly had the right to be supported by the churches he established and in which he labored. But for sake of the gospel, he chose not to claim this right.

---

2. Ernest Burton comments, "The fact that those who receive instruction are called upon to contribute to the support of the teacher shows that such teaching in all probability was not undertaken merely as a voluntary and relatively light avocation . . . but occupied in preparation for it and the work itself, if not the teacher's whole time, yet enough so that it was necessary to compensate him for the loss of income which he thus sustained. In short, it is a class of paid teachers to which this verse refers" (*A Critical and Exegetical Commentary on the Epistle to the Galatians*, ICC [Edinburgh: T and T Clark, 1921], 335). H. W. Beyer maintains that this verse "establishes the claim of the teacher to support, and therewith confirms the validity and necessity of a professional teaching ministry in the congregation" ("κατηχέω," in *TDNT*, 3:639).

Just like Paul, there are many elders who are self-supported in the sense that they draw a salary from outside the church. They spend much of their free time in helping to shepherd the congregation, but they are not paid for their labors. Some churches have difficulty financially supporting one or more elders. By having elders who do not receive monetary compensation for their work, the church is able to include more men as elders without the extra burden of supporting them financially. This situation allows the elders to shepherd the congregation more effectively.

Summary

The Bible clearly teaches that those who work for the church deserve to be paid (Matt. 10:10; Luke 10:7; 1 Cor. 9:8–10; Gal. 6:6; 1 Tim. 5:17). This does not mean that all elders have the right to demand pay from the church but that those who give most of their time and energy to shepherding and teaching the congregation should be compensated for their labor. At the same time, those elders who do not work "full-time" for the church or who are not "staff" should not be viewed as having less authority than those who are officially employed by the church. Non-staff elders provide support for the other elders by helping to shepherd the congregation without adding to the church's burden by requiring financial support.

Reflection Questions

1. What verses would you use to demonstrate that elders have the right to be paid?
2. Why does Paul quote Deuteronomy 25:4 to prove that leaders should be paid for the work they do (see 1 Cor. 9:9; 1 Tim. 5:18)?
3. When Paul states in 1 Timothy 5:17 that elders who rule well are worthy of double honor, what does he mean by the phrase "double honor"?
4. What does Jesus mean when He states that "the laborer deserves his wages" (Luke 10:7)?
5. Why is it important to understand that not all elders must receive a salary or work "full-time" for the church?

What Should Be Done
If an Elder Is Caught in Sin?

The main reason this question is addressed is because Scripture speaks directly to such a situation. In 1 Timothy 5:19–25, Paul gives authoritative instructions concerning what should be done if an elder is caught in sin and stresses the importance of making sure that those who are appointed as elders are truly qualified.

The Proper Method of Disciplining Elders

> Do not admit a charge against an elder except on the evidence of two or three witnesses. As for those who persist in sin, rebuke them in the presence of all, so that the rest may stand in fear. In the presence of God and of Christ Jesus and of the elect angels I charge you to keep these rules without prejudging, doing nothing from partiality. (1 Tim. 5:19–21)

Paul makes it clear to Timothy what should be done if an elder is accused of a particular sin. He first mentions that a charge or accusation against an elder is not to be accepted without proper testimony—at least two or three witnesses. This principle is based on an Old Testament law: "A single witness shall not suffice against a person for any crime or for any wrong in connection with any offense that he has committed. Only on the evidence of two witnesses or of three witnesses shall a charge be established" (Deut. 19:15). This principle is also found in the context of Jesus' teaching on church discipline: "If your brother sins against you, go and tell him his fault, between you and him alone. If he listens to you, you have gained your brother. But if he does not listen, take one or two others along with you, that every charge may be established by the evidence of two or three witnesses" (Matt. 18:15–16).

The purpose of having two or three witnesses is to substantiate the charge with proper evidence. These additional witnesses have either personally witnessed the sin or are present to verify another's accusation.

Paul continues by stating that those (elders) who sin are to be rebuked in the presence of all (1 Tim. 5:20). This verse raises a number of difficult interpretative issues. The first concerns whether Paul is still giving instruction about sinning elders. Some suggest that in verse 20, Paul shifts from speaking about an elder caught in sin to members of the congregation. The evidence for this view is found in the fact that Paul uses the singular "elder" in verse 19 but shifts to the plural ("those who persist in sin") in verse 20. Consequently, those who hold this view maintain that the "laying on of hands" in verse 22 refers to an act of restoration after discipline and repentance. This position, however, is most likely not correct. The context before verse 20 clearly refers to elders. Furthermore, the laying on of hands in verse 22 almost certainly refers to the public appointment of an elder to office. The laying on of hands is never used in the New Testament as a symbolic act of restoration but is commonly used in reference to appointing or commissioning someone (1 Tim. 4:14; 2 Tim. 1:6; also see question 31). It is best, then, to interpret the phrase "those who persist in sin" as still referring to elders.

Paul tells Timothy to "rebuke" these elders. Earlier Paul warned Timothy *not* to "rebuke" an "older man" (1 Tim. 5:1). The word translated "older man" (*presbuteros*) is the same word translated "elder" in 1 Timothy 5:17. However, there are two clear indicators that Paul is not contradicting himself. First, the Greek term *presbuteros* can mean either "older man" or "elder" (i.e., an officeholder)—the context must decide. In 1 Timothy 5:1, it is clear that the office of elder is not in view because the following verses refer specifically to age categories ("younger men," "older women," "younger women"). Second, the verbs translated "rebuke" in verses 1 and 20 are actually two different Greek words. In verse 1 Paul uses *epiplēssō*, which is a stronger word than *elenchō* in 5:20. The idea in the latter text is not reprimanding and chiding, but correcting and reproving those who are in sin.

"Those who persist in sin" (*tous hamartanontas*, present active participle) are to be rebuked "in the presence of all." Because the participle is present tense, many commentators and Bible versions emphasize the ongoing, progressive nature of the action. It is "those who continue or persist in sin" who are to be publicly rebuked. If the participle is interpreted as stressing the progressive aspect, a question then arises concerning those elders who sin only once or are repentant for their sins. Are they not to be rebuked publicly? Is Paul's point that only those elders who stubbornly refuse to heed private warnings and persist in sin are to be rebuked before all? A more likely interpretation is that all elders who are found guilty of sin are to be rebuked.[1]

There is also debate whether the sinning elder is to be rebuked in front of all the other elders or, more broadly, in front of the whole congregation. Some argue that if we limit those who are sinning to only elders, then "all" should also be limited to all the elders. But it is also possible to read the verse as follows: "Those (elders) who sin rebuke in the presence of all (the congregation), that the rest (of the elders) also may fear." This interpretation fits Jesus' teaching on church discipline, where the final step is "tell it to the church" (Matt. 18:17).

A public rebuke is necessary due to the serious nature of the sin committed. Also, a public sin has public consequences and therefore needs a public rebuke. It is probable that Paul has a specific case or cases in mind as he writes to Timothy.[2] Furthermore, based on the content of the letter, the sin most likely involves false teaching. This type of public sin (embracing and teaching false doctrines) would naturally require a public rebuke so that the members of the Ephesian church would understand why a former elder is no longer in leadership. Another reason for a public rebuke is "so the rest may stand in fear" (1 Tim. 5:20). "The rest" probably refers to the rest of the elders, not the entire congregation. By publicly rebuking a sinning elder, the church administers discipline, and at the same time, this act causes the other elders (and by implication the other church members) to fear the same punishment. The other elders would fear the shame of such public humiliation. Thus, church discipline serves as a deterrent for sin in the church. If public sin goes unpunished, especially among the elders, many in the church might begin to think that sin is not that serious and may give in to sin in their own lives.

Finally, in verse 21 Paul solemnly charges Timothy to oversee this whole process without prejudging or showing partiality. He gives Timothy this charge "in the presence of God and of Christ Jesus and of the elect angels."

---

1. So Alexander Strauch, *Biblical Eldership: An Urgent Call to Restore Biblical Church Leadership*, 3rd ed., rev. and expanded (Littleton, CO: Lewis and Roth, 1995), 218.

2. Gordon Fee states that the "urgency of this appeal is what makes one think that these are not simply general instructions in dealing with elders, but reflect the specific, historical situation" (*1 and 2 Timothy, Titus*, NIBCNT [Peabody, MA: Hendrickson, 1984], 131).

Timothy is not to make up his mind before hearing the facts but is to be completely just and fair in dealing with elders who sin.

The Importance of Appointing Qualified Elders

> Do not be hasty in the laying on of hands, nor take part in the sins of others; keep yourself pure. (No longer drink only water, but use a little wine for the sake of your stomach and your frequent ailments.) The sins of some men are conspicuous, going before them to judgment, but the sins of others appear later. So also good works are conspicuous, and even those that are not cannot remain hidden. (1 Tim. 5:22–25)

This section continues Paul's teaching on elders. The main theme is that elders should not be appointed too quickly. As mentioned earlier, the "laying on of hands" refers to the appointing or commissioning of someone. Thus, Timothy is cautioned not to be too quick to appoint someone to the eldership.[3] Choosing the correct elders the first time will spare the church from many problems in the future. Just as deacons are to "be tested first" (1 Tim. 3:10), elders also must be tested to see whether they are really who they appear to be.

Timothy's role as Paul's apostolic delegate carries with it much responsibility as he oversees the affairs of the church. If he appoints the wrong person to office, Timothy is, in a sense, taking part in the sins of others (1 Tim. 5:22). By prematurely appointing someone to office, he is condoning the sins that person commits.

This text again stresses the importance of an elder meeting the biblical qualifications. An elder must be a person with proven character. The true character of a person, however, is not always immediately visible. Some might look qualified but are not. Paul reminds Timothy that although the sins of some men go before them, "the sins of others appear later" (1 Tim. 5:24). Some people's sins are not evident, and therefore it is wise not to appoint them as elders until they have proven themselves. Others might not

---

3. It is difficult to know whether Paul's command not to lay hands on someone too hastily is meant to be understood retrospectively or prospectively. If he is speaking retrospectively, then he is stating that the current problems in the church are largely due to ordaining elders who had not yet displayed proven character. If he is speaking prospectively, then Paul has in mind appointing new elders after some are dismissed from their office.

look qualified but are (1 Tim. 5:25). There is a danger in refusing to appoint someone as an elder based on one's initial impression. Over time his good works will prove themselves. In this case, Timothy should not be afraid to appoint him as an elder. Therefore, Timothy should not turn anyone down too hastily.

Summary

Because elders have a public role, they are more open to accusations of sin. Paul, therefore, instructs Timothy and the Ephesian congregation, in accordance with the Old Testament and the teaching of Jesus, that sufficient testimony is needed before such charges will be considered. In addition, Paul reminds Timothy not to appoint elders too hastily so that such accusations can be avoided in the future.

Reflection Questions

1. How might having a plurality of elders be helpful when an elder needs to be disciplined?
2. Why is it important to have at least two or three witnesses before an accusation against an elder is accepted? Might there be some situations when witnesses are not necessary?
3. What is the role of the congregation in disciplining elders?
4. What should be done with an elder who continues to live in sin?
5. What steps can be taken to help ensure that those who are appointed as elders are truly qualified?

PART 3

The Office of Deacon

What Is the Background of the New Testament Deacon?

D eacon" is a translation of the Greek term *diakonos*, which normally means "servant" or "messenger." Only context can determine whether the term is being used in its ordinary usage or as the technical designation of a church officer. The Greek term is used twenty-nine times in the New Testament, but only three or four of those occurrences refer to an office-holder (Rom. 16:1[?]; Phil. 1:1; 1 Tim. 3:8, 12). Whereas there are some parallels between the Jewish elder and the Christian elder, there does not seem to be a parallel to the role of deacon in Jewish or Greek society (although the term is often used to describe different occupations in the Greek world).

Acts 6 as a Model for Deacons

The origin of the deacon is not known for certain, but many scholars believe that the seven chosen in Acts 6 provide the prototype of the New Testament deacon. The reason many are hesitant to call the Seven the first "deacons" is because the noun *diakonos* does not occur in the text. Only the related verb *diakoneō* ("to serve") is found (Acts 6:2). Another dissimilarity is that the text mentions the apostles but not elders. Therefore, a direct correlation is difficult to make. Still, Acts 6 does provide a pattern or paradigm that seems to have been continued in the early church. It is necessary, then, to investigate this passage in more detail.

> Now in these days when the disciples were increasing in number, a complaint by the Hellenists arose against the Hebrews because their widows were being neglected in the daily distribution. And the twelve summoned the full number of the disciples and said, "It is not right that we should give up preaching the word of God to serve tables.

Therefore, brothers, pick out from among you seven men of good repute, full of the Spirit and of wisdom, whom we will appoint to this duty. But we will devote ourselves to prayer and to the ministry of the word." And what they said pleased the whole gathering, and they chose Stephen, a man full of faith and of the Holy Spirit, and Philip, and Prochorus, and Nicanor, and Timon, and Parmenas, and Nicolaus, a proselyte of Antioch. These they set before the apostles, and they prayed and laid their hands on them. (Acts 6:1–6)

The Problem (Acts 6:1–2)

The need for the Seven to be chosen arose from growth in the church. As the church grew, there arose more spiritual and physical needs among the new converts. Widows, for example, were usually dependent on others for their daily needs. One problem that emerged in the early church was that the Greek-speaking Jewish widows were being neglected. When the twelve apostles received news of this problem, they knew that something must be done. They understood the importance of providing for the physical needs of the people. They understood that allowing this problem to continue could cause division in the church.

But there was another problem. Although the apostles realized the gravity of the situation before them, they also realized that for them to get distracted with serving tables would divert them from their primary calling of preaching the Word of God. The apostles were not indicating that it would be too humiliating for them to serve widows. Jesus had taught them that being a leader in His kingdom is very different from being a worldly leader (Matt. 20:25–27), and He had washed their feet to demonstrate servant leadership (John 13:1–18). Rather, the apostles wanted to remain faithful to the calling and the gifts they received from God. For them to leave the preaching of the Word to serve tables would have been a mistake. Instead, they proposed a better solution to this problem.

The Solution (Acts 6:3–6)

The apostles decided to call all the disciples together and present a solution to the problem. The disciples were to choose seven men to be appointed to the task of overseeing the daily distribution of food. The members of the congregation, however, were not to simply choose anyone who was willing to serve; they had to select men who had good reputations and were Spirit-filled. By appointing these men to help with the daily distribution of food, the apostles took this need seriously but did not get distracted from their primary calling. With the Seven appointed to take care of this problem, the apostles were able to devote themselves "to prayer and to the ministry of the word" (v. 4).

The primary spiritual leaders of the congregation were the apostles. They were appointed to a "ministry of the word." As the church grew, the number of problems grew with it. As a result, other factors began to distract them from their calling. The Seven were needed to allow the apostles the freedom to continue with their work. This is a similar paradigm to what we see with the offices of elder and deacon. Like the apostles, the elders' primary role involves preaching the Word of God (Eph. 4:11; 1 Tim. 3:2; Titus 1:9). Like the Seven, deacons are needed to serve the congregation in meeting whatever needs may arise. Thus, although the term *diakonos* does not occur in Acts 6, this passage provides a helpful model of how godly servants can assist those who are called to preach the Word of God.[1]

References to "Deacons" in the New Testament

Romans 16:1

Surprisingly, the Greek term *diakonos* only occurs three or four times as a designation of an officeholder. In Romans 16:1 Phoebe is called a *diakonos* "of the church at Cenchreae." It is debated as to whether Paul is using the term *diakonos* here as a general term for "servant" or as a more technical term for a "deacon" (i.e., a church officer). Most English Bible versions choose the more neutral term "servant," but the RSV renders it "deaconess" and the NRSV renders it "deacon."

In the New Testament the term is applied to governments (Rom. 13:4), Christ (Rom. 15:8; Gal. 2:17), and Christians who are in some sort of leadership position. Besides referring to Phoebe and to himself as a *diakonos*,[2] Paul also applies the term to Apollos (1 Cor. 3:5), Tychicus (Eph. 6:21; Col. 4:7), Epaphras (Col. 1:7), and Timothy (1 Tim. 4:6). Based on this data, it

---

1. Wayne Grudem comments, "It seems appropriate to think of these seven men as 'deacons' even though the name *deacon* had perhaps not yet come to be applied to them as they began this responsibility" (*Systematic Theology: An Introduction to Biblical Doctrine* [Leicester: InterVarsity Press; Grand Rapids: Eerdmans, 1994], 919).
2. 1 Cor. 3:5; 2 Cor. 3:6; 6:4; Gal. 2:17; Eph. 3:7; Col. 1:23, 25.

is possible that Paul refers to Phoebe as a *diakonos* because, like Apollos, Tychicus, Epaphras, and Timothy, she had some leadership responsibilities among the people of God. It is difficult to be certain, however, whether Paul is using the term as a technical reference to an officeholder (see questions 38 and 39).

Philippians 1:1

The term *diakonos* clearly refers to a church office in Paul's opening greeting in his letter to the Philippians. He addresses "all the saints in Christ Jesus who are at Philippi, with the overseers and deacons" (Phil. 1:1). This is the only place where Paul greets church officers in the salutation of a letter and is perhaps the clearest indication of a distinction between church members and church leaders in Paul's early writings. Some, however, object to the idea that Paul is referring to any organized church office. Rather, they maintain that the terms refer to function and not office since no definite article is given in the Greek. They contend that Paul is not referring to officers but to those who are merely engaged in watching over others and serving. Thus, it is argued that the terms are merely used functionally to designate those who are ministering to the saints.

There is a problem with this analysis, however. If Paul is merely greeting all those who serve freely and spontaneously, why is it necessary for him to greet those people separately? Is Paul merely addressing those who sometimes function as overseers or perform acts of service, or does he have a definite group of individuals in mind? Hawthorne rightly notes, "Paul mentions the [overseers and deacons] in such a way as to distinguish them from the congregation. This implies that he considered them to be persons with some kind of official status."[3] It is simply not convincing to argue that Paul is naming anyone who might function as a supervisor or servant without referring to some definite group of people.[4] The absence of the definite articles

---

3. Gerald F. Hawthorne, *Philippians*, WBC (Waco, TX: Word, 1983), 43:7. E. Best affirms this position with even stronger words when he writes, "I say 'officials' because ἐπίσκοπος at any rate could not have been used in any other way than as a designation of an office. The word was widely employed for officers in different types of societies and organisations including religious groups, and for (though less widely) civil officials; a first century Greek could not have used it in a purely functional sense without suggesting that the person who exercised oversight held 'official' status" ("Bishops and Deacons: Philippians 1,1," in *Studia Evangelica*, Texte und Untersuchungen 102, ed. F. L. Cross [Berlin: Akademie-Verlag, 1968], 4:371).

4. Alexander Strauch comments, "The interpretation . . . that assigns merely a functional sense to Paul's usage of *overseers* and *deacons* in this instance is confusing and nearly meaningless"

does not prove that these groups are indefinite since the context suggests otherwise.

Apart from the introductory greeting in Philippians 1:1, we would have no indication of church leaders and an organized ministry in the Philippian church. Nevertheless, the presence of such leaders does not change Paul's writing style of addressing the entire congregation. Paul links the overseers and deacons with all the saints since they are not to be treated as believers on a higher level. Yet, they are, for reasons unknown, distinguished within the greeting. A. T. Robertson aptly comments, "Paul does not ignore the officers of the saints or church, though they occupy a secondary place in his mind. The officers are important, but not primary. The individual saint is primary. Church officers are made out of saints. . . . Paul does not draw a line of separation between clergy and laity. He rather emphasizes the bond of union by the use of 'together with.'"[5]

1 Timothy 3:8, 12

The final two occurrences of *diakonos* as a reference to a church office are found in 1 Timothy 3, where Paul lists the requirements for "deacons." It is striking that Paul does not explain the duties of this office, which suggests that the Ephesian church already had experience with deacons. Paul simply lists the qualifications and assumes the church will use these officers in the appropriate manner. The fact that deacons do not need to be "able to teach" is a feature that sets them apart from the elders (cf. 1 Tim. 3:2; 5:17). Because

(*Biblical Eldership: An Urgent Call to Restore Biblical Church Leadership*, 3rd ed., rev. and expanded [Littleton, CO: Lewis and Roth, 1995], 176). Peter T. O'Brien likewise states, "[Paul] has in view particular members of the congregation who are specifically described and known by these two titles; otherwise the additions seem to be meaningless. . . . That Paul should refer to two definite groups in the prescript of his letter suggests that they have special, self-evident authority" (*The Epistle to the Philippians*, NIGTC [Grand Rapids: Eerdmans; Carlisle, U.K.: Paternoster, 1991], 48). Bengt Holmberg comments that "it is clear from all these texts [Rom. 16:1–21; 1 Cor. 16:16; Phil. 1:1; 1 Thess. 5:12] that the apostle is thinking of particular persons or groups known to him and to his readers and who perform functions specific enough to single them out for mention" (*Paul and Power: The Structure of Authority in the Primitive Church as Reflected in the Pauline Epistles* [Philadelphia: Fortress, 1980], 99).

5. A. T. Robertson, *Paul's Joy in Christ: Studies in Philippians* (New York: Revell, 1917), 42–43. Hawthorne likewise states, "Paul did not address himself to these 'officers' over the head of the congregation. Rather, as was his custom elsewhere in his letters, he addressed the congregation; he addressed the bishops and deacons second and only in conjunction with the congregation" (*Philippians*, 7–8). Similarly, Gordon D. Fee writes, "When they [i.e., overseers and deacons] are singled out, as here, the leaders are not 'over' the church, but are addressed 'alongside of' the church, as a distinguishable part of the whole, but as part of the whole, not above or outside it" (*Paul's Letter to the Philippians*, NICNT [Grand Rapids: Eerdmans, 1995], 67).

Paul does not list any of the duties deacons should perform, it is likely that the early church understood the Seven chosen in Acts 6 to be a model for their own ministry. That is, as deacons they were responsible for caring for the physical needs of the congregation and doing whatever was needed so that the elders could focus on their work of teaching and shepherding.

Summary

The office of the Christian deacon does not have a close parallel to leaders found in either Jewish or Greek society. The seven men chosen in Acts 6, while not specifically called deacons, provide the closest parallel to the Christian office. Just as the Seven were needed to attend to the physical needs of the Greek-speaking Jewish widows, so deacons are needed to look after the physical needs of the church. By being responsible for the oversight of such concerns, the deacons allow the elders to focus their efforts on attending to the spiritual needs of the congregation.

Reflection Questions

1. Do you think Acts 6:1–6 provides the prototype for the New Testament deacon? Why or why not?
2. What was the problem the early church was facing in Acts 6:1–6?
3. What was their solution to this problem?
4. Was it arrogant of the apostles to refuse to serve tables and instead get others to do this menial task?
5. Why do you think the office of deacon is not mentioned as much as the office of elder in the New Testament?

What Are the Qualifications for a Deacon?

The only passage in Scripture that mentions the qualifications for deacons is 1 Timothy 3:8–13. Paul lists the qualifications for elders in both 1 Timothy 3 and Titus 1, but he makes no mention of deacons in his letter to Titus. The similarities of the qualifications for deacons and elders/overseers are striking in 1 Timothy 3. Like an elder, a deacon must not be addicted to much wine (cf. 1 Tim. 3:3, "not a drunkard"), not greedy for dishonest gain (cf. 1 Tim. 3:3, "not a lover of money"), blameless (cf. 1 Tim. 3:2, "above reproach"), the husband of one wife, and one who manages his children and household well. Furthermore, the focus of the qualifications is on the moral character of the person who is to fill the office. "Both the office of a church leader and the office of church worker require the same type of person: a mature Christian whose behavior is above reproach."[1] The main difference between an elder and a deacon is a difference of gifts and calling, not character.

In 1 Timothy 3, Paul gives an official, but not exhaustive, list of the requirements for deacons. Consequently, if a *moral* qualification is listed for elders but not for deacons, that qualification still applies to deacons. The same goes for those qualifications listed for deacons but not for elders. For example, simply because it is not listed in the requirements for elders, an elder is not permitted to be double-tongued (1 Tim. 3:8). Paul already stated that elders must be "above reproach," which would include this prohibition. The differences in the qualifications, then, signify traits that are either particularly fitting for the officeholder to possess in order to accomplish his duties or especially needed in light of particular problems in the location to which Paul writes (in this case, Ephesus). Most likely, Paul is giving descriptions

---

1. William D. Mounce, *Pastoral Epistles*, WBC (Nashville: Nelson, 2000), 46:195.

that counter the descriptions of the false teachers in Ephesus. Thus, these descriptions mostly involve personal characteristics, not duties. Because many of the requirements for deacons are the same as those for elders, we will focus our attention on those requirements that are unique to deacons.

Dignified (1 Tim. 3:8)

The first requirement that Paul lists for deacons is that they must be dignified. The Greek word translated "dignified" (*semnos*) occurs only four times in the New Testament (Phil. 4:8; 1 Tim. 3:8, 11; Titus 2:2). The term normally refers to something that is honorable, respectable, esteemed, or worthy and is closely related to "respectable" (*kosmios*), which is given as a qualification for elders (1 Tim. 3:2). In Philippians 4:8, Paul exhorts the believers to meditate on things that are true, *honorable*, just, pure, lovely, commendable, excellent, and worthy of praise. In Titus 2:2, Paul commands the older men to be "dignified." The other two occurrences are found in 1 Timothy 3—one as a requirement for a deacon (v. 8) and the other for his wife (v. 11). Thus, a deacon and his wife must be characterized as people who are honored and respected by those who know them. The work of a deacon is service oriented. This does not mean, however, that the leadership a deacon provides is not important. Such work is often crucial to the life of the church and requires someone who is respected.

Not Double-tongued (1 Tim. 3:8)

The second requirement is that a deacon must not be double-tongued. The Greek word (*dilogos*) literally means "something said twice," and it occurs only here in the New Testament. People who are "double-tongued" say one thing to certain people but something else to others, or they say one thing but mean another. They are two-faced and insincere. Their words cannot be trusted, and thus they lack credibility. "Deacons thus must be the type of people who are careful with their tongues, not saying what they should not, being faithful to the truth in their speech."[2] They must be those who speak the truth in love. They cannot be slippery with their words, seeking to manipulate situations for their own personal good.

---

2. Ibid., 199.

Sound in Faith and Life (1 Tim. 3:9)

Paul also indicates that a deacon must "hold the mystery of the faith with a clear conscience." The reference to "the mystery of the faith" is another way for Paul to speak of the gospel (cf. 1 Tim. 3:16). Consequently, this statement refers to the doctrinal beliefs of a deacon. Unlike those who have suffered shipwreck regarding the faith (1 Tim. 1:19) and whose consciences are seared (1 Tim. 4:2), deacons are to hold firm to the true gospel without wavering. Yet, this qualification does not merely involve one's beliefs, for he also must hold these beliefs "with a clear conscience." That is, the behavior of a deacon must be consistent with his beliefs. If it is not, his conscience will speak against him and condemn him. Thus, this requirement speaks not only to the doctrine of a deacon but also to his behavior. "It is not sufficient to have a grasp on the theological profession of the church; that knowledge must be accompanied with the appropriate behavior, in this case a conscience that is clear from any stain of sin."[3] Similarly, Paul instructs older men to be "sound in faith" (Titus 2:2). False teachings were rampant in Ephesus and were wreaking havoc in the church. Paul, therefore, stresses the need for deacons to be sound in their faith. One might think that this requirement is not necessary because deacons are not responsible for teaching in the church. Yet, as church officers and leaders, they have influence on the lives and beliefs of others. Furthermore, simply because deacons are not required to teach does not mean they are not permitted to teach.

Tested (1 Tim. 3:10)

Another qualification not specifically mentioned in the list for elders is the need for deacons to be tested before they can serve the church in an official capacity. Paul writes, "And let them also be tested first; then let them serve as deacons if they prove themselves blameless" (1 Tim. 3:10). Paul states that those who prove themselves to be "blameless" are qualified to serve as deacons. The word translated "blameless" is a general term referring to the overall character of a person's life (cf. Titus 1:6, where the same word is used) and is similar to the word used for the qualification of elders in 1 Timothy 3:2 ("above reproach"). Although Paul does not specify what type of testing is to take place, at a minimum, the candidate's personal background, reputation, and theological positions should be examined. But not only should the moral, spiritual, and doctrinal aspects be tested; the congregation also must

---

3. Ibid., 200.

consider the person's actual service in the church. A person with a deacon's heart is one who looks for opportunities to serve. As a person is given more responsibilities in the church, his ability to serve in a responsible manner and his ability to relate to others should be examined. Allowing someone who has not been tested to become a deacon can later lead to many problems. As with the elders, time is needed to assess the candidate because the sins of some are not immediately apparent (1 Tim. 3:6; 5:24). Thus, a hasty appointment to office is unwise and contrary to the intent of the qualifications. A specific length of time, however, is not given and should be left up to the local church to decide.

Godly Wife (1 Tim. 3:11)

It is debated whether this verse refers to the wife of a deacon or to a deaconess (see questions 38 and 39). For the sake of this discussion, we will assume the verse is speaking about the qualifications of a deacon's wife. According to Paul, the wives of deacons must "be dignified, not slanderers, but sober-minded, faithful in all things." First, like her husband, the wife must be dignified, or respectable. Second, she must not be a slanderer or a person who goes around spreading gossip. Later, Paul warns younger widows to remarry so that they do not learn to become idle, "going about from house to house, and not only idlers, but also gossips and busybodies, saying what they should not" (1 Tim. 5:13; cf. 2 Tim. 3:3; Titus 2:3). A deacon's wife also must be sober-minded, or temperate. The same word is used for elders in 1 Timothy 3:2. Thus, the deacon's wife must be able to make good judgments and must not be involved in things that might hinder such judgment. Finally, she must be "faithful in all things" (cf. 1 Tim. 5:10). This requirement is general in nature and functions similarly to the requirement for elders to be "above reproach" (1 Tim. 3:2; Titus 1:6) or for deacons to be "blameless" (1 Tim. 3:10). The wife of a deacon must be a trustworthy person. The character of a deacon's wife is important to the success of his ministry. She must be committed, self-controlled, and faithful like her husband. Paul does not mention that the wives first must be tested, however, since it is not they, but their husbands, who are appointed to the office.

Summary

The character of a potential deacon and his wife should be examined before he is put into office. The high standard required for deacons should not be minimized simply because they do not normally teach or lead the church. As officers of the church, they represent the church in some capacity, handling important and sometimes sensitive tasks.

Reflection Questions

1. How do the qualifications for a deacon differ from those for an elder/overseer?
2. Do you think the qualifications in 1 Timothy 3:8–13 are exhaustive? Why or why not?
3. How might it be determined whether a candidate for the office of deacon holds to the mystery of the faith with a clear conscience (1 Tim. 3:9)?
4. If the office of deacon is merely an office of service (and not an office that carries authority), why does Paul state that deacons first must be tested?
5. Why is it important for a deacon to have a godly wife?

What Is the Role of a Deacon?

Whereas the office of elder is often ignored in the modern church, the office of deacon is often misunderstood. In many churches, the board of deacons provides the spiritual leadership in the church in partnership with the pastor. They are involved in making the important decisions of the church and often are involved in teaching and shepherding. But based on the New Testament data, the role of the deacon is mainly a servant role. Deacons are needed in the church to provide logistical and material support so that the elders can concentrate their efforts on the Word of God and prayer.

Differences with Elders

The New Testament does not provide much information concerning the role of deacons. The requirements given in 1 Timothy 3:8–13 focus on the deacon's character and family life. There are, however, some clues as to the function of deacons when their requirements are compared with those of the elders. Although many of the qualifications are the same or very similar, there are some notable differences.

Perhaps the most noticeable distinction between elders and deacons is that deacons do not need to be "able to teach" (1 Tim. 3:2). Deacons are called to "hold" to the faith with a clear conscience, but they are not called to "teach" that faith (1 Tim. 3:9). This suggests that the deacons do not have an official teaching role in the church. D. A. Carson rightly comments, "Deacons were responsible to serve the church in a variety of subsidiary roles, but enjoyed no church-recognized teaching authority akin to that of elders."[1] Again, this

---

1. D. A. Carson, "Church, Authority in the," *EDT*, ed. Walter E. Elwell [Grand Rapids: Baker, 1984], 229. Wayne Grudem likewise states, "It is significant that nowhere in the New Testament do deacons have ruling authority over the church as the elders do, nor are deacons ever required to be able to teach Scripture or sound doctrine" (Wayne Grudem, *Systematic Theology: An Introduction to Biblical Doctrine* [Leicester: InterVarsity Press; Grand Rapids: Eerdmans, 1994], 920).

does not mean that deacons cannot teach in any capacity but simply that they are not called to teach or preach as a matter of responsibility related to their office as deacon.

Like elders, deacons must manage their house and children well (1 Tim. 3:4, 12). But when referring to deacons, Paul does not compare managing one's household to taking care of God's church (1 Tim. 3:5). The reason for this omission is most likely due to the fact that deacons are not given a ruling or leading position in the church—a function that belongs to the elders.

Other differences provide us with less information. Some maintain that the omission for deacons to be gentle and not quarrelsome (1 Tim. 3:3) may indicate that the elders were often put in situations that required such characteristics. Knight, for example, suggests that this omission "may reflect the fact that the deacon is not in the role of one who must give oversight and direction, as well as discipline, in sometimes difficult situations that make such qualifications imperative."[2]

Although Paul indicates that a person must be tested before he can hold the office of deacon (1 Tim. 3:10), the requirement that he cannot be a new convert is not included. Paul notes that if an elder is a recent convert, "he may become puffed up with conceit" (1 Tim. 3:6). One implication of this distinction could be that those who hold the office of elder—because they possess leadership over the church—are more susceptible to pride. On the contrary, it is not as likely for a deacon—someone who is in more of a servant role—to fall into this same sin.

The fact that Paul includes the character of a deacon's wife also might reveal an important distinction (1 Tim. 3:11). Because the role of a deacon is focused toward serving and not leading, a wife could easily be involved. The wife of an elder would be more limited since Paul forbids women "to teach or to exercise authority over a man" (1 Tim. 2:12). Finally, the title "overseer" (1 Tim. 3:2) implies general oversight over the spiritual well-being of the congregation, whereas the title "deacon" implies one who has a service-oriented ministry.

Duties of Deacons

We have discussed some distinctions between elders and deacons, but we have yet to specify the precise duties of deacons. We already have indicated

2. George W. Knight, *The Pastoral Epistles*, NIGTC (Grand Rapids: Eerdmans; Carlisle, U.K.: Paternoster, 1992), 167.

that deacons are not responsible to teach or lead the congregation. They are not the spiritual leaders of the church. Instead, the deacons provide leadership over the service-oriented functions of the church. The Bible, however, does not clearly indicate the function of deacons. But based on the pattern established in Acts 6 with the apostles and the Seven, it seems best to view the deacons as servants who do whatever is necessary to allow the elders to accomplish their God-given calling of shepherding and teaching the church.[3] Just as the apostles delegated administrative responsibilities to the Seven, so the elders are to delegate responsibilities to the deacons so that the elders can focus their efforts elsewhere. Newton rightly concludes, "In the servant role, deacons take care of those mundane and temporal matters of church life so that elders are freed to concentrate upon spiritual matters. Deacons provide much needed wisdom and energy to the ample physical needs in the church, often using such provision as opportunities to minister as well to the spiritual needs of others."[4] As a result, each local church is free to define the tasks of deacons based on its particular needs.

There are some clues as to the function of deacons based on the requirements in 1 Timothy 3. Grudem offers some possibilities.

> [Deacons] seem to have had some responsibility in caring for the finances of the church, since they had to be people who were "not greedy for gain" (v. 8). They perhaps had some administrative responsibilities in other activities of the church as well, because they were to manage their children and their households well (v. 12). They may also have ministered to the physical needs of those in the church or community who needed help [Acts 6]. . . . Moreover, if verse 11 speaks of their wives (as I think it does), then it would also be likely that they were involved in some house-to-house visitation and counseling, because the wives are to be "no slanderers."[5]

We must note, however, that some of the requirements could have been given to counter the characteristics of false teachers and were not so much

---

3. The role of the Seven should not be compared too closely with the role of the deacons since Steven was also a miracle-worker (Acts 6:8) and preacher (6:8–10) and Philip was an evangelist (Acts 21:8).
4. Phil A. Newton, *Elders in Congregational Life: Rediscovering the Biblical Model for Church Leadership* (Grand Rapids: Kregel, 2005), 41.
5. Grudem, *Systematic Theology*, 919.

directed toward deacons' duties. Mounce maintains that the requirements listed suggest that a deacon would have substantial contact with people: he must not be double-tongued, must have a dignified wife, be faithful in marriage, and have a well-managed family.[6] Although such a conclusion is possible, it cannot be given too much weight.

What are some duties that deacons might be responsible for today? Basically they could be responsible for any item not related to teaching and ruling the church. Below is a list of possible duties.

- *Facilities.* The deacons could be responsible for the basic management of the church property. This would include making sure the place of worship is prepared for the worship service. Other items may include cleanup, sound system, etc.
- *Benevolence.* Similar to what took place in Acts 6 with the daily distribution to the widows, the deacons should be involved in administrating funds for the needy.
- *Finances.* Some believe that matters of finance should be handled by the elders since the famine-relief money brought by Paul and Barnabas was delivered to the elders (Acts 11:30). But while the elders can oversee the financial business of the church, it is probably best left to the deacons to handle the day-to-day matters. This would include collecting and counting the offering, record keeping, helping to set the church budget, etc.
- *Ushers.* The deacons could be responsible for distributing bulletins, seating the congregation, preparing the elements for communion, etc.
- *Logistics.* Deacons should be available to help in a variety of ways so that the elders are able to concentrate on teaching and shepherding the church.

At the end of this chapter is a flow chart diagramming the various ministries of elders and deacons.

Summary

The role of a deacon is different from the role of an elder. Whereas elders are charged with the tasks of teaching and shepherding the church, deacons

---

6. William D. Mounce, *Pastoral Epistles*, WBC (Nashville: Nelson, 2000), 46:195.

are given a more service-oriented function. That is, they are given the task of taking care of matters related more to the physical or temporal concerns of the church. For example, they might have responsibility over areas such as facilities, benevolence, finances, and other matters related to the practical logistics of running a church.

Reflection Questions

1. What are the roles of the deacons in your church?
2. In one sentence, how would you describe the main function of the deacons from a biblical perspective?
3. What are the main differences between the elders and the deacons?
4. Are there any clues given in the qualifications for deacons that might shed light on their duties?
5. What are some needs deacons might fill in your church?

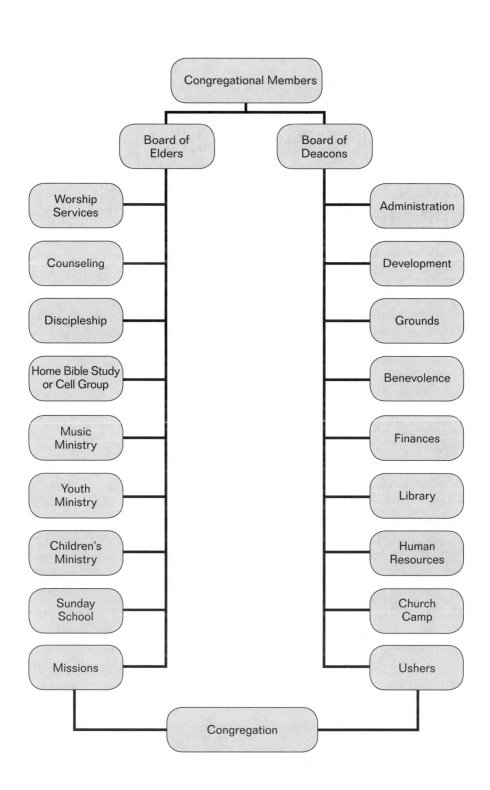

What Is the Relationship Between the Office of Deacon and the Office of Elder?

The relationship between the office of elder and the office of deacon is often assumed but rarely articulated. In this chapter we will analyze the New Testament data and seek to answer the question of whether the deacons hold a lower office than the elders and, if so, how the two offices should relate to each other.

It Is a Lower Office

There are a number of factors in Scripture that indicate that the office of deacon is, in one sense, a lesser office than that of the elder. First, the function of the deacons is to provide support for the elders so that they can continue their work without being distracted by other matters. Just as the apostles appointed seven men to care for the physical needs of the congregation in the daily distribution of food (Acts 6:1–6), so the deacons are needed so that the elders can attend to the spiritual needs of the congregation. The title "deacon" also suggests one who has a secondary role as one who comes beside and assists others. Deacons are not involved in the important tasks of teaching (cf. 1 Tim. 3:2; 5:17; Titus 1:9) and shepherding (cf. Acts 20:28; Eph. 4:11; 1 Peter 5:1–2). These tasks are reserved mainly for the elders. Rather, the deacons provide assistance and support so that the work of the church can continue effectively and smoothly.

Second, the office of deacon is mentioned after the office of elder/overseer. There are two examples in the New Testament. In Philippians 1:1, Paul not only greets the entire congregation (as was his normal practice), but he also greets the "overseers and deacons." Later, when Paul lists the needed qualifications for overseers and deacons in 1 Timothy 3, the qualifications for over-seers are listed first. Although such ordering does not necessarily indicate order of priority, it at least may emphasize the importance of those who teach and lead the church.

Third, references to the office of deacon are far less frequent than refer-ences to the office of elder. Although the general use of the Greek term *diako-nos* occurs quite frequently, the more specific use of the term as a reference to an officeholder is found only three or four times in the New Testament (Rom. 16:1[?]; Phil. 1:1; 1 Tim. 3:8, 12). On the other hand, the terms *presbuteros* ("elder") and *episkopos* ("overseer") as references to officeholders occur more than twenty times.[1] Again, these numbers are not conclusive by themselves, but they add to the point that deacons held a lesser office.

Fourth, elders were appointed to new churches before deacons were. The early church in Jerusalem had elders before they had deacons—assuming the Seven appointed in Acts 6 could not technically be considered "deacons." During Paul's first missionary journey, he and Barnabas appointed elders in the churches of Asia Minor (Acts 14:23). Yet, nowhere does Luke indicate that deacons were appointed. While this omission does not prove that dea-cons did not exist in the churches at that time, the fact that they are not men-tioned indicates that they were not as important to the progress of the gospel in the mind of Luke. Later, Paul commands Titus to appoint elders in every city on the island of Crete (Titus 1:5), but he says nothing about deacons. If deacons were as important to the life of the church, it would seem that he also would have included instructions to appoint deacons and included the needed qualifications as he did in 1 Timothy.

It Is a Distinct Office

There is some danger in describing the office of deacon as a lower office than the office of elder. Misconceptions concerning the two offices are common, so it is important to clarify what was not intended in our previous discussion. For example, there is no indication in Scripture that the office of deacon is a lower office in the sense that one must become a deacon before he can serve as an elder. These offices are distinguished by their function in the church and the gifts of the individual. Similar, yet distinct, qualifications are given for elders and for deacons. Paul does not indicate in his qualifications for elders

---

1. Elder: Acts 11:30; 14:23; 15:2, 4, 6, 22, 23; 16:4; 20:17; 21:18; 1 Tim. 5:17, 19; Titus 1:5; James 5:14; 1 Peter 5:1; 5; 2 John 1; 3 John 1. Overseer: Acts 20:28; Phil. 1:1; 1 Tim. 3:2; Titus 1:7.

that one first must have been a deacon. As a matter of fact, his comment that an elder must not be a recent covert (1 Tim. 3:6) would make little sense if he expected a person to be a deacon before he could move up to the position of an elder. Furthermore, it is likely that many churches did not have deacons at the beginning of their existence. The distinction between elders and deacons is not a distinction of rank but a distinction of function. Unlike elders, deacons do not teach and shepherd the congregation (1 Tim. 3:2, 5). If a person is a gifted teacher and meets the qualifications listed in 1 Timothy 3:1–7, he should seek to become an elder. On the other hand, if someone does not have the gift of teaching but enjoys serving in other areas, he might consider becoming a deacon. Becoming a deacon is not a stepping-stone to becoming an elder. The two offices are distinct in that they require a different set of gifts.

Deacons are also distinct from elders in the sense that they are not merely the personal assistants of the elders. Deacons are not called to serve the elders. Rather, they are called to serve the church. The Seven in Acts 6 were not enlisted to serve the apostles. They were selected and appointed to help solve a critical issue in the life of the congregation. Although it is necessary for the elders to work closely with the deacons, the deacons are not there simply to answer the call of the elders but should be given freedom to serve the church. Moreover, it is inappropriate for the deacons to be chosen by the elders alone. The congregation as a whole should be involved in the process. Again, the reason is that the deacons do not exist to serve the elders but are called to serve the entire congregation.

It Is an Important Office

To say that the office of deacon is, in some sense, a lower office than the office of elder is not to minimize its importance in the life and health of the church. The appointing of the seven men in Acts 6 saved the church from potential disaster. Because the Hellenistic widows were being overlooked by the church, some Hellenistic Jews may have been tempted to form their own congregations. The result would have been devastating to the unity of the church. Thus, what began as a minor issue could have turned into a massive problem if left unchecked. The church could have experienced its first split and been stifled in its progress to proclaim the gospel message to all the nations. Wisely, however, the apostles appointed the Seven to solve this problem. In a similar manner, deacons are needed in the church to care for the "physical" life of the church.

Neither are deacons less than elders in the sense that they are lesser Christians or are lesser in God's eyes. All gifts are from God and are given according to His will (1 Cor. 12:11). Paul uses the analogy of a body to illustrate the point that all members that make up a body are needed. The foot, hand, eye, and ear—although they have different functions—are all integral parts of the body and cannot be ignored. As a matter of fact, Paul states that those who receive less honor because of their gifts and use in the church should not be neglected. He states,

> The parts of the body that seem to be weaker are indispensable, and on those parts of the body that we think less honorable we bestow the greater honor, and our unpresentable parts are treated with greater modesty, which our more presentable parts do not require. But God has so composed the body, giving greater honor to the part that lacked it, that there may be no division in the body, but that the members may have the same care for one another. (1 Cor. 12:22–25)

All members are needed, and this is especially true for the important work of the deacons.

Summary

Scripture seems to indicate that the office of deacon is a secondary office to that of the elder. This distinction is primarily due to the ruling and teaching functions of the elders. The deacons, on the other hand, are primarily servants who handle the details of the church, allowing the elders to do their work more effectively and efficiently. The role of the deacons, however, is vital to the life and health of the church. Although deacons work closely with the elders, they are not there to serve the elders but to serve the church. Also, a person does not need to become a deacon before he is qualified to become an elder.

Reflection Questions

1. What New Testament evidence is there to support the notion that the office of deacon is, in one sense, a lower office than the office of elder?

2. Why is it wrong to think that someone must become a deacon before he can serve as an elder?
3. What is the appropriate relationship between the deacons and the elders?
4. Why is the office of deacon such a crucial office in the church?
5. Does your church celebrate the work of the deacons? What could be done to show appreciation to them for their work?

What Are the Reasons for Affirming That Women Can Be Deacons?

The question of whether women can be deacons must be considered independently of whether they can become elders. While many Christians believe the Bible forbids women to hold the office of elder, some of these same Christians also are convinced that women can hold the office of deacon. In the following pages, we will consider the most common arguments given in favor of allowing women to be deacons. In particular, we will present the arguments related to three crucial texts: 1 Timothy 3:11; 1 Timothy 2:12; and Romans 16:1–2.

1 Timothy 3:11

In 1 Timothy 3:8–13, Paul lists the qualifications needed for a man to become a deacon. In verse 11, however, he introduces the requirements needed for "women." According to the NRSV, Paul states, "Women likewise must be . . ." The ESV, on the other hand, reads, "Their wives likewise must be . . ." The question is whether Paul is speaking of the requirements for the wife of a deacon or for a woman deacon. The following arguments suggest that Paul has the latter in mind:

1. The Greek term *gunaikas* (from the word *gunē*) can refer either to "women" or, more specifically, to "wives"—the distinction can be determined only by the context. If Paul was referring to the wives of the deacons, he could have indicated his intention by adding the word "their" ("*Their* wives likewise . . ."). Because the Greek does not contain the word for "their" (although it is included in many English translations), it is best to translate the original text simply as "women." In this case, Paul is introducing another office and is not merely referring to the wives of deacons.

2. Paul begins verse 11 in a manner similar to verse 8, which introduces a new office. In verses 1–7, Paul identifies the qualifications needed for anyone aspiring to the office of overseer. When Paul begins the next section, which introduces the office of deacon, he states, "Deacons likewise . . ." (v. 8). The point to be made is that verse 11 begins in the same manner, which suggests that another office (deaconess) is being introduced. The flow of Paul's writing then becomes evident: ". . . an overseer must be [v. 2] . . . deacons likewise must be [v. 8] . . . women [deacons] likewise must be [v. 11] . . . ." Verses 12 and 13, which refer again to qualifications for male deacons, include additional information that Paul adds as an afterthought, causing a disjointed unit.

3. Another reason that suggests that Paul is not speaking about deacons' wives but rather about women deacons is that the qualifications for overseers do not include any reference to their wives. It does not seem likely that Paul would add a special requirement for the wife of a deacon when the more important office of overseer has no such requirement. Thus, it does not seem likely that Paul would have stricter requirements for deacons than he does for elders.

1 Timothy 2:12

Many Christians are opposed to allowing women to become deacons because, according to 1 Timothy 2:12, Paul forbids a woman "to teach or exercise authority over a man." And because all offices in the church, including the office of deacon, possess an inherent authority, women are not permitted to hold such offices. There are two main responses to this dilemma that would still allow women to be deacons. First, Paul's prohibition could be limited due to cultural reasons. That is, Paul prohibits women from teaching and having authority over men because the women of Ephesus were either uneducated or were teaching false doctrine (or both). Therefore, in the case of women who are educated and are not teaching false doctrine, Paul's prohibition does not apply.

A second response is that the ministry of deacons is by nature a ministry of service that does not require women to teach or exercise authority over men and thus would not violate Paul's prohibition. Unlike the elders, deacons do not need to be "able to teach" (1 Tim. 3:2) because their ministry does not involved teaching. Furthermore, it could be argued that the office of deacon is not an authoritative office due to the nature of their service-oriented ministry. Deacons are not called to lead the church but to serve the church. Therefore, the two prohibitions given by Paul in 1 Timothy 2:12 are not violated by allowing women to become deacons.

Romans 16:1–2

In this text, Paul commends Phoebe to the church at Rome and calls her a *diakonos* "of the church at Cenchreae." There are at least three reasons that support the translation of *diakonos* here as "deacon," referring to an office-holder and not merely one who is a "servant."

1. Paul uses the masculine form *diakonos* to refer to a woman. Thus, it can be argued that Paul is not using the term generally to refer to one who is a servant but that he has a specific office in mind. The masculine form of *diakonos* used to reference a woman suggests that the term became standardized when referring to an office.

2. When the generic meaning of *diakonos* (i.e., "servant") is intended, the text usually reads, "servant *of the Lord*" or something similar. This is the only place Paul speaks of someone being a *diakonos* of a local church. Tychicus is called a "minister [or servant] in the Lord" (Eph. 6:21), Epaphras is named a "minister [servant] of Christ" (Col. 1:7), and Timothy is labeled a "servant of Christ Jesus" (1 Tim. 4:6). Because only Phoebe is specifically said to be a servant of a local congregation (the church at Cenchreae), it is likely that she was a "deacon" of her church.

3. Phoebe is sent to perform an official task on behalf of the apostle Paul and her church. Paul commends her to the church at Rome and urges the Roman Christians to aid her since she is about the important business of the church. He asks that they "welcome her in the Lord in a way worthy of the saints, and help her in whatever she may need . . . , for she has been a patron of many and of myself as well" (Rom. 16:2). Such an official task, it is argued, requires an official office.[1]

---

1. Many scholars posit that Phoebe was in fact the bearer of the letter of Romans, so C. E. B Cranfield, *A Critical and Exegetical Commentary on the Epistle to the Romans*, ICC (Edinburgh: T and T Clark, 1979), 3:780; John Murray, *The Epistle to the Romans*, NICNT (Grand Rapids: Eerdmans, 1968), 226; Douglas J. Moo, *The Epistle to the Romans*, NICNT (Grand Rapids: Eerdmans, 1996), 913; Peter Stuhlmacher, *Paul's Letter to the Romans*, trans. Scott J. Hafemann (Louisville: Westminster/John Knox, 1994), 246; and F. F. Bruce, *The Letter of Paul to the Romans*, rev. ed., TNTC (Leicester: InterVarsity Press; Grand Rapids: Eerdmans, 1985), 6:252.

Summary

The conclusion drawn from the above data is that women can be deacons in the church. In 1 Timothy 3:11, Paul gives the qualifications for women deacons and in Romans 16:1 specially names Phoebe, a sister in the Lord, a "deacon of the church at Cenchreae." Furthermore, allowing women to become deacons does not violate Paul's prohibition in 1 Timothy 2:12 since a deacon does not "teach or exercise authority" in the church.

Reflection Questions

1. Are you persuaded that 1 Timothy 3:11 refers to a woman deacon and not simply the wife of a deacon?
2. What individual arguments do you find the most persuasive?
3. Do you agree with those who maintain that the office of deacon is not an authoritative office and therefore does not violate 1 Timothy 2:12?
4. What are the reasons for affirming that Phoebe was a deacon of her church?
5. Why do you think that many churches who do not allow women to be elders will allow them to be deacons?

What Are the Reasons for Affirming That Women Cannot Be Deacons?

We will now offer the reasons in favor of not allowing women to be deacons. It must be acknowledged, however, that while many of the following arguments suggest that women were not deacons in the New Testament, such conclusions must be tentatively held due to the paucity of information. As with the previous question, we will discuss the arguments related to 1 Timothy 3:11; 1 Timothy 2:12; and Romans 16:1–2.

1 Timothy 3:11

Although the Greek text is ambiguous as to whether Paul is referring to the wives of deacons or to women deacons, the following reasons favor the former reading.

1. In the immediate context, the Greek term *gunē* is translated "wife." For example, in verse 2, Paul states that overseers must be the "husband of one wife [*gunē*]" and in verse 12 he similarly writes that deacons must each "be the husband of one wife [*gunē*]." Therefore, because the usage of *gunē* in the preceding context (v. 2) and the usage of *gunē* in the following verse (v. 12) has the meaning of "wife," it is consistent with the context to translate *gunē* as "wife" in verse 11.

2. In the context, the possessive article "their" is not required to make the passage understandable as referring to the wives of deacons. It is obvious that if "wives" are referred to in verse 11, they could only be the wives of potential candidates for the office of deacon. On the other hand, if Paul switches to the qualifications for a separate office of female deacon, we would expect a clear indication—such as "women *who serve as deacons*." Furthermore, in verse 12 Paul shifts

back to speaking about male deacons without giving any indication that he ever left the topic. Thus, if the text referred to women deacons, it would disrupt the natural flow of the text, lacking a clear transition back to male deacons in verse 12.

3. If Paul is referring to women deacons in verse 11, we would expect some reference to their marital status and fidelity. In every other list of qualifications (for elders/overseers, deacons, and church-supported widows), Paul includes such a reference. In 1 Timothy 3:2 and Titus 1:6, an elder/overseer must be "the husband of one wife"; in 1 Timothy 3:12 a deacon must be "the husband of one wife"; and in 1 Timothy 5:9 a widow supported by the church must have been "the wife of one husband." In verse 11, however, Paul makes no mention of a woman's marital status or fidelity.

4. The argument that the "likewise" in verse 11 must introduce a new office is not compelling based on other uses of the same term in 1 Timothy. For example, in chapter 2 Paul states, "I desire then that in every place the men should pray, lifting holy hands without anger or quarreling" (v. 8). In the next verse, he adds, "likewise also that women should adorn themselves in respectable apparel, with modesty and self-control, not with braided hair and gold or pearls or costly attire" (v. 9). Paul links his injunctions to men and women with "likewise," but his comments are very different. He states that men are to pray . . . likewise women are to dress appropriately. He does not say, "Men are to pray . . . likewise, women also are to pray." Therefore, to maintain that the "likewise" in 3:11 must introduce a new office interprets the word too narrowly. Rather, Paul is saying that just as deacons are to be dignified, likewise, so are their wives.

5. It would be strange for Paul to give the qualifications for male deacons in verses 8–10, interrupt himself to introduce a new office of female deacon in verse 11, and then return to the qualifications for male deacons in verses 12–13. If verse 11 refers to the wife of a deacon, however, then verse 11 fits nicely in the flow of the section. Verses 11 and 12 form the second half of a deacon's qualifications. Verses 8–10 speak of a deacon's personal and moral qualifications, whereas verses 11–12 refer to his family and home life. That is, his wife is to be dignified, he is to be faithful to his wife, and he is to govern his home and children well. Thus, verses 11 and 12 form a common theme of

the deacon's family. These verses are dealing with the same topic and naturally belong together.[1]

6. It is also unlikely that verses 12 and 13 are an afterthought, being listed after the requirements for female deacons. Why would Paul forget to mention that a deacon must be the husband of one wife or a good manager of his household? Such requirements are very significant to the office and ones that Paul had just mentioned in relation to the qualifications for overseers. Therefore, the idea that Paul simply forgot to mention some qualifications and then returns to them after he introduces the qualifications for women deacons is not persuasive.

7. If Paul had intended to establish an additional office (female deacons), it is more likely that he would have done so explicitly, rather than incidentally. For Paul to provide only one sentence with only four requirements seems unlikely. He lists fifteen requirements for overseers and nine (or ten) requirements for deacons, whereas female deacons would be given only four requirements. Such a short list would be surprising, especially since we know that women were being led astray by the false teachers (1 Tim. 5:13; 2 Tim. 3:6–7).

8. Although it is true that nothing is said concerning the wife of an elder, one cannot base too much on this argument from silence. It must be remembered that the lists of requirements in 1 Timothy 3 are not formal lists but are ad hoc in the sense that they are directed at countering specific problems prevalent in the church at Ephesus. It is entirely possible that, for reasons we do not know, Paul deemed it necessary and important that the wife of a deacon meet a certain standard. Furthermore, it is likely that the deacons' wives participated in their husbands' ministry of serving in a way that elders' wives did not. Since the deacons were not involved in a teaching and ruling ministry (which was forbidden for women, 1 Tim. 2:12) but in a serving ministry, their wives could easily be involved in their ministry. The Seven chosen in Acts 6 were all men. What is interesting is that their ministry involved ministering to widows. It seems reasonable to assume that the wives of the Seven could have been involved in such a ministry, whereas the wives of the apostles would not have assisted their husbands in preaching the Word.

---

1. See Wayne Grudem, *Systematic Theology: An Introduction to Biblical Doctrine* (Leicester: InterVarsity Press; Grand Rapids: Eerdmans, 1994), 919n. 25, for similar arguments.

1 Timothy 2:12

In 1 Timothy 2:12, Paul forbids a woman "to teach or to exercise authority over a man." As we have seen, many argue that because the office of deacon is not a teaching office or an office that exercises authority, a woman is allowed to become a deacon. Such an argument, however, is unconvincing for the following reasons.

1. Although it is true that deacons are not given a teaching ministry, it is a mistake to assume that deacons do not exercise any authority in their ministry. Deacons are servants but they are also leaders in the church, and as leaders they possess authority. The Seven chosen in Acts 6 were given oversight over the daily distribution of food—a responsibility that certainly involved exercising authority over others. Deacons exercise authority in the physical/logistical realm, which would be inappropriate for women.

2. It would seem that by definition an office assumes a certain amount of authority. If no authority is involved, then the office is, in a sense, irrelevant. Other features related to the concept of office also indicate that authority is involved. Those appointed to the office of deacon are usually officially appointed before the congregation and are given the designation "deacon," which sets them apart for their office. If they are merely servants who by virtue of their office have no authority over others, then why is it necessary to set them apart and give them a distinct title?

3. If deacons do not exercise authority, then why is it necessary for them to meet so many qualifications? If the Seven chosen in Acts 6 had no authority, then why was it necessary that they had a good reputation and were full of the Holy Spirit and wisdom? If deacons have no authority, then why is it necessary that they not be greedy for dishonest gain, manage their household well, and are first tested?

4. Even if having women deacons does not violate 1 Timothy 2:12, it does not follow that women can or should be deacons. Nowhere in Scripture is there a clear example of women being deacons—except perhaps Romans 16:1. When the early church had an issue related specifically to women, they appointed men to handle the problem. Because there is no indication that women were appointed to any of-

fice in the New Testament church, it would be wise for the church today to follow God's designed pattern of leadership.

Romans 16:1–2

In Romans 16:1, Paul commends Phoebe to the church at Rome and calls her a *diakonos* "of the church at Cenchreae." While it is possible that Paul's use of *diakonos* is used in the more technical sense of a church office, the evidence for that conclusion is weak.

1. Although it is true that the masculine form *diakonos* is used to describe Phoebe, this may be because the feminine form did not exist at that time. Thus, the use of the masculine form has no real significance here. On the other hand, Paul could have created a Greek word for a female deacon if he had wanted to make it clear that Phoebe held the office of a deacon. Elsewhere in his writings, Paul sometimes created his own words when necessary to convey his intentions.

2. That Phoebe is described as a *diakonos* "of the church at Cenchreae" does not prove the term is used as a designation for an office. Since she was sent on an official mission by Paul (most scholars assume that Phoebe was the bearer of the letter to the church at Rome), it could be that he needed to describe the church from which she was sent. Thus, the term is used in a more specific sense, not as a designation of a church office, but as a designation of someone who is sent on an official task on behalf of Paul.[2]

Summary

Although the grounds for not allowing women to become deacons is not as strong as those for not allowing women to be elders, there is still sufficient evidence that such was not God's design for the church. It is unlikely that in 1 Timothy 3:11 Paul is listing qualifications for the office of a female deacon. Rather, he is identifying the traits needed for the wife of a deacon. Allowing women to be deacons also violates 1 Timothy 2:12, which states that women are forbidden to exercise authority over men. The closest evidence that the

---

2. John Murray notes, "If Phoebe ministered to the saints . . . then she would be a servant of the church and there is neither need nor warrant to suppose that she occupied or exercised what amounted to an ecclesiastical office comparable to that of the diaconate" (*The Epistle to the Romans*, NICNT [Grand Rapids: Eerdmans, 1968], 2:226).

early church had women deacons is found in Romans 16:1–2 with the example of Phoebe. This text, however, is not conclusive, and basing an office on one verse or passage is never a good practice. Therefore, it is best to not allow women to hold the office of deacon.

Reflection Questions

1. What are the reasons for affirming that 1 Timothy 3:11 does not refer to women deacons?
2. What individual arguments do you find most persuasive?
3. What are some reasons for believing the office of deacon is an authoritative office?
4. Are you convinced that Phoebe was a deacon? Why or why not?
5. Do you think women should be deacons?

Is It Important to Use the Titles "Elder" and "Deacon"?

Many churches that have leaders who essentially function as elders and deacons have been described in this book, but these leaders are not called "elders" and "deacons." Thus, the question before us is whether it is essential that each congregation employ this terminology or whether other terms will work just as well. In this section, I will seek to demonstrate that although the terminology used is not as important as the actual role of church leaders, there are good reasons for employing biblical terminology.

Titles Are Not Essential

Although titles often are used for church leaders, Jesus warns against seeking after them. In contrast to the scribes and Pharisees, Jesus instructs us, "But you are not to be called rabbi, for you have one teacher, and you are all brothers. And call no man your father on earth, for you have one Father, who is in heaven. Neither be called instructors, for you have one instructor, the Christ" (Matt. 23:8–10). There is a real danger of men seeking leadership in the church simply for the title or the recognition that the title brings. Jesus warns against such motivation by stating, "The greatest among you shall be your servant. Whoever exalts himself will be humbled, and whoever humbles himself will be exalted" (Matt. 23:11–12). Leadership in the church is not about acquiring titles but about becoming a servant.

The particular title used to describe a church leader is not the central issue. The more important issue is the role that person is fulfilling. As we have seen, the apostle Paul sometimes uses titles to describe particular church leaders. It should be noted, however, that Paul is more interested in service than he is with any office.[1] It is the one who *teaches* the Word who receives some sort of compensation (Gal. 6:6). It is those who *labor, lead*, and *admonish* who are to be respected *because of their work* (1 Thess. 5:12). The church is to be subject to those who *devote themselves to ministry* (1 Cor. 16:15–16). Epaphras is called a faithful *servant* who has *labored earnestly* for the gospel (Col. 1:7; 4:12 NASB). Archippus is exhorted to fulfill his *ministry* (Col. 4:17). Although at times Paul more specifically speaks of office (Eph. 4:11; Phil. 1:1; 1 Tim. 3:1–2, 8, 12; 5:17; Titus 1:5, 7), his main concern is that the gospel is advanced. In one sense, then, titles are not essential to the Christian ministry. Paul emphasizes the importance of a leader's function more than the particular title a leader bears.

Titles Are Important

Simply because titles are not essential to the Christian ministry, however, does not mean they have no importance or relevance. Some churches purposefully avoid the biblical terminology because it is perceived as possibly being divisive. Some people in the church prefer one title, while others prefer another. To stay clear of any controversy, all biblical titles are avoided. Other churches simply use the titles that have been passed down from one generation to another, giving no thought to whether such titles are accurate. Thus, the tradition of the church or denomination takes precedence over the biblical usage of the terms. There are at least three reasons why I believe it is beneficial for churches to faithfully use the titles given in Scripture.

Before I go into the various reasons why certain titles should be used, it is first necessary to explain that the title itself, without the appropriate role, is counterproductive. For example, the office of deacon is consistently found in many churches, although the duty of deacons varies widely. In many churches, the deacons function like elders in the sense that they are involved in leading and shepherding the church. In other circumstances, the deacons do not really serve but are simply elected or chosen to make important decisions. In some denominations, a deacon is an entry level ministerial position that is the first step up the ecclesiastical ladder.

---

1. Bengt Holmberg states, "The general impression we get when reading Paul's letters is that the local offices were rather unimportant ... even if the apostle seems to appreciate them" (*Paul and Power: The Structure of Authority in the Primitive Church as Reflected in the Pauline Epistles* [Philadelphia: Fortress, 1980], 112). Some reasons for this phenomenon are (1) Paul's own authority was still preeminent; (2) the presence of prophets and teachers limited the need for other leaders; (3) the young churches were not in a position to be self-governed; and (4) Paul normally addressed his letters to whole congregations, not simply the leadership.

The office of elder is more complex due to the number of terms that can be used. Which title is to be preferred: elder, overseer, bishop, or pastor? Here we must allow for some flexibility because the Bible does not employ one term consistently. While the title "elder" is more common than "overseer," both refer to the same officeholder and therefore can be used. If the title "pastor" is used, it should be used consistently. That is, some of the elders should not be given the additional title of "pastor" simply because they work full-time for the church or are on staff. If one elder is also called a pastor, then it is appropriate that all the elders be called pastors. The title "bishop" has the same essential meaning as "overseer," but it is often avoided by evangelical churches due to the connotations the term took on after the New Testament. This is also why most modern English Bible versions prefer to translate the Greek term *episkopos* "overseer" rather than "bishop."

The first reason it is helpful for church leaders to use the terms as they are used in Scripture is that it bases our authority on the Bible and not human wisdom. By using titles that are not found in Scripture, the congregation may begin to doubt the basis of authority for the church leaders. But when it is shown that elders or overseers are responsible for shepherding and teaching the church based on the model of the New Testament churches, it gives authority and credibility to their office. Many churches today model their organizational structure after a successful business model. The church, however, should not be run like a business, and it is dangerous to organize the church based on whatever works in society. God has provided the church with a basic structure that should be closely followed. To stray from that structure is, in a sense, to say that our way is better than God's way. By using biblical terminology, as well as performing biblical roles, the leaders communicate to the congregation that the Bible is the final authority for all faith and practice.

A second reason it is best to use the titles for leaders given in Scripture is that it allows the congregation to know what to expect from the leadership. If other terms are used, the congregation either has to guess what the responsibilities of the leaders are or read their individual job descriptions (which they may or may not have access to). If the biblical terms and functions are used, however, the congregation will know immediately that the deacons are not in charge of preaching and teaching or ruling the church. Rather, they are responsible for the menial and service-oriented tasks of the church.

Finally, it is beneficial to employ the biblical terminology for church leaders because it holds leaders to the biblical qualifications. If the ruling and teaching leaders of the church are simply called "council members," or are given some other title not found in Scripture, then it is difficult to hold such leaders to the biblical qualifications. When one of them is questioned as to whether he meets the qualifications for elders or deacons, he can simply reply, "You cannot hold me to those qualifications because I am not an elder or a deacon. I am a council member." If the qualifications are going to be consistently applied to the leaders of the church, it is best for those leaders to bear the titles given at the head of the qualifications. If the appropriate titles are not used, it confuses the congregation and provides a way of escape for unqualified officeholders. Using the titles found in Scripture avoids such confusion. In fact, as church members read their Bibles and the qualifications given therein, they just might begin to examine their own hearts to see how they measure up to such a standard. If they aspire to hold a particular office, they will know precisely what is expected of them based on the qualifications given in Scripture.

Summary

Titles are not essential to the Christian ministry, but they are important. They demonstrate that the church's basis for authority is not found in human wisdom, but in God's. They also allow the congregation to know what to expect from their leaders. Finally, they link a particular office with a particular set of qualifications that must be met before someone can appropriately take the title.

Reflection Questions

1. Why did Jesus warn us against seeking after titles?
2. Do you agree that titles are not as important as the role the person who holds the title is fulfilling?
3. How does using the scriptural titles for church offices demonstrate that our authority is based on the Bible and not human wisdom?
4. How does using the scriptural titles help the congregation know what to expect from its leadership?
5. How does using the scriptural titles help hold the leaders to the biblical qualifications?

Selected Bibliography

Brand, Chad Owen, and R. Stanton Norman. *Perspectives on Church Government: Five Views of Church Polity*. Nashville: Broadman and Holman, 2004.

Dever, Mark. *Nine Marks of a Healthy Church*, expanded ed. Wheaton, IL: Crossway, 2004.

Dever, Mark, and Paul Alexander. *The Deliberate Church: Building Your Ministry on the Gospel*. Wheaton, IL: Crossway, 2005.

Engle, Paul E., and Steven B. Cowan, eds. *Who Runs the Church? 4 Views on Church Government*. Grand Rapids: Zondervan, 2004.

Newton, Phil A. *Elders in Congregational Life: Rediscovering the Biblical Model for Church Leadership*. Grand Rapids: Kregel, 2005.

Piper, John. *Biblical Eldership*. Minneapolis: Desiring God Ministries, 1999.

Strauch, Alexander. *Biblical Eldership: An Urgent Call to Restore Biblical Church Leadership*. Revised and expanded. Littleton, CO: Lewis and Roth, 1995.

Scripture Index

Also available

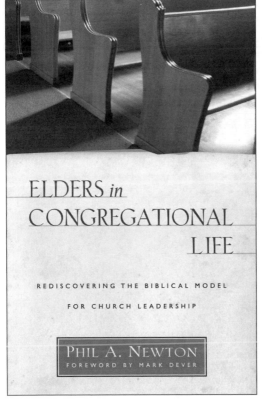

ISBN 978-0-8254-3331-3 | 176 pages | paperback

A biblically functioning church requires much more than skillful organization and clever techniques. It calls for intentional devotion to the New Testament model of the church, and church leadership stands at the heart of the model. In this practical book, experienced pastor Phil Newton gives a definitive and biblical answer to the current debate in many churches and church associations over elder-based leadership in independent congregations.

> "You can tell by the wealth of information in these chapters that Phil has lived through the process, and he's willing to share his own experiences—good and bad—in order to help us have even better experiences in our churches."
>
> —From the foreword by **Mark Dever**